THE ANTI-DOPING CRISIS IN SPORT

D0082633

The sense of crisis that pervades global sport suggests that the war on doping is still very far from being won. In this critical and provocative study of anti-doping regimes in global sport, Paul Dimeo and Verner Møller argue that the current system is at a critical historical juncture.

Reviewing the recent history of anti-doping, this book highlights serious problems in the approach developed and implemented by the World Anti-Doping Agency (WADA), including continued failure to accept responsibility for the ineffectiveness of the testing system, the growing number of dubious convictions, and damaging human-rights issues. Without a total rethink of how we deal with this critical issue in world sport, this book warns that we could be facing the collapse of anti-doping, both as a policy and as an ideology.

The Anti-Doping Crisis in Sport: Causes, Consequences, Solutions is important reading for all students and scholars of sport studies, as well as researchers, coaches, doctors and policymakers interested in the politics and ethics of drug use in sport. It examines the reasons for the crisis, the consequences of policy strategies, and it explores potential solutions.

Paul Dimeo is a Senior Lecturer in the Faculty of Health Sciences and Sport at Stirling University, UK.

Verner Møller is a Professor in the Department of Public Health at Aarhus University, Denmark.

THE ANTI-DOPING CRISIS IN SPORT

Causes, Consequences, Solutions

Paul Dimeo and Verner Møller

Routledge
Taylor & Francis Group

LONDON AND NEW YORK

First published 2018
by Routledge
2 Park Square, Milton Park, Abingdon, Oxon OX14 4RN

and by Routledge
711 Third Avenue, New York, NY 10017

Routledge is an imprint of the Taylor & Francis Group, an informa business

British Library Cataloguing-in-Publication Data
A catalogue record for this book is available from the British Library

Library of Congress Cataloging-in-Publication Data
A catalog record for this book has been requested

ISBN: 978-1-138-68165-1 (hbk)
ISBN: 978-1-138-68167-5 (pbk)
ISBN: 978-1-315-54567-7 (ebk)

Typeset in Bembo
by HWA Text Data Management, London

CONTENTS

CONTENTS

PREFACE

The sense of crisis that pervades global sport in the late 2010s has an undercurrent of pessimism that the war on doping might never be won. The policy to retest samples from suspected athletes who were not caught when they successfully competed in the Olympics has done little more than shown that the World Anti-Doping Agency (WADA) and the International Olympic Committee (IOC) have collectively failed to prevent doping through the 2000s. WADA investigations and media coverage of the highly organised Russian doping programme, which has been proven to operate in secrecy from 2010 to 2015, shows that the most determined cheats can beat the testers. This is precisely what the sports world learnt from the 2012 investigation into professional cycling led by the United States Anti-Doping Agency (USADA), which focused on Lance Armstrong but revealed an epidemic of doping problems. Similar lessons were learnt from the 2006 raid in Madrid on the clinic run by doping doctor Fuentes. Twenty years since the crisis precipitated by the 1998 Tour de France which helped usher in the creation of WADA, there is little sense that progress has been made to stop the most ambitious athletes and their support personnel from taking the logic of sport to a degree that transgresses the rules laid out in the World Anti-Doping Code (WADC). The anti-doping discourse presents doping as a crisis of sport and its perceived values.

However, the crisis is not limited to the act of using a banned substance to enhance performance. It has been exacerbated by the uniquely excessive ways in which doping has been interpreted, responded to, and policed. The anti-doping crisis is not just caused by consumers and suppliers, but by regulators and their implementers, and by moral arbitrators who over-emphasise the scandalous nature of doping, and under-emphasise or ignore the failings of, and harms caused by, anti-doping policies. Such criticisms of policy can be found in debates on the policing and regulation of illicit drugs where, in some countries and for some drugs, it has become accepted that a more tolerant approach to users can facilitate a more rational channelling of resources towards policing suppliers and high-risk drug cultures. Sports have yet to catch up with these developments, as the emphasis remains firmly upon 'clean sport' or 'drug-free sport'.

This absolutist approach means that anti-doping has unique characteristics. The expectation that all athletes be 'clean' at all times means that policies are not just targeted at users or those at risk of using a banned substance. All athletes are subject to a testing system that invades their privacy in ways that would not be tolerated in any other walk of life. Moreover, the list of banned substances (the List of Prohibited Substances and Methods, hereafter the 'Prohibited List') is so lengthy and complex that athletes are not always fully informed of all the potential ways they could be sanctioned before they are tested. The list includes many drugs that are not performance-enhancing or a risk to health, such that the focus and purpose of anti-doping is sometimes lost within the need to follow rules and punish those who transgress them (deliberately or not). The implementation of policy is so tough that innocent athletes have been sanctioned, stigmatised and often given little opportunity for legal recourse. And yet, the moralising narratives continues unabated: cheats are seen to be undermining sport, any doping violation should be punished, all athletes should support WADA, and all athletes should be treated as potential cheats. The empowerment of anti-doping in response to over 30 years of scandals has paradoxically increased the drastic consequences for clean athletes and disproportionately punished unintended cases of doping, led to irrational stigmatisation of anyone caught doping, while at the same time consistently failed to crack down on doping.

This book is a critical assessment of policy. We begin with a selection of unintended consequences (Chapter 1), a description of the crisis. From there, we explore the historical reasons and policy decisions that have led to the contemporary malaise (Chapters 2 and 3). The consequences are described and explained by focusing upon the failure to catch cheats (Chapter 4), the inevitable and unethical outcome of regularly punishing the wrong people (Chapter 5), dilemmas and failings over medical and science issues (Chapter 6) and the de-humanisation inherent in anti-doping (Chapter 7). These themes collectively point towards the need for reform, both to address ongoing doping contexts and to improve the humanity and ethics of anti-doping policies and practices. We review the proposals for reform which have previously been suggested by academics (Chapter 8), before outlining several of our own ideas for change (Chapter 9).

Our intention is not to promote cultures of doping or a simplistic liberalisation agenda. We merely argue that the past and present of anti-doping point to the need for a different type of approach for the future. Of course, we should note that the future of sport might be revolutionised if the spectre of gene doping becomes a reality, though for the moment we have no evidence that it will. Should new undetectable gene-based technologies emerge then anti-doping will become obsolete. Since we have not yet reached that point, we shall explore the state of the system in its current form.

Our thinking on this subject has benefitted immensely from dialogue with humanities researchers, scientists, students, athletes, coaches, doctors, policy makers, journalists, whistle-blowers – too many to thank individually, but we are grateful for their insights and time. The ongoing work of the International Network of Doping Research is an important collective enterprise for understanding anti-doping through detached analysis and empirical research. We are inspired by those athletes whose lives have been drastically impacted by anti-doping, and who have fought personal battles against the inhumane and immoral ways in which the system treated them. Behind the headlines of international scandals there are hidden tragedies: lives ruined by a rigid approach to drug use. Our aim is to encourage rational debate based on preserving fundamental human rights and dignities in the context of modern sports culture.

ACRONYMS AND ABBREVIATIONS

AAF	adverse analytic finding
ADAMS	Anti-Doping Administration Management System
ADHD	attention deficit hyperactivity disorder
ADRV	anti-doping rule violation
AEPSAD	National Anti-Doping Organization of Spain (Agencia Española de Protección de la Salud en el Deporte)
AIGCP	International Association of Professional Cycling Groups (Association International des Groupes Cyclistes Professionels)
BALCO	Bay Area Laboratory Co-operative
BOA	British Olympic Association
CAS	Court of Arbitration for Sport
CCES	Canadian Centre for Ethics in Sport
CONADE	National Physical Culture and Sports Commission (Mexico) (Comisión Nacional de Cultura Física y Deporte)
CPA	Association of Professional Cyclists (Cyclistes Professionels Associés)
DCO	drug control officer
DHEA	dehydroepiandrosterone
EPO	erythropoietin
FBI	Federal Bureau of Investigation
FIFA	International Association Football Association (Fédération Internationale de Football Association)
Global DRO	Global Drug Reference Online
IAAF	International Association of Athletics Federations (until 2001 International Amateur Athletic Federation)
IF	international federation
iNADO	Institute of National Anti-Doping Organisations

IOC	International Olympic Committee
JADCO	Jamaica Anti-Doping Commission
NADO	national anti-doping agency
NBA	National Basketball Association (USA)
NFL	National Football League (USA)
NGB	national governing body
NHL	National Hockey League (USA)
PAG	Pan-Arab Games
RADO	regional anti-doping organisation
RUSADA	Russian Anti-Doping Agency
TUE	therapeutic use exemption
UCI	International Cycling Union (Union Cycliste Internationale)
UKA	UK Athletics
UKAD	United Kingdom Anti-Doping
UNESCO	United Nations Educational, Scientific and Cultural Organization
USADA	United States Anti-Doping Agency
USATF	USA Track & Field
WADA	World Anti-Doping Agency
WADC	World Anti-Doping Code
WCA	World Championships in Athletics
WCF	World Curling Federation

1

THE INADVERTENT CONSEQUENCES OF ANTI-DOPING

Few would disagree that equality, fair play, and the protection of health are sporting ideals worth protecting and this is what the world anti-doping campaign has been and still is working to achieve. So, unsurprisingly the establishment of the World Anti-Doping Agency (WADA) in 1999 was lauded and supported. The revelation of extensive use of medical products for performance enhancing purposes at the Tour de France in 1998 and the bad press that followed made the sporting community realise that something needed to be done to oppose it. The consensus around WADA brought the world together with a view to end an unhealthy and corrupt sporting practice and to restore the positive image of sport. But over the course of time it has become evident that the mission was impossible.

This is not the same as saying that what WADA has achieved within twenty years is unimpressive. The negotiation of the World Anti-Doping Code (WADC), that has been signed by 139 governments and around 550 international sports federations, is a remarkable accomplishment. And so is the institutional setup. WADA registers 124 national anti-doping agencies that are responsible for testing and code compliance in their respective countries. However, a decentralised system faces problems in ensuring harmonisation and that all athletes are treated in the same way. It has been argued that the nature of anti-doping testing means that the prerequisite for fair and equal conditions is not in place (Hanstad *et al.* 2010). Some countries have more resources and a better infrastructure to set up an effective surveillance system than others. Some have built highly efficient bureaucratic systems whereas others have slow and ineffective bureaucracies. It is also a cause for concern that some have bribery as an integral part of how their economy works, which creates a higher risk the doping control officers could be bribed. Thus, another type of inequality emerges as countries with little corruption tend to play by the rules.

The fact that the rules are not implemented to the same standard and speed in all countries is unsurprising given the different governmental traditions, economic resources, and levels of bureaucratic organisation. But this is something that could be levelled out by WADA via funding, counselling, and harmonisation work. If lack of harmonisation were the only challenge the situation would be solvable. However, there are more problems that are direct consequences of the anti-doping campaign which increase as the campaign intensifies. These adverse effects of anti-doping cannot be easily remedied by the system, as they are logical consequences of the system, as this chapter will show. The more intensive anti-doping becomes the more its bureaucracy loses the sense of the purposes of fairness and health. Perhaps it is for these reasons that the inadvertent consequences are neglected; indeed, that athletes who fall victim to the inequities of the system can find themselves blamed for their inability to 'follow the rules'.

Dopers are evil but hopefully not *that* evil

It is often claimed by anti-doping authorities that it has become harder for the cheats to beat the system. In spite of that some athletes have continued to dope if positive tests can be taken as reliable indications. In 2016, ten athletes tested positive for the synthetic anabolic steroid clostebol. That number was three times higher than the previous year and also higher than in 2013 when six athletes were banned for using the substance (Bergan 2017). And if cases of clostebol use are not enough evidence of elite level athletes' continuation of intentional doping , the Portuguese cyclist André Cardoso's erythropoietin (EPO) positive test on 18 June 2017 while he was preparing for the Tour de France should suffice (MacLeary 2017). Apparently, athletes' win-at-all-costs mentality makes some of them accept the increased risk of being caught. Naturally, they do what they can to avoid detection, but they are not deterred from doping. They, and their support personnel, are commonly presented as unscrupulous people who are not the least concerned about the level playing field and the harm it does to their sport in case they get caught. This was exemplified when WADA Director General David Howman, in the wake of the Lance Armstrong case, explained why the standard ban for first-time doping offences was increased from two to four years in 2013:

> We have got a budget of not even the salary Wayne Rooney earns at Manchester United. I think what you have to do is say, 'Right, how do you make the bucks you have go as far as they possibly can to get rid of those rotten apples?'
>
> *(MacMichael 2013)*

The comparison between a single professional football player and WADA's entire budget is also an indication that Howman concedes that anti-doping has little effect due to sparse resources. Even if we can assume that they had enough money to create a system so efficient that even the most nefarious athletes were deterred from using drugs, would that mean the fight against doping would finally be won? Would the rights of clean athletes to participate in doping free sport be guaranteed, and the level playing field restored? Most probably not.

The win-at-all-cost mentality might instead make the most unprincipled athletes find ways to make the anti-doping system work in their favour. If doping was no longer a viable way to get the desired edge, their evil minds could lead them to organise ways to get their fiercest rivals to fall into the anti-doping trap. As the testing system becomes more effective the easier it would become to get athletes trapped. But anti-doping policy leaders have to stop short of entertaining that line of thinking. Athletes such as Lance Armstrong, Marion Jones, Ben Johnson, and Michelle Smith may have violated the rules, and therefore been exposed in media as cheats, but if we think of them as unprincipled enough to turn the anti-doping system against their naturally superior clean rivals, the belief in the fairness of the anti-doping system would be undermined. So, we may think of athletes as evil but anti-doping leaders cannot allow themselves to think of doping athletes and their entourage as *that* evil.

Nonetheless it is not a new idea that such fraudulent behaviour can take place in sport. The five-times Tour de France winner Belgian cyclist Eddy Merckx, who failed a doping test in Savona during the Tour of Italy in 1969, claimed that his doping positive test was a result of sabotage:

> In more than one interview since his retirement, he has blamed but refused to name a particular individual who, Merckx has said, 'bows his head when I see him'. 'I know what happened. I know who spiked my water bottle' he told the journalist Gianpaolo Ormezzano in 1982.
>
> *(Freibe 2012 p. 309)*

It is not only cyclists who have claimed to be victims of sabotage. On a very hot day at the FIFA World Cup in Italy 1990 Argentina beat Brazil in the round of 16. During an injury break Branco, one of Brazil's best players, was handed a water bottle by Argentina's physiotherapist Miguel di Lorenzo. After the game Branco complained he felt dizzy and ill after drinking from the bottle, sparking speculation that the water had been spiked. The incident was at the time interpreted as a colourful conspiracy theory in the endless rivalry between the two dominant football powers of South America. However, in 2005, the story resurfaced after Diego Maradona had referred to the incident in a TV interview and jokingly claimed that he had encouraged the Brazilians to drink from the bottle. When subsequently Carlos Bilardo, then Argentina coach, was asked about the story he replied: 'I'm not saying it didn't happen' (Bellos 2005). The person at the centre of the controversy, di Lorenzo, has denied the story claiming it was nothing but made up lies. It is impossible to know who is telling the truth. But imagine if anti-doping reached a point where the testing programme is of such high quality that WADA can rightfully boast it is virtually impossible for dopers to go undetected and top-level athletes continue to fail tests occasionally. We are so familiar with athletes who plead innocence and explain positive results as a consequence of contamination of various kind. The current situation is that doping testing is so poor that it seems fairly accurate of Howman to say: 'We are catching the dopey dopers but not the sophisticated ones' (Cyclingnews 2011). Thus, it is easy to dismiss high-profile athletes' explanations after they fail a test as unreliable. But if the system became virtually unbeatable and athletes still got caught it would be harder to rebuff pleas of innocence because in that scenario it would be irrational to dope. Of course, it could still be argued that even athletes who have not doped on purpose have been negligent and hence responsible. But how far does this argument go? Athletes go to restaurants and cafés where food or drinks can be spiked.

When in 2015 the 46-year-old British amateur cyclist Robin Townsend, tested positive for the stimulant modafinil, he maintained that his drink was spiked by a rival. During his hearing Townsend presented a threatening text the person suspected of the spike had sent to his partner. He further explained that the person he suspected had been aggressive and invited him to a fight in a car park. Nevertheless, Townsend was given a four-year ban from participating in all sports. After the verdict UK Anti-Doping's (UKAD) Director of Legal, Graham Arthur, explained:

> Under the World Anti-Doping Code all athletes, whether amateur or professional, must follow the principle of "Strict Liability". They are solely responsible for any banned substance which is found in their system, whether or not there is an intention to cheat.
>
> *(Cary 2016)*

Athletes could be advised not to eat in restaurants or other places where they have no control of who prepares the food to avoid the risk of malicious food tampering. This, however, does not protect athletes from being unknowingly doped by people they trust. It is almost impossible for athletes to protect themselves from people close to them. An unprincipled sport manager, for instance, could easily spike a water bottle to get rid of an expensive athlete who does not live up to expectations.

When Luxembourgish cyclist Fränk Schleck tested positive for the diuretic xipamide during the Tour de France 2012 he claimed he was victim of sabotage. He said:

> The medical world states that this product, when performing in extreme conditions such as in a cycling tour, is very dangerous; it can even cause death. Therefore I really need to find the cause that clarifies how this product ended up in my system: since I didn't take anything, I assume it must have been given to me by someone.
>
> *(Cyclingnews 2012)*

Unfortunately, the reputation cyclists now have for denying all doping, even when they were doing so, means that their credibility is low. Sports leaders and the public often assume an 'excuse' for doping is simply a cover-up. However, that should make us more concerned. If we do not believe any doping excuse then sabotage becomes much easier.

Interestingly, the deputy director of the WADA-approved laboratory in Cologne, Hans Geyer, prepared a report in relation to the Schleck case in which he concluded that: 'it cannot be excluded that an effective dose of xipamide has been administered for manipulation purposes between the 6th and the 14th of July'. Geyer substantiated this assessment by explaining three effects of the banned product that makes it irrational to use the product during the race: first 'the application of a diuretic at a stage race leads to a decline in performance'; second 'during the Tour de France many doping controls can be expected, where diuretics can be detected'; and third 'the use of diuretics for weight loss reasons makes no sense during a stage race' (Cyclingnews 2013). In light of this it is understandable that Schleck was given only half the then maximum sanction of two years. Still, if he was indeed a victim of a spiked water bottle, losing one year of his career, losing his contract, and having his reputation tarnished for good is a harsh fate. The only way athletes can be protected against this risk is to offer them the same legal protection as in the court of law and change the burden of proof. But removing the strict liability rule would spell the end of anti-doping, so that is unlikely to happen. Hence athletes have to live with the risk of being framed. That is, even in the unimaginable situation that anti-doping became 100 per cent efficient in catching those who cheat, justice and fairness for the athletes would still not be guaranteed. The fact that the system can be abused by unscrupulous individuals is a grave inadvertent consequence that has been largely overlooked in the anti-doping debate and never taken into account by the anti-doping system.

A clear case of sabotage occurred in September 2017. Japanese canoeist Yasuhiro Suzuki admitted to spiking the drink of his rival, Seiji Komatsu, with a muscle-building supplement containing the banned steroid methandienone, during the national championships. The perpetrator was banned for eight years (*Japan Times* 2018).

Doping doctors in demand

Another inadvertent effect of anti-doping is that as testing methods improve, and it gets harder to beat the system, experts able to provide effective and undetectable doping programmes will see their market value increase. We saw the first unambiguous example of this in 2006, in the wake of Spanish civil guard's criminal investigation into a Spanish doping network that led to the exposure of a doping clinic in Madrid run by Dr Eufemiano Fuentes (Hardie 2011). This action, known as Operación Puerto, revealed that elite athletes from different countries and different sports were clients of Fuentes.

More than 150 different code names were found on many more blood bags in the clinic.

Hitherto only the cyclists involved have been named. During the court case against Fuentes, which took place in Madrid in 2013, judge Julia Patricia Santamaria ordered that 211 blood bags related to 35 unidentified athletes be destroyed (ESPN 2013). And even though this order was repealed in 2016 by the appeal court, which also overturned Fuentes' suspended one-year prison sentence and €4,500 fine for endangering public health, no athletes outside cycling have yet been exposed (Tremlett 2016). Nevertheless, the names revealed are sufficient to demonstrate the point that doctors who are able to work around the doping controls – in the case of Fuentes by facilitating autologous blood doping – are attracting top athletes whether or not the same doctor is also treating their fiercest rivals. Thus, the two favourites to win the Tour de France 2006 after Lance Armstrong's retirement, Jan Ullrich and Ivan Basso, riding for Team T-Mobile and Team CSC respectively, were both precluded from the race due to their connections to Fuentes.

One could be forgiven for believing that the riders were unaware that rivals from other teams were consulting the same doctor for the same purpose, but this is unlikely. As a consequence of the short-term contracts in cycling riders often move from one team to another and bring experience gathered in their former teams with them. Tyler Hamilton, for instance, describes in his autobiography *The Secret Race* that during his time at Team CSC his then sports director Bjarne Riis introduced him to Fuentes (Hamilton and Coyle 2012). So, when Hamilton decided to accept an offer from Team Phonak, it could come as no surprise to him that Ivan Basso, his successor as team captain of CSC was introduced to the same facility in Madrid that Hamilton continued to use after he ended his collaboration with Riis.

Fuentes' diverse clientele of athletes was not unique. Danish cyclist Michael Rasmussen – perhaps best known for his dramatic removal from the Tour de France in a winning position in 2007 for having misled the anti-doping authorities by providing incorrect whereabouts information – reveals in his 2013 autobiography *Gulfeber* (*Yellow Fever*) a similar arrangement in Austria run by the private company HumanPlasma. After his impressive performance in the Tour de France 2005, where he won the king of the mountains jersey, his position within the Dutch-based team Rabobank was improved. As a consequence, he was introduced to Rabobank's arrangement with HumanPlasma. Rasmussen reveals that he got a phone number to the Austrian clinic from his Dutch team captain Michael Boogerd, who in turn had learned about this facility at the Olympic games in Athens in a conversation about various doping practices with Dutch middle-distance runner Simon Vroeman. HumanPlasma, run by Dr Paul Hoecker, was also aiding athletes with blood doping. The athletes paid €1,800 per visit which covered blood extraction and storage. When Rasmussen first visited the clinic accompanied by Boogerd, they were collected at the airport by Walter Mayer a former cross-country skier who was now coaching the Austrian cross-country and biathlon national team. During the same visit he also met Vroeman and other athletes (Rasmussen 2013). Rasmussen's description bears witness to the attraction of competent doping doctors and the word-of-mouth spread of information among top-level athletes about who to go to for qualified assistance.

The 2002 revelation about the California-based sport nutrition company Bay Area Laboratory Co-operative (BALCO), founded by Victor Conte, shows that such doping operations were not exclusively a European phenomenon. Behind the scenes Conte ran a doping programme and was, among other things, involved in the invention of the synthetic steroid tetrahydrogestrinone (THG). Among those who benefitted from Conte's services were a number of famous athletes from various sports including American football player Bill Romanowski, track and field sprinters Marion Jones, Tim Montgomery, Kelli White and Dwain Chambers, boxer Shane Mosley, and baseball player Barry Bonds (CNN 2016).

These three examples refer to doping providers who were all found out, but it is hard to believe there are no other experts in the market who know how to give athletes a competitive edge with minimal risk of being found out. The improved anti-doping effort with added emphasis on intelligence may have resulted in greater vigilance among doping doctors. In all likelihood, they will have learned that it is too risky to have many customers and consequently limit their clientele to a trusted few who are willing and able to pay more for cutting-edge doping programmes. If this is true, anti-doping has worked to the opposite effect of what it was established to achieve. It is often argued that doping makes the playing field uneven; that it should not be possible to take medical shortcuts to victory; and that sport should not be a competition between medical doctors by proxy. In pre-WADA times doping was not so stigmatised, relatively easily accessible, the role as provider of doping expertise was basically risk-free. But the riskier it gets to provide doping services, the fewer will run the risk. As a result, it becomes harder to get expert assistance. So, paradoxically, those athletes who still dare to dope, and have the economic resources and personality to establish a trusting relationship with doping experts, will have a much higher chance of success than they would have had in pre-WADA times.

The increasing risk of punishing innocent athletes

A major challenge for the fight against doping is the advances in medical science. New products with potentially performance-enhancing effects are regularly introduced. New improved generations of older well-known drugs may suddenly be harder to detect. In addition to this, doping experts will search for ways to beat the test by combining different drugs or administer drugs in unexpected ways. An example of this was when subcutaneous EPO injections were replaced by intravenous injections. This significantly reduced the time the hormone could be detected with available tests. When blood profiling was introduced as an indirect way to reveal blood manipulation, micro-dosing was invented so the athlete's blood profiles did not change sufficiently to be flagged by the biological passport (Ashenden *et al.* 2011).

If anti-doping aims to be potent it is obvious that the efficacy of testing must constantly improve. Not only must anti-doping authorities work to ensure there is a reliable test for all the banned substances on the ever-growing Prohibited List, they must also work towards increased sensitivity of the test in order to minimise athletes' chances of evading the testing system. However, the adverse effect of the expansion of drugs tested for and improvements of the tests' sensitivity is that athletes who have never taken a banned substance and never been negligent in a reasonable sense of this word, will have an increasing risk of falling victim of a false positive (Pitsch 2011).

An equally unfortunate consequence relates to the introduction of the biological passport. It is clear that those who are doping will monitor their blood values more closely than those who do not dope. Consequently, non-dopers' risk of being caught, because they are unaware that their blood values, for whatever reason, have turned suspicious, are higher than the dopers' risk. Speed skater Claudia Pechstein's two-year suspension in 2009 is a disturbing example.

Pechstein, who has five Olympic gold medals to her name, never tested positive but the International Skating Union's (ISU) introduction of the blood profile monitoring system proved fatal for her. From February 2000 to April 2009 she submitted blood samples for the programme. Despite her record of negative doping tests blood experts found her blood profile atypical. This, together with her outstanding performances, raised suspicion about blood manipulation. According to the ISU, 0.4–2.4 per cent reticulocytes are considered the normal range. Reticulocytes are immature red blood cells not yet ready to carry oxygen. The hormone EPO stimulates the bone marrow to produce red blood cells which enter the blood stream in immature form. Injections of EPO will boost the production of reticulocytes and, on the day before the beginning of the ISU World Championship, her reticulocyte count was at 3.54 per cent. This was significantly above the normal range so they required a second test later that same day which showed a slight decline to 3.38 per cent in reticulocytes. Yet, this was also outside the normal range so after experts reviewed her blood profile, and the medical advisor Harm Kuipers had been consulted, the German Speed Skating organisation decided to withdraw Pechstein from the Championship despite her haematocrit level being below the 'no-start' threshold. A week later she was tested again and this time her reticulocytes count was only 1.37 per cent almost three times lower than the previous tests. The fluctuations identified in her blood profile were above the 95 per cent probability threshold that ISU had established in their biological passport programme. Hence, ISU filed a case against Pechstein with the ISU Disciplinary Commission who handed her a two-year suspension (CAS 2009). Pechstein appealed the case to the Court of Arbitration for Sport (CAS) on the grounds that the ISU's biological passport model was inconsistent with the

Biological Passport Guidelines drafted by WADA, which proposed a 99.9 per cent probability in order to minimise the risk that innocent athletes were being punished. Had Pechstein's profile been evaluated in accordance with the WADA guidelines which were finalised only a week after CAS published its verdict, she would have been safe. However, because the WADA guidelines had not yet taken effect CAS upheld the two-year suspension. The arbitration panel seemed unconcerned that the statistical likelihood of potentially sanctioning an innocent athlete under the ISU model is as high as 1 to 20 whereas WADA's threshold reduces that to 1 in 1000. And it should be noted that WADA, who pride themselves of protecting the clean athletes, did not do anything to defend Pechstein, although the agency's guidelines indicate that they considered the ISU's 95 per cent probability indefensible.

The problem of innocent convictions is perhaps even bigger in relation to the ability to detect banned substances. The Spanish cyclist Alberto Contador's positive test for clenbuterol in 2010 illustrates this problem. When, in September 2010, it was revealed that Contador tested positive for clenbuterol during the Tour de France two months earlier, he maintained his innocence. The minuscule amount of clenbuterol found in Contador's urine was as low as 50 picograms. This was 40 times below the amount laboratories should be able to detect in order to get WADA accreditation (Birnie 2010). But WADA had no minimum threshold level for clenbuterol. Contador claimed that the positive doping test was a result of eating a contaminated steak.

Contador had tested negative on the 20 July, the day before he provided the sample that proved positive. Clenbuterol is a β_2-agonist that has been found to augment muscle bulk in cattle. In humans it can contribute to increased strength in certain muscle fibre types (Spann and Winter 1995). That is why it is on the Prohibited List. But, since the amount of clenbuterol was so small, there is little chance Contador took it during the race to enhance his performance level. It would make no sense for a cyclist to risk a ban for a small amount of a muscle-building product during a race. But WADA presented an alternative explanation for the occurrence of clenbuterol when lodging an appeal with the CAS against the Spanish Cycling Federation's initial decision to clear Contador of charges. WADA suggested that Contador had used clenbuterol in preparation for the Tour de France and extracted a bag of blood for transfusion in the race while still having traces of the substance in his bloodstream. That is, according to WADA, the positive test was a combined result of pre-race doping and in-race blood doping (Barak et al. 2012). WADA based this speculation on the fact that in the sample provided on 20 July the Cologne lab found traces of plastic residue that might turn up after a blood transfusion. Contador's sample exceeded eight times the normal amount of plasticiser. The arbitrators considered both explanations and found them equally improbable. Hence, they came up with a third possibility, which they found more likely, namely that Contador had eaten a food supplement containing clenbuterol. Thus, based on their own speculation, the arbitrators ruled that Contador had been negligent and banned him for two years. In any case, had the equipment at the Cologne laboratory not been extraordinarily sensitive, Contador would not have faced any charges.

We will probably never get to know for sure how the banned substance got into Contador's body, but the possible explanations are all cause for concern. If the adverse analytical finding was a result of the consumption of a polluted steak Contador cannot fairly be said to have been negligent. Thus, he was a victim of anti-doping. The will to protect clean athletes' right to participate in doping-free sport had backfired, with an innocent athlete being suspended for two years.

If the CAS's explanation is true, it could be fairly argued that Contador had been negligent as it is common knowledge within elite sport that food supplements can contain banned ingredients not mentioned on the product label. If this were indeed the case it is obvious that the producer of the food supplement was to blame for selling an impure product. The producer was directly responsible for the positive test, while Contador was punished, not because he was an intentional doper but because he either was ill-advised or naively trusted a legal company's content declaration. Even if this outcome is necessary for the anti-doping sanction system to not be undermined by positive tests being explained away due to food-supplement contamination, it is still draconian to hand out lengthy bans to athletes for naivety and negligence. This is another adverse effect of anti-doping.

Finally, if the scenario suggested by WADA is what happened, Contador was intentionally doping and deserved punishment. But in that case, it speaks volumes about the ineffectiveness of the testing system because Contador was then exposed for a blunder, namely having blood extracted at a time when his pre-season doping regime was still traceable, whereas his direct in-competition blood doping went undetected. The ineffectiveness also shows in that he, despite being subject to out-of-competition testing supported by a rigid whereabouts reporting system, was able to use clenbuterol in preparation for the Tour without being caught. Whichever scenario is true, Contador's positive test should be compared with other cases in which clenbuterol contamination had led to bans of other innocent athletes.

The Chinese cyclist Li Fuyu is perhaps the most obvious example. Fuyu, the first Chinese rider to race with an elite ProTour team, rode as a domestique in Lance Armstrong's team Radioshack. In spring 2010, he tested positive for clenbuterol after a one-day race in Belgium, where he finished 122nd in the race, nine minutes behind the winner. Li's reaction sounds familiar:

> I have no idea how the clenbuterol came into my body. All I know is that I have never taken doping products in my entire career. My role at team RadioShack was one of a humble helper, nothing more. I am 31 years old and I know I could not move up to a leading role in the team.
>
> *(Lin 2010)*

Despite experts arguing that the dosage found in Li's sample was so small it probably was a case of food contamination, the failed test led to a two-year suspension. Had it not been for the outbreak of a veritable clenbuterol 'epidemic' in China and Mexico in 2010, Li, together with Contador, would probably have been written off as yet another doped athlete who responded to a positive test by feigning innocence. However, the seriousness of the problem was confirmed when a team of athletes returned from competition in China. All athletes were tested within the first two days after their return and every single sample was positive for low amounts of clenbuterol (Guddat *et al.* 2012). Previously, in 2009, scientists working in the Cologne laboratory where Contador's sample was tested had published a paper in which they concluded that with use of the newest superfine instruments clenbuterol could be detected at such low levels that positives could be due to consumption of trace amounts present in meat or even in the water supply (Leicester 2011). In 2010 this study was confirmed when the German youth national football team returned from the FIFA Under-17 World Cup tournament in Mexico and everyone in the squad subjected to routine doping tests was found positive. That the tournament took place in Mexico shows that the problem of contaminated meat is not limited to China. In fact, a total of 109 players representing 19 of the 24 squads involved tested positive during the tournament. In an attempt to find out just how grave the problem was, a follow-up study with people living in China and with tourists staying in China for various lengths of time and in various locations was conducted. Based on current anti-doping regulations, 22 of the 28 volunteers tested positive (Thevis and Schänzer 2014). From an anti-doping perspective, such widespread meat pollution is critical as it basically means that every meat-eating athlete's career in certain countries is at risk.

The same year in which Contador was handed a two-year suspension, Italian rider Alessandro Colo was banned for a year after testing positive for the same substance after a race in Mexico. The reduced sentence was due to the possibility that he was a victim of food contamination. The Danish rider Phillip Nielsen took part in the same race, lived and ate at the same hotel and he also tested positive for clenbuterol. However, the Danish disciplinary committee exonerated Nielsen and in this case WADA did not appeal the decision to CAS.

Despite proof that detection of very small traces of clenbuterol found in doping tests can be a result of food contamination, WADA has not introduced a threshold value for this substance. So, in effect, WADA accepts that innocent athletes may be banned for eating meat.

If the problem was limited to clenbuterol, a threshold might have been a solution. But there are a number of cases where athletes have tested positive after, allegedly, having used a product they thought was safe. The fact that nutritional supplements can be contaminated has been known for quite some time (van der Merwe and Grobbelaar 2005). Hence it can be argued that athletes who use such products should know they are gambling with their careers. But if athletes can go to another country and buy a nasal spray they have used for years as a cold remedy it is no longer negligence in a meaningful use of this word if they end up testing positive because the content in the apparently identical product is not the same as in their home country. Nevertheless, this situation caused the Scottish skier Alain Baxter to test positive in 2002 after he, as the first Briton ever, won a medal in alpine skiing at the Winter Olympics. Despite the chemical he was positive for, levomethamphetamine, was not mentioned on the product and was an isomer of methamphetamine without any stimulating effect, he was required to return his bronze medal.

It is true that Baxter's situation is exceptional, but he is not the only athlete who has tested positive for a drug clearly without intention to dope and without negligence in any meaningful sense of the word and still suffered the consequences of an anti-doping system that prides itself on zero tolerance. Another obvious example is the Danish footballer, Jesper Münsberg who in 2008 tested positive for salbutamol. The then 31-year-old left back, representing Næstved Boldklub in the Danish second division, is an asthmatic. After having played a pre-season friendly anti-doping officers turned up and requested a urine test. Münsberg had a therapeutic use exemption (TUE) to use an inhaler that contained salbutamol, so it was no surprise that he provided a doping positive. The Danish Sports Confederation (DSC) and the Danish Football Federation were both convinced Münsberg had done nothing wrong and decided not to pursue the case. Unfortunately for Münsberg, WADA appealed this decision to CAS because the content found in his sample was 2,460 ng/ml, more than double of the threshold of 1,000 ng/ml WADA has set, based on the assumption that a person cannot exceed this limit from using an inhaler. So they suspected Münsberg of having taken advantage of his TUE to take salbutamol pills for performance-enhancing purposes. In accordance with the strict liability rule it was now up to the player to prove he had not taken salbutamol pills.

As a semi-professional footballer, Münsberg did not have the financial resources to fight WADA, but the DSC and the Danish Football Players' Association decided to support the player and agreed to share the costs related to the case. This included an independent test in Oslo, Norway where Münsberg underwent a three-day-long series of experiments under the supervision of Norwegian WADA representatives. These experiments confirmed that when Münsberg was puffing his inhaler according to the prescription, he surpassed the WADA threshold by nearly one hundred per cent (Wivel 2010). Despite this indisputable falsification of WADA's reason for the 1,000 ng/ml threshold CAS handed the blameless Münsberg a six-month suspension. The case is an unsettling example of an athlete who was punished by the anti-doping system despite having committed no rule violation. The Münsberg case gives reason to assume that the more fine-tuned the doping controls get, the more athletes with a clean conscience will get caught. This case bears similarities to that of Chris Froome, who was found to have exceeded the allowable limit in 2017.

Violation of athletes' privacy

There are a great number of examples of athletes who have benefitted from advanced doping programmes for years before their doping was revealed. When they were finally exposed, leading sports officials have publicly celebrated this as proof that cheating does not pay. Sebastian Coe for instance:

> welcomed the announcement that 23 athletes from the London Olympics have failed drugs tests after their defrosted urine and blood samples were reanalysed, saying it sent out a strong message to all cheats that they will eventually be caught.
>
> *(Ingle 2016)*

The truth of the matter, though, is that the test system's inefficiency in catching organised cheats and not just the 'dopey dopers' is frustrating for those in charge. So, in order to improve the efficacy of the system, the demands upon the athletes have steadily increased.

The sports authorities had realised long ago that in-competition testing was an impotent way to fight doping. By the 1970s some countries introduced out-of-competition testing and in the 1980s it was implemented in the majority of the countries in the developed world (Houlihan 1999). Unannounced testing meant that athletes could no longer feel safe even if they stopped doping early enough in advance of competition to ensure that the drugs had been metabolised and could no longer be traced in their urine. This improvement had its limits, of course. Athletes soon realised the risk of no-notice out-of-competition testing and started to train at secret places while they were gaining strength and stamina by illegal means. This problem was not resolved until the publication of the WADC in 2003, in which WADA obliged some athletes to provide updated information on their whereabouts. WADA explained the necessity of this requirement:

> Unannounced Out-of-Competition Testing is at the core of effective Doping Control. Without accurate Athlete's location information such Testing is inefficient and sometimes impossible.
>
> *(WADA 2003)*

The rationale is impeccable, but the consequence for the athletes is controversial because it involves further restrictions on their privacy. The intrusion into athletes' privacy had already gone far. One thing is to be requested to go to the toilet and produce a urine sample which you subsequently hand to a control officer who waits discreetly at a distance, as was the case when anti-doping originally was introduced. The problem with this procedure is that some athletes took advantage of this considerate approach and used the controllers' respect for their privacy to beat the test. In 1978, for instance, cyclist

Michel Pollentier was accidentally exposed after he had pumped urine from a rubber container (a condom) hidden in his armpit via a hose into the urine bottle (Hamilton 2013). In 1992 German sprinters Katrin Krabbe, Silke Möller and Grit Breuer were found to have provided urine samples during a training session in South Africa that 'bore such similarity it led to the allegation that they had been provided by the same person' (Verroken 1996 p. 25).

Such incidences convinced those in charge of anti-doping that tougher action was needed. Hence, they insisted athletes fully expose their genitals so the controllers can ensure the urine leaves their body and that no device is used to substitute samples. Many athletes feel the extent of exposure required by the policy to be embarrassing. For some it has led to shy bladder syndrome or in clinical terms 'paruresis' which is 'a general state of psychogenic urine retention involving inability to urinate when other people are around' (Elbe and Overbye 2015 p. 329). Psychologist Anne Marie Elbe offers an insight into the gravity of the problem. A 17-year-old German athlete was selected for a random doping test after she had competed in the German championship, but was unable to urinate while the doping control officer looked at her genitals. She hoped that drinking water would persuade her bladder to let go so in the course of three hours she drank more than six litres of water. All she got out of this was increasing pain. The doping controllers could not let her off as it would count as a doping violation, so they kept the girl's ordeal going until she pleaded for a blood test instead which finally persuaded the officers to call off the control (Elbe *et al.* 2012).

Luxembourgian triathlete, Elisabeth May, gives another vivid description how she felt harassed by an enthusiastic doping control officer. Having competed at a World Cup race in Japan she was picked for random doping control. The Japanese officer asked May to lift her shirt up to her neck. Then the officer grabbed her arms and forced them away from her torso without explaining why. After the officer let go, May provided the sample while the officer stood bending over her with her head 30 centimetres away from May's. The experience led May to think that her right as an athlete to participate in fair competition was less important than her right to dignity (Nielsen 2011a). Being a law student she started in vain to inquire about an ethical code for testing. Interviewed about the situation, Jens Evald, then head of Anti-Doping Denmark (ADD) and now a CAS arbitrator explained: 'If you suspect somebody is trying to forge the control you cannot have an ethical rule that dictates a minimum distance of 50 centimetres between controller and athlete' (Nielsen 2011a). The anti-doping crusaders' neglect of athletes' dignity and privacy was further amplified when former WADA vice-president, Brian Mikkelsen was asked, with reference to May's experience, if anti-doping had gone too far. Speaking in the capacity of Danish Minister for Culture, which oversees sport, Mikkelsen emphasised that the current regime is necessary for the credibility of sport:

> Methods develop constantly. If this means that athletes one day have to be body searched with rubber gloves then you may have to do that [...] if

you consider what cheaters have done in previous times it is necessary to have a strict control.

(Nielsen 2011b)

Athletes have complained about anti-doping officials lack of respect for their privacy for many years, but only the Danish cyclist Michael Rasmussen has exposed the full extent of the harassment he suffered. On two occasions, he had control officers ringing his doorbell moments after he had been to the toilet. The rules say that when an athlete has been notified the athlete must remain within direct observation of the doping control officer at all times until the completion of the sample collection procedure. Rasmussen had to accept that a stranger followed him into his kitchen where he was having breakfast. After finishing his porridge and coffee Rasmussen was still unable to urinate. Instead he felt his bowels beginning to work. So he told the officer that he needed a moment in private. The officer could not allow that. He informed Rasmussen that if he insisted on being alone he would have to report a doping rule violation. Rasmussen had to accept the humiliation of allowing the stranger to be present in the toilet while he was defecating. In his autobiography, he offers his sentiment:

> On three occasions I have had to defecate in front of people I did not know. Twice in my own house. It is totally unacceptable conditions and the most degrading thing I have done in my entire life.
>
> *(Rasmussen 2013 p. 320)*

Since this has happened to the same athlete three times, it is unlikely that he is the only one who has had this experience. This reflects an unprecedented harassment of one particular athlete and shows how mortifying this degrading anti-doping request is.

Perhaps the whereabouts system can be accepted as a normal part of athletes' lives to support clean sport, as is often claimed by anti-doping agencies. It is nevertheless worth considering if the whereabouts requirement is justified by the aim. As sports sociologist Ivan Waddington observes, convicted paedophiles and criminals on parole are required to provide less information about their whereabouts to the state authorities than athletes are to the anti-doping authorities (Waddington 2010). The fact that the whereabouts requirement comprises all athletes in the registered testing pool, including those who have not broken the rules – that is 98 per cent according to the official statistics – adds to the privacy concerns which, according to sports philosopher Oskar MacGregor include:

> WADA subjecting affected athletes to a form of forced interrogation in the stipulation that they submit quarterly whereabouts reports to their ADOs; the aggregation of the athletes' whereabouts data with other sources of

information, in order to provide more complete individual athlete doping risk profiles; the potential risk of data insecurity [exposed in 2016 by the hacker group Fancy Bears], breaches of confidence, or even blackmail, in relation to their aggregated whereabouts data; or the public disclosure of whereabouts information entailed by three whereabouts failures within any 18-month period.

(MacGregor 2015 p. 313f)

In addition to the general whereabouts requirement introduced in the first version of the WADC, the updated 2009 version further required the athletes to specify one 60-minute time slot between 6 a.m. and 11 p.m. each day where they would be available and accessible for testing at a specific location. The explanation of the benefit of this demand is worth reflection: 'The 60-minute time slot "anchors" the Athlete to a certain location for a particular day' (WADA 2009).

Being anchored means that the athletes must be at home, in a hotel, at a training facility or any other place of their choosing. But wherever the athletes say they will be they will have to stay put for one hour. If we say an elite sports career is twelve years that means that the athlete if he/she is in the registered testing pool during those years must accept to be 'anchored' for a total of 4,380 hours, equalling 182 full days, which is more than six months. So, the price honest athletes have to pay for their elite sports career is six months of house arrest. And it is waking hours. They do not even get the same rebate as ordinary prison inmates who sleep away a third of the time being served.

The end of winning

The final, and from a sporting point of view, perhaps most significant adverse effect of anti-doping we want to mention relates to Article 6.5 of the WADC which says that a sample may be reanalysed at any time at the request of the anti-doping organisation that collected the sample or WADA. In the International Standard for Testing it was specified that the test sample should be stored for a maximum of eight years (WADA 2009). In the 2015 revision of the Code this was prolonged to a maximum of ten years. Once again, the rationale is immediately clear. Because it takes time to develop reliable and effective drug tests anti-doping laboratories will often be unable to detect new doping products when they first occur. Mandatory storage of samples, so retesting can be done when detection methods for new drugs are in place, addresses the problem because athletes who beat the test while competing will thereby risk being exposed years later.

Prior to the Olympic Games in Rio 2016, the IOC retested 1,243 samples taken at the Beijing 2008 and London 2012 Olympics. According to the IOC these reanalyses resulted in a total of 98 doping positives that went undetected when the samples were originally provided (Wilson 2016). As a consequence some athletes were stripped of their medals, while others got an unexpected medal or an upgrade like the Indian wrestler Yogeshwar Dutt who, four years after he won his bronze medal, got it replaced by one of silver (Selvaraj 2016).

Such retrospective actions give the impression that justice is done. The awareness that samples will be stored in a freezer waiting for new tests to be developed may deter some from doping. However, the deterrence effect is limited, otherwise we would not have seen so many doping incidents. After all, the possibility for retesting was included in the first version of the WADC.

Athletes who finish second and learn up to ten years later that they lost to doped rivals may get some satisfaction out of this and feel justice is done, especially if the promoted athletes were not doping themselves. However, the excitement one gets from being declared winner of a competition years after it took place is probably not so big that it is worth the bother; especially not if we take into account that retesting is no guarantee for justice. Andy Schleck's reaction to the news that he would be crowned the winner of the Tour de France 2010 after Alberto Contador's demotion after the above mentioned clenbuterol incident is striking:

> If now I am declared winner of the 2010 Tour de France it will not make me happy. I battled with Contador in that race and I lost. My goal is to win the Tour de France in a sporting way, being the best of all competitors, not in court. If I succeed this year, I will consider it my first Tour de France victory.
>
> *(Gallagher 2012)*

What matters to athletes are the results of a competition when it takes place. A retrospective desktop victory is joyless. There will be no podium celebration and no national anthem played. And if the doping is uncovered years after it took place, the culprit has probably reaped the economic benefits of his or her sporting success at the expense of the defeated. The positive test will not take any of this away from the victor or compensate the victim. Hence the only proper argument for reanalysing samples is that it delivers sporting justice.

Reanalyses have usually been organised in the lead up to the Olympic Games with athletes potentially participating in the games a primary target. Thus, in May 2016, the IOC announced that retesting of 454 selected doping samples from the 2008 Beijing Olympics had resulted in adverse analytical findings leading to 30 athletes from six sports being banned from competing at the Olympic Games in Rio (IOC 2016). At first it appears right to prevent athletes who were found doping eight years ago from participating in the forthcoming Olympics in order to protect clean athletes, but it rests on the uncertain assumption that their rival athletes were clean. If, say, two weightlifters were competing in Beijing and it was only the winner of the competition who was selected for testing, then only the winner's urine was stored for future reanalysis. The other athlete may have used the same drug and still be able to participate in Rio, with a better chance of success because his or her winning rival had been banned. Or both athletes were originally tested and both had used the same drug but only the medal winners; sample were retested meaning that the other doped athlete could take part in Rio. In this case retesting was not protecting clean athletes but mediocre athletes. Or alternatively they were both originally tested and then retested but they were using different types of drugs. One was using the drug that the reanalysis was targeting, while the other used a drug that was or could not be tested for. In that case retesting benefitted the lucky or more advanced doper rather than the clean athlete. These scenarios go to show that even where the reanalyses of tests is apparently serving the protection of clean athletes, there is no guarantee that this is the outcome in reality. And the overall consequence of anti-doping retesting is devastating because it puts an end to the very *raison d'être* of sport.

The most common question put to people who return from the stadium or have just seen the Olympic final of the women's 100-metre sprint is: 'Who won?' Every sporting competition is designed to single out a winner. The podium, medals, champagne, and fireworks are all testament to that. Retesting makes all this provisional. Spectators who witness a person cross the finish line first will not know if they have won. They will not have certainty of the outcome the next day, week, or month. They may have forgotten all about the competition and the athletes involved may even be retired when the news breaks that a winner they vaguely recall was doping and a runner-up whose name they have forgotten is declared the rightful winner. Equally as important, they will not know if he or she was indeed a rightful winner. The only thing they will know for sure is that the revised result list will stand if the competition took place ten years, or longer, ago. Live sport is reduced to meaningless spectacles.

In Chapter 2, we will describe how this came about.

References

Ashenden, M., C. E. Gough, A. Garnham, C. J. Gore and K. Sharpe (2011). "Current markers of the Athlete Blood Passport do not flag microdose EPO doping". *European Journal of Applied Physiology* 111(9): 2307–2314.

Barak, E., Q. Byrne-Sutton and U. Hass (2012). UCI v. Alberto Contador Velasco and RFEC; WADA v. Alberto Contador Velasco and RFEC. CAS 2011/A/2384, CAS 2011/A/2386 C. o. A. f. Sport. Lausanne: Court of Arbitration for Sport.

Bellos, A. (2005). "Brazil revive drug row after 15 years". *The Guardian* 21 January. Retrieved 2 January 2018 from https://www.theguardian.com/football/2005/jan/21/newsstory.sport5

Bergan, A. E. (2017). "More athletes used clostebol in 2016 than before". Retrieved 26 June 2017 from https://antidopingworld.wordpress.com/2017/05/24/more-athletes-used-clostebol-in-2016-than-before/

Birnie, L. (2010). "Alberto Contador, the clenbuterol, the beef excuse and the traces of plastic." *Cycling Weekly*, October 5. Retrieved 15 August 2016 from http://www.cyclingweekly.co.uk/news/latest-news/alberto-contador-the-clenbuterol-the-beef-excuse-and-the-traces-of-plastic-56988

Cary, T. (2016). "UK amateur cyclist Robin Townsend handed four-year ban by UK Anti-Doping after testing positive for modafinil". *The Telegraph* 21 January. Retrieved

2 January 2018 from http://www.telegraph.co.uk/sport/othersports/cycling/12112458/ UK-amateur-cyclist-Robin-Townsend-handed-four-year-ban-by-UK-Anti-Doping-after-testing-positive-for-modafinil.html

CAS (2009). CAS 2009/A/2012 Claudia Pechstein v. International Skating Union. Court of Arbitration for Sport. Lausanne: Court of Arbitration for Sport.

CNN (2016). "BALCO fast facts". 17 April. Retrieved 15 August 2016, from http://edition.cnn.com/2013/10/31/us/balco-fast-facts/

Cyclingnews (2011). "Howman: Reform needed in anti-doping fight". Retrieved 3 February 2016 from http://www.cyclingnews.com/news/howman-reform-needed-in-anti-doping-fight/

Cyclingnews (2012). "Fränk Schleck doping positive confirmed". Retrieved 20 June 2016 from http://www.cyclingnews.com/news/frank-schleck-doping-positive-confirmed/

Cyclingnews (2013). "Schleck doping use of Xipamid unlikely, expert says". Retrieved 20 June 2016 from http://www.cyclingnews.com/news/schleck-doping-use-of-xipamid-unlikely-expert-says/

Elbe, A. M. and M. Overbye (2015). "Implications of anti-doping regulations for athletes' well-being". In V. Møller, I. Waddington and J. Hoberman (eds), *Routledge Handbook of Drugs and Sport* (pp. 322–336). London: Routledge.

Elbe, A. M., M. M. Schlegel and R. Brand (2012). "Psychogenic urine retention during doping controls: Consequences for elite athletes". *Performance Enhancement & Health* 1: 66–74.

ESPN (2013). "Fuentes sentenced as Puerto case closed". 30 April. Retrieved 3 August 2016 from http://en.espn.co.uk/cycling/sport/story/204973.html

Freibe, D. (2012). *Eddy Merckx: The Cannibal*. London: Random House.

Gallagher, B. (2012). "Andy Schleck expresses sadness for Alberto Contador as he prepares to be crowned 2010 Tour de France winner". *The Telegraph*, 6 February. Retrieved 20 September 2016 from http://www.telegraph.co.uk/sport/othersports/cycling/9065201/Andy-Schleck-expresses-sadness-for-Alberto-Contador-as-he-prepares-to-be-crowned-2010-Tour-de-France-winner.html

Guddat, S., G. Fußhöller, H. Geyr, A. Thomas, H. Braun, N. Haenelt, A. Schwenke, M. Klose, M. Thevis and W. Schänzer (2012). "Clenbuterol – regional food contamination a possible source for inadvertent doping in sports". *Drug Testing and Analysis* 4: 534–538.

Hamilton, R. (2013). *Le Tour de France: The Greatest Race in Cycling History*. Chichester: Summersdale Publishers.

Hamilton, T. and D. Coyle (2012). *The Secret Race: Inside the Hidden World of the Tour de France: Doping, Cover-ups, and Winning at all Cost*. New York: Bantam.

Hanstad, D. V., E. Å. Skille and S. Loland (2010). "Harmonization of anti-doping work: myth or reality?" *Sport in Society* 13(3): 418–430.

Hardie, M. (2011). "It's not about the blood! *Operación Puerto* and the end of modernity". In M. McNamee and V. Møller (eds), *Doping and Anti-Doping Policy in Sport: Ethical, Legal and Social Perspectives* (pp. 160–182). London: Routledge.

Houlihan, B. (1999). *Dying To Win: Doping in Sport and the Development of Anti-doping Policy*. Strasbourg: Council of Europe Publishing.

Ingle, S. (2016). "Olympics: 23 athletes caught out after London 2012 drug retests". *The Guardian* 18 September. Retrieved 2 January 2018 from https://www.theguardian.com/sport/2016/may/27/olympics-23-athletes-caught-out-london-2012-drug-retests

Japan Times (2018) "One of Japan's top sprint canoeists banned for spiking rival's drink to cause positive drug test", 9 January. Retrieved 12 Janury 2018 from https://www.japantimes.co.jp/news/2018/01/09/national/one-japans-top-sprint-canoeists-banned-spiking-rivals-drink-cause-positive-drug-test/

IOC (2016). "The IOC takes decisive action to protect the clean athletes – doped athletes from Beijing, London and Sochi all targeted". Retrieved 20 September 2016 from https://www.olympic.org/news/the-ioc-takes-decisive-action-to-protect-the-clean-athletes-doped-athletes-from-beijing-london-and-sochi-all-targeted

Leicester, J. (2011). "Bad food can harm innocent athletes". Retrieved 16 August 2016 from http://www.stuff.co.nz/sport/other-sports/4578193/Bad-food-can-harm-innocent-athletes

Lin, R. (2010). "China: Li Fuyu claims innocence – experts agree." Retrieved 16 December 2017 from http://archive.is/xdvP

MacGregor, O. (2015). "WADA's whereabouts requirements and privacy". In V. Møller, I. Waddington and J. Hoberman (eds), *Routledge Handbook of Drugs and Sport* (pp. 310-321). London: Routledge.

MacLeary (2017). "Andre Cardoso suspended by his Trek-Segafredo team after testing positive for EPO ahead of making Tour de France debut in support of Alberto Contador" *The Telegraph* 27 June. Retrieved 2 January 2018 from http://www.telegraph.co.uk/cycling/2017/06/27/tour-de-france-rider-andre-cardoso-suspended-trek-segafredo/

MacMichael, S. (2013). "WADA to vote next week on doubling doping bans to 4 years". Retrieved 3 February 2016 from http://road.cc/content/news/98525-wada-vote-next-week-doubling-doping-bans-4-years

Nielsen, M. K. (2011a). "Triatlet blev nøgenchikaneret i Japan" ["Triathlete was naked harassed in Japan"]. Retrieved 15 September 2016 from http://www.bt.dk/oevrig-sport/triatlet-blev-noegenchikaneret-i-japan

Nielsen, M. K. (2011b). "Slut med nøgen-chikane ved dopingtest" ["The end of naked harassment at doping tests"]. Retrieved 15 September 2016 from http://www.bt.dk/oevrig-sport/slut-med-noegen-chikane-ved-dopingtest

Pitsch, W. (2011). "Caught between mathematics and ethics: some implications of imperfect doping test procedures". In M. McNamee and V. Møller (eds), *Doping and Anti-Doping Policy in Sport* (pp. 66–83). London: Routledge.

Rasmussen, M. (2013). *Gul feber*. Copenhagen: People's Press.

Selvaraj, J. (2016). "How medals change metals: Why athletes are retested for doping". *Indian Express*, 1 September. Retrieved 20 September 2016 from http://indianexpress.com/article/sports/sport-others/yogeshwar-dutt-bronze-medal-to-silve-2012-london-olympics-r-besik-kudukhov-dope-test-3006842/

Spann, C. and M. E. Winter (1995). "Effect of clenbuterol on athletic performance". *Annals of Pharmacotheraphy* 29(1): 75–77.

Thevis, M. and W. Schänzer (2014). "Clenbuterol testing in doping control samples: drug abuse or food contamination? " *Lab&More* 1: 20–23. Retrieved 2 January 2018 from http://www.int.laborundmore.com/archive/884010/Clenbuterol-testing-in-doping-control-samples%3A-drug-abuse-or-food-contamination%3F.html

Tremlett, G. (2016). "Operation Puerto blood bags must be released to authorities, judge orders". *The Guardian*, 14 June. Retrieved 2 January 2018 from https://www.theguardian.com/sport/2016/jun/14/operation-puerto-blood-bags-must-be-released-judge-madrid

van der Merwe, P. J. and E. Grobbelaar (2005). "Unintentional doping through the use of contaminated nutritional supplements". *South Africa Medical Journal* 95: 510–511.

Verroken, M. (1996). "Drug use and abuse in sport". In D. R. Mottram (ed.), *Drugs in Sport* (pp. 18–55). London: E & FN Spon.

WADA (2003). *World Anti-Doping Code*. Retrieved 20 August 2007 from https://www.wada-ama.org/sites/default/files/resources/files/wada_code_2003_en.pdf

WADA (2009). *World Anti-Doping Code: International Standard for Testing*. Retrieved 21 August 2010 from https://www.wada-ama.org/en/resources/world-anti-doping-program/international-standard-for-testing-and-investigations-isti-0

Waddington, I. (2010). "Surveillance and control in sport: a sociolgist looks at the WADA whereabouts system". *International Journal of Sport Policy and Politics* 2: 255–274.

Wilson, S. (2016). "45 more athletes test positive for doping in retests of 2008, 2012 Olympic samples". Retrieved 20 August 2016 from http://globalnews.ca/news/2841250/45-more-athletes-test-positive-for-doping-in-retests-of-2008-2012-samples/

Wivel, K. (2010). "CAS-seret". *Weekendavisen*, 7 May.

2

ORIGINS AND EMERGENCE OF THE ANTI-DOPING CRISIS

There is no single point of origin for anti-doping policy or ideas. The latest research in the field of sports history points us to the late nineteenth century, when American and British newspapers reported comments that stimulant use might be regarded as a form of cheating. We do not know if these comments are representative of broader schools of thought, or were being reported due to their unusual challenge to social acceptance of drugs. However, those early debates indicate growing awareness of the benefits and unknown harms of drugs. There was very little governmental policy on social drugs at this time: individuals had more freedom of choice and opportunity to experiment. Stimulants were treated as potentially useful for combating fatigue, in the body and mind (Bell *et al.* 2012), and thus had some social cachet. It was not until the 1920s that regulation appeared in Europe and North America.

Early attitudes of some sports leaders towards drug use appears to have been influenced by the use of drugs in animal sports, especially horse racing (Gleaves and Llewellyn 2014). That would account for the terminology used as the word dope usually refers to something slow or stupid: if a horse was doped it would slow down and thus lose a race. Organised betting rings predicted outcomes based on insider knowledge of which horse had been doped. There is an obvious rationale to stopping such underhand deception as it makes the event predictable and gives an unfair financial advantage to punters and bookies in the know. Moreover, the fact that it was associated with organised criminals lent an air of corruption to the very word doping.

It is far from clear how, where, when and why the word dope was transferred to human sport when the purpose of drug use was the opposite: to boost performance and triumph over a non-drug using rival. Many early debates use the words 'stimulants' or 'tonic', but by the mid-twentieth century doping and anti-doping were the official and populist lexicon of drug use and regulation. Not only was the most salient word somewhat amorphous, it would become something of a challenge to define what was meant by doping (Gleaves 2015b). The first list of banned substances was published in the late 1960s and expanded rapidly through the subsequent decades, and the commonly used words were increasingly incapable of summarising the huge variety of drugs, methods and techniques used to enhance performance. In fact, by the 2000s, WADA had no specific definition but instead determined eight forms of doping, later to become ten, that included trafficking and assisting someone else to dope. It might be the case that a strict definition would have constrained anti-doping efforts, as policy organisations demanded the flexibility to put new substances and methods on the list. Yet, it remains remarkable that a global policy lacks a foundational definition and thus a clearer vision of its purpose.

The use of stimulants by athletes was the reason for public controversies at the 1904 and 1908 Olympics marathons, with the latter providing the first written statement that athletes were forbidden to use drugs during the race. This did not prevent the Italian Dorando Pietri from doing so, even though he was not punished for this apparent transgression (Dimeo 2007). We do not know how common it was at this time to use stimulants like strychnine and cocaine; the evidence has not yet been produced to draw any substantive conclusions. We can see though that some medical experts working within sport saw no problem with drug use. When Thomas Hicks used strychnine in the 1904 Olympic marathon, Charles Lucas wrote for the official IOC report on the Games to say that drugs were of much benefit to athletes (Lucas 1905).

By the 1920s there appears to be competing strands of interest in doping. Scientists conducted experiments on a range of drugs, vitamins and procedures such as ultra-violet light to see what might reduce fatigue and improve performance (Hoberman 1992). This was not just about sport, the research using athletes as subjects for experiments was often contextualised with reference to the benefits of reducing fatigue in the workplace and for the military (Dimeo 2007). These interests also coincided with the progress of the pharmaceutical industry in relation to both infrastructure and commercial opportunity (Chandler 2009). On the other hand, sports administrators were expressing their concerns that these developments were not welcome; somehow sport ought to be protected from what Conrad (2007) called the medicalisation of everyday life. It might be the case the ideology of amateur sports culture mitigated against drug use. The fact that the International Association of Athletics Federations (IAAF) (which at this time was called the International Amateur Athletics Association) outlined a rule against doping in 1928, followed by the International Olympic Committee (IOC) in 1936, suggests that it was the leaders of organisations with only amateur members that took offence to such unnatural interventions in the preparation for competitions. The vagueness in definition was evident, with the IAAF proposing that the use of drugs or artificial stimulants of any kind should be condemned (Gleaves 2015b).

The lack of clarity can be explained by the fact that doping was part of a wider milieu of modernisation that some sports officials considered to be intuitively wrong. Such concerns resonate with criticisms from amateur sports leaders that the use of coaches was contrary to the values of sports, and was associated with professional sports like cycling and marathon running (Day 2013). There is a social-class dimension here, as sport could simply be a hobby for wealthy middle- and upper-class athletes, a distraction from the demands of elite society that should not be sullied by money or drugs. Doping was in a broad sense contrary to their perceptions of what sport means, but the details were much harder to pin down. As one observer put it in 1908, doping was simply not the English thing to do (Dimeo 2007).

This stratum of British society was taught that sport was a means of instilling discipline into social groups at home and in colonial outposts (Mangan 2013). It was also a preparation for war. Yet, the emergence of sports clubs was often gender exclusive, class-based and in colonial contexts racially exclusive (Mills 2005). Being naturally good at sport was a symbol of health and discipline that was passed down through generations. The meaning of sport was complex, varied and contextually situated. For a progressive doctor like Charles Lucas who saw health benefits in combatting fatigue for marathon runners, a well-organised approach to drugs was logical and to be valued. In the 1930s and 1940s scientists were openly arguing that drug taking might be no different to systematic training or psychological coaching (Bøje 1939). Some searched for hormonal treatments to counter fatigue and build muscle strength (De Kruif 1945). For IOC members and others like them, who had a sense of tradition and amateur values, sport should be different to the rest of society: purer, cleaner, nobler. The social-class distinctions were part of the early discourses on anti-doping, the privileged did not need to make money from sport so felt no compulsion to cheat or artificially enhance their performances. It is less clear why they were so motivated to impose their world-view upon others.

Anti-doping was initially driven by a handful of men who held powerful elite positions, had careers within and outside sport, and had a sense of entitlement and leadership. Some of them had an interest in horse racing, and no doubt took offence to the criminal underworld masterminding the corruption of races for the sake of material gain. They constructed doping as immoral, hoping perhaps it would disappear, but they failed to appreciate the appetite for performance enhancement among competitive athletes, and that without a definition and sufficient detection methods, the problem would only get worse.

A façade of morality

An important legacy of the mid-twentieth century construction of doping as antithetical to sport is the ideology of morality that was introduced and instilled as the reason to ban drugs. By setting the frame of reference in this way, it has ever since become difficult to challenge the basis for anti-doping and to publicly sympathise with any athlete found guilty of doping (intentionally or purposefully). There is a profound stigma associated with doping that is the by-product of the moralisation process begun many decades ago, and arguably is hampering any reform in the current crisis.

As example of this is the IOC President Henri de Baillet-Latour who provided a useful illustration of the perceived interrelationship of values and the threat of doping in 1937: 'amateur sport is meant to improve the soul and the body therefore no stone must be left unturned as long as the use of doping has not been stamped out' (Gleaves and Llewellyn 2014). Almost three decades later, the sports administrator and physician who was asked to develop the IOC's first anti-doping policy, Sir Arthur Porritt, wrote that doping is 'an evil – it is morally wrong, physically dangerous, socially degenerate and legally indefensible' (Porritt 1965).

While we do not have enough evidence to prove how widely accepted this paradigm was, there were sufficient highly placed individuals willing to commit to the idea that doping was immoral to allow the frame of reference to develop in this way. It became intertwined with the second rationale for anti-doping, that drugs could lead to health harms. However, the health argument developed only after a number of high-profile incidents in the late 1950s and 1960s. The morality of anti-doping predates any concerns over health. In 1956, Pope Pius XII was quoted in the IOC Bulletin denouncing the use of 'gravely noxious substances' (Hunt 2011 p. x)

By defining doping as immoral, the leaders of anti-doping could portray themselves as the guardians of the purity of sport, willing to expend personal and organisational resources expelling the forces of evil that would corrupt sport. Yet the question emerges as to the motivation for this attack on stimulant use: was it a real concern for the athletes? Was it some form of self-aggrandisement, an opportunity to build a power base? Or was it an assertion of historical claims of power, privilege and position in society on behalf of the 'officer class' in a world that was quickly becoming more democratic?

Historiographies of other social movements include critical accounts of elite minorities who use the language of morality to assert their authority over subordinates. In colonial contexts, the idea of civilisation was a veneer under which the rulers could brutalise, instil fear, convert heathens and promote cultural imperialism. Morality is a concept which can be manipulated and controlled for the purposes of those in power. One of the most notorious examples is provided by Hitler:

> We want to burn out all the recent immoral developments in literature, in the theatre, and in the press – in short, we want to burn out the *poison of immorality* which has entered into our whole life and culture as a result of *liberal excess* during the past ... (few) years
>
> *(Hitler 1942 p. 871)*

Returning to anti-doping, there is no objective reason why taking a pill before or during a race in order to counter fatigue and stimulate the body and mind needed to be considered an act of immorality with such profound resonance for the very meaning of sport. The consensus around that idea was invented and manufactured over time using myth, propaganda and fear. Yet we still need to consider why drugs were seen in such highly symbolic terms.

One interpretation is that the act of swallowing a pill demeaned the purpose of sport, which is to make the most of natural talent and show determination. The immorality argument was related to the need to protect some form of understanding about the natural body, sport and the artificiality of drugs. It could quite easily have gone the other way, sport could have been construed as the cultural field in which human performance is pushed forward in a controlled manner using natural and man-made initiatives. This seems to be highly dependent on localised situations and the interests of either individuals, team managers or governments. In the late nineteenth century European scientists experimented upon athletes to find the best ergogenic aids (Hoberman 1992). The interwar period saw clinical research on stimulants emerge on both sides of the Atlantic, particularly in countries with some pharmaceutical industries, such as Germany and the USA. In the 1970s East Germany had sports academies to train young athletes, elite coaches using new technologies, and doctors controlling the use of the anabolic steroid Oral-Turinabol as a supplemental aid to performance (Franke and Berendonk 1997). In the twenty-first century athletes train at altitude or in hypoxic chambers, and optimise diets up to (and sometimes beyond) what is considered legal. Thus, to propose that the handful of anti-doping pioneers represented an essential or universal understanding of sports ethics and purpose is a gross over-simplification.

A second interpretation is that swallowing a pill was seen as the thin end of a thick wedge relating to human enhancement more generally. Modern societies have wrestled with the impact of new technologies and the Promethean fear that opening the door to artificial changes would start an irreversible wave of change with highly unpredictable outcomes (Møller 2004). Again certain developments in the Western world were important: in postwar Europe, scientific modernism was being challenged in the aftermath of nuclear technologies and medical tragedies such as the emblematic thalidomide disaster.

A third interpretation is that the arrival of more consistent patterns of drug use in sport coincided with increasing (and uncontrollable) drug use in wider society, particularly among troublesome youth cultures. There was a perceived need to protect the healthiness of sport, the separation of sport from other more stressful aspects of modern life, and to encourage young people to take part in a healthy and constructive activity. The purported benefit of sport to wider society might become undermined if participants felt the need to consume stimulants in order to keep up with the competition.

A broader perspective on this matter leads us to analysing the changes occurring in sport and society, the generational shift that the leaders wanted to resist. The postwar period had created some disarray, especially for the Olympic movement. The international peaceful cooperation intended by Baron Pierre de

Coubertin could only be pursued if sport led the way for reintegrating former enemies, and by avoiding concerns about ongoing political rivalries. By the mid-1950s it was clear that the Olympic Games had become a battleground, ideologically and symbolically but still very visibly and corporeal, between the East and West. By the 1960s, media coverage had made sport more attractive to commercialisation. Ironically, the politicised nature of sport combined with lack of doping controls worked as a catalyst to widespread doping, but at the same time made international sport more appealing. Sportive nationalism and doping went hand-in-hand during this time period (Hoberman 1986, Hunt 2011).

Anti-doping pioneers were trying to stand firm on at least controlling athletes' behaviours, if they could not control the wider political and economic revolutions. If doping represented modernity at this stage, anti-doping was an attempt, albeit futile, to hold on to the idealism and romance of sport in a chaotic and fast-changing world. In that sense, the traditionalism of anti-doping, the harking back to a 'purer past' was in fact a strategy of anti-modernity (Møller 2004). It was a veneer to show that the IOC and other sports bodies had an ethical view of sport despite the politicised Cold War battles, the boycotts and the increasing commercialisation. Anti-doping, even if it failed, propped up the idealistic vision of the Olympics as having a sound ethical basis. As Ritchie showed:

> by the early 1970s, amateur ideals were formally abandoned and relevant rules and restrictions were removed from the Charter. But drug use was one aspect of sport that could be controlled, or at least certain members of the IOC perceived it could, and so rules were put in place and procedures for detection and punishment were implemented, and these continue to this day, albeit with greater scientific sophistication and the commitment of greater money and infrastructural resources. But because 'ethics' per se was never considered – because the IOC was trying to 'turn back the clock' and preserve images of Olympic purity in light of dramatic and embarrassing cases – the anti-doping movement was faced with a series of contradictions in its policies that, arguably, continue to the present day.
>
> *(Ritchie 2015 p. 28)*

The enhancement of anti-doping policy also had the effect of empowering those who positioned themselves as ethical and righteous, and subjugating those who were caught doping, regardless of the circumstances. Most often we are encouraged to think of anti-doping as protecting the clean athletes, but in actual fact it was about protecting the image of sport by punishing athletes and having monitoring systems so that sports organisations can maintain the illusion to fans, sponsors, media and governments that their product is ethical and attractive (Møller 2009).

Losing the drugs war, winning the public-relations campaign

Anti-doping policy was formed by the IOC in the 1960s when a list of banned substances was developed and testing introduced. It was a workable and achievable policy, as the only drugs being used were stimulants that had a short-term effect on performance. Testing could detect their presence in urine and thus the authorities could identify which athletes had been doping to cheat. The logic was sound, testing the top finishers would ensure that no medal was awarded to someone who had gained an artificial advantage over their opponents (Dimeo 2016).

Even so, there were several questionable underlying assumptions. The system would only work if the scientists could detect all the drugs on the banned list, which meant the list could only develop after the science was firmly in place. But scientists had to uncover the current patterns of drug use in order to know which drugs to test for (Beckett *et al.* 1967). Thus, it would be quite simple for an athlete to beat the tests by finding an alternative form of stimulant drug that had not yet been researched, for which there was no test. This strategic response to doping controls would haunt anti-doping organisations for decades. It would also fail to deliver the ambition of drug-free sport, as not all potentially performance-enhancing drugs were on the banned list. It is hard to tell if the anti-doping leaders were so naïve that they did not imagine the range of responses undertaken by those seeking an edge over their rivals, or if they simply hoped the impression of an effective policy would be enough to prove they were taking it seriously. Regardless of which, it was obvious that the idealistic view of drug-free sport was never going to be achievable.

Another assumption was that doping was restricted to a minority of cheats who deliberately sought to fix the result, which resonates with the horse-racing scenario even if the ergogenic effect is the opposite. Cheating to win was seen as caddish behaviour that did not give all participants the same chance of success. Some scientists and administrators described doping as immoral and contrary to the values of sport. However, some sports had a tacitly accepted doping culture, and once it becomes normalised the doped athlete is merely levelling the playing field, not creating an advantage for themselves over others. And of course, if an event did not have testing there was no way to know if it was clean or not. Having created a suspicion that all athletes might dope, there was no conceivable method of ensuring that they did not, the fertile ground was laid for increasing demand for doping and a vast underground supply network. The vision of drug free sport was not deliverable in reality. Indeed, it had the most profound consequence that was not just unintended but was the opposite of what was intended.

There is no evidence that the dilemmas, challenges and potential consequences were discussed. Anti-doping was an edict, handed down from IOC President Avery Brundage, who inherited it from de Baillet-Latour, the objective of which was a simple idea of drug-free sport. From the start, there were arguments about who would fund testing, with Brundage insisting that international federations find the resources. With limited resources, doping controls were focused on the priority contexts, including the Olympic Games, cycling, football and other athletics events. Some federations were not supportive of these measures, and in cycling many of the established riders actively resisted being drug tested claiming that as professionals they should be allowed to choose to dope.

By the end of the 1970s the evidence clearly shows a major gulf between the pretence that anti-doping was working and the reality of systematic doping cultures in a wide set of sports and countries. Anti-doping had failed before it had really got started, but the public-relations propaganda would hide the full scale of the problem such that the Olympics and other sports could pursue commercial ambitions and allow professionalisation among athletes. By the mid-1970s the steroid boom had changed the face of sports, and there was absolutely nothing the IOC or others could do about it. In part, this was about resources and politics. However, the shift in landscape from in-competition stimulant use to out-of-competition steroid use made the ambition of clean sport even more unrealistic.

One option must have been to back track on earlier promises and accept that athletes would seek performance-enhancing drugs. Research on drugs, and information openly provided to users, could have led to transparency. However, the morality underpinning anti-doping meant that no form of artificial enhancement could be condoned. The paradox was that the IOC created a situation that soon was uncontrollable but still felt the need to show the wider world that they were solving it. After every Games from 1968 through to 1996, the chair of the IOC Medical Commission, Prince Alexandre de Mérode, would reiterate the success of anti-doping measures in a bid to reassure the public that the Olympics were clean (Dimeo et al. 2011). The use of new technology was hailed as the solution, even in the case of the Moscow 1980 Olympics when subsequent analysis of the samples collected showed widespread doping use. The propaganda was further evident when some positive tests were allegedly covered-up during the 1984 Games. If doping was motivated by the Cold War, neither side had the inclination to stop it. On the other hand, if doping was motivated by athletes' desire for success, the end of the Cold War would make no difference to the continuity of doping.

Confusion and scandals

It is no exaggeration to say that international sport was fuelled by steroids in the 1980s, even though evidence is incomplete regarding the full scope of the problem. We know that East Germany doped most of its elite athletes. West Germany, USSR, and the USA, had well-organised doping. Perhaps on a smaller scale, Canada, the UK, Australia and other European countries, all had athletes and coaches prepared to dope for success. When Ben Johnson was caught for stanozolol use in the 1988 Seoul Olympics, the major surprise for those close to the action was not that he was using banned substances, but that the drug testers had actually succeeded in catching a high-profile doper (Francis 1990). However, the image of clean sport was promoted in the media coverage of that case which reflected the moral framework instilled in a previous generation, with Johnson being labelled evil, a disgrace and having publicly embarrassed his country. The stigma still hangs over him and there have been very few opportunities for him to recover his career in sport or his personal reputation.

Signs of the lack of progress in anti-doping had emerged slowly since the early 1980s. The retesting of samples from the 1980 Olympics showed that many athletes were misusing testosterone including females (Hunt 2011). Scientists had set a generous ratio of testosterone:epitestosterone that allowed some usage as long as the threshold was not breached. Evidently, clean sport meant abiding by the rules which were in part dictated by the available testing methods. Indeed, steroid use was not banned until a test was developed in 1975, so anyone using those type of drugs prior to then had not broken any rules. Several insider accounts from the early 1980s showed that athletes and their support staff knew how to beat the testing system (Francis 1990).

One method was to time the dosages such that there would be no trace of the drug in their system when they came to be tested. At this time, there was no out-of-competition testing, so a 3–4 week wash-out period was often sufficient. Another method would be to swap urine samples for either another person, or one they had produced while not using the drug. Some of this knowledge was openly distributed (Duchaine 1989), while a number of countries operated internal testing of athletes ahead of their participation in events. In circumstances where doping was supported by medical staff and laboratories, athletes would be tested before leaving their country to ensure they would be 'clean' (Franke and Berendonk 1997). Any risk of a positive test might lead to an invented excuse for their withdrawal. A third approach would be to consume diuretics which help to mask the presence of steroids, and over time many such drugs would be placed on the list of banned substances. A consequence of the desire to control a complex pharmacology of mixed drug use and masking agents would lead to some athletes testing positive for the masking agent when there was no evidence they were using the steroids for which the masking drug was supposedly used to conceal. So, by its willingness to fight steroid use the IOC had opened a Pandora's box of regulation.

The first case of surprise testing came in 1983 ahead of the Pan American Games in Caracas, Venezuela. When the organisers informed athletes of their intention to drug test, there were numerous last-minute withdrawals and a total of 16 were tested positive. In Canada there was an open debate when one of the weightlifters explained that many of the countries' athletes were using steroids (Ritchie and Jackson 2014). The American weightlifter, who subsequently became a university professor, Terry Todd wrote for *Sports Illustrated* that steroid use offered a 'predicament' (Todd 1983). Another scandal broke in 1985 when *Rolling Stone* magazine told its readers that the USA cycling team from the 1984 Olympic Games, including five medal winners, had been using a blood doping technique that was not banned or detectable (Gleaves 2015a). The sense of outrage led to a decision to ban blood doping, but that was largely on the grounds of risk from unhygienic needle sharing during the heightened anxieties over HIV/AIDS. Much like the challenge of steroids and endogenous testosterone, the authorities faced a dilemma of how to control a procedure for which there was no test. The superficial ban did not prevent usage, and systematic blood doping was common in cycling, track and field and other sports through the 1990s and 2000s. By the 1980s, however, we can say that the failure to prevent doping, allied with an unrealistic vision of clean sport and a flawed public-relations campaign that avoided scandal, meant that users sought new and creative ways to both dope and to cheat the testing system.

Sections of the media saw doping as a good story, an interesting exposé of the tension between sport for health and sport for success. Writing for *Sports Illustrated* in 1969, Brad Gilbert had brought the issue to the attention of the American public (Gilbert 1969). A *New York Times* exposé in 1971 took a similarly scandalising approach. A year later, a BBC Panorama documentary featured interviews with bodybuilders using steroids. The track and field coach, Wilf Paish said on that programme that drugs were an inevitable part of sport (Dimeo 2007). However, such stories were rare and despite the efforts of reporters to bring attention to the widespread doping practices, very little response emerged from the world's leading sports authorities. An authoritative account of the problem was published by sports writer Les Woodland (1980) reviewing stimulants, steroids and related health issues, but there was little to suggest at this time that the IOC or other organisations were fully committed to anti-doping, and thus doping was an open secret.

Other publications also scandalised drug use, emphasising the health and performance enhancement impacts of various types of doping substances. William Taylor was an early proponent of the idea that steroids were a crisis that needed more attention. In his book *Macho Medicine* he criticised the American College of Sports Medicine (ACSM) for their denial that steroids were an effective performance-enhancing drug (Taylor 1991). It would not be until 1983 that the ACSM recognised this fact, but took a dim view of any usage or any form of clinical research. Some bodybuilding experts over-emphasised the health risks, for example in the 1984 book *Death in the Locker Room*, which includes case studies and anecdotes meant to scare readers into avoiding all forms of doping (Goldman *et al.* 1984). The other side of the story was manifest in the power of Olympic athletes, who looked extremely healthy and were breaking world records in many sports. And somewhat less visibly, steroid use was becoming more common among young athletes, keen to find ways to build muscle and improve their sporting prospects (Terney and McLain 1990). The discourses of denial and fear were inadequate to prevent the curious and the ambitious from trying out these muscle drugs (Hoberman 2005).

By the mid-1980s various interweaving narratives and perspectives emerged that would set the tone for later problems. Many athletes saw doping as an opportunity to help them succeed, sometimes they were supported by coaches and even governments. Consequently, there were many innovations and suppliers willing to help athletes in their pursuit of success. Market forces were in play. It was very clear that the ethics of anti-doping, and all the emphasis on doping as cheating and immoral, were not discouraging cultures of drug use. In response to demand, quite a number of suppliers found a profitable enterprise. Not only were individual entrepreneurs helping to promote doping, but some countries paid lip service to anti-doping while either actively encouraging their athletes to dope or turning a blind eye to the extent of doping. There was very little appetite to address and resolve this problem (Wilson and Derse 2001).

Nonetheless, we see moral activists proclaiming the need to improve anti-doping and reasserting the arguments made in earlier historical periods. For example, a conference held in London in 1985 saw many speakers agonising over the dreadful effects of doping and demanding more action from the broader sports community (Dimeo 2007). A number of countries appeared to be leading this charge, not least the UK and Canada, but the image promoted by their vocal anti-doping campaigners belied a pattern of doping among some of their athletes. Elsewhere, the sterling work by scientists like Manfred Donike in Cologne, and David Cowan in London, helped to enhance the prospect of better testing methods. However, they became embroiled in arguments about resources showing that anti-doping was far from immune from internal politics (Krieger 2016).

When Ben Johnson was caught in the summer of 1988, it seemed to validate the anti-doping effort and make it appear successful, although this created a dilemma. The IOC wanted the appearance of ethics and anti-doping but did not want large-scale scandals influencing the image of their product. There were competing interests and those inside the anti-doping industry were not able to catch the cheats nor could they handle the negative publicity of too many sanctioned athletes. If the full scale of doping through the 1970s, 1980s and 1990s had been known to the watching public, it is questionable whether the Olympics would have survived the scandal and the disappointment of those who wanted their sporting heroes to be 'pure'. By the late 1980s, the sporting and medical worlds were dramatically different to the conditions of the 1960s when anti-doping was formulated. There was a much wider pharmacology and globalised methods of distribution; sport was much less amateur, personal obsession with success coincided with nationalistic ambitions and corporate interests to create more commercial opportunities; the health of the athletes was a much more contested idea, not least because sports medicine and science had helped to bring the expertise required to safely dope. However, the IOC and others maintained a traditionalist sense of 'purity' despite, or perhaps because of, a rapidly changing global environment. The desire to protect sport from the troubles brought by drugs could be seen as noble and ambitious, it seems to have reflected public, media and 'official' medical expectations; even though it would prove impossible to deliver and the intensity of policy itself would eventually cause a wider range of harms.

The impotence of anti-doping

The consequences of the Ben Johnson case were far-reaching and meaningful. The Canadian government set up an independent inquiry led by Charles Dubin, who found evidence of widespread doping in Canada and elsewhere. Witness after witness told stories that exposed the failings of the anti-doping system. Dubin saw doping as an affront to the essence of sport, to the values that sport conveyed to young people, and a threat to government support for healthy sports endeavours (Dubin 1990). His conclusions caused Canada to focus much more on recreational sport and to withdraw funding from the elite, win-at-all-costs, Olympic focused projects that Ben Johnson and his coach Charlie Francis had come to symbolise. In essence, Dubin both represented and reinforced the ideological purpose of anti-doping rooted in amateurism, premised on simplistic notions that sport provides healthy exercise and good community relations. He wanted Canada to return to imagined traditional sporting cultures, where the core values were life-affirmingly positive (Ritchie 2013).

Just as Dubin pronounced the need to reorient the emphasis of sport, the fall of the Berlin Wall and reunification of Germany led to revelations of East Germany's doping system that would become notorious for both the role of the state, and the exploitation of children. The worst excesses of doping cultures were now linked to the crimes against citizens undertaken by the Stasi; steroid use now had sinister overtones. When testimonies were presented in court during the reunification trials (1995–1999), the world's media reported upon the scandalous 'evil' that had occurred in the name of sport. East German officials had systematically doped Olympic athletes, including some girls as young as 12 years old, and while many people had cast doubt on their performances during that time the IOC had failed to gather any form of evidence from 1972 through to 1988 that doping was occurring (Franke and Berendonk 1997). This was a monumental failure. The confluence of Canadian evidence and ideological retrenchment, alongside the perceived evils of corruption and abuse of power on a scarcely believable scale in East Germany, made doping seem unavoidably problematic. The more open debate of the late 1970s and early 1980s had given way to the twin ideas of the need to stop doping, and the need to reassert the fundamentalist dogma of the pure essence of sport.

However, the East Germany case would distract attention from what had been, and continued to happen, in Western countries. By having a focal point with the accompanying political criticism of totalitarianism, East Germany became a soft target for accusations. Evidence from the USA showed organised doping, cover-ups and risky doping behaviours among the wider population including high-school children (Assael 2007). Later interviews with British athletes would suggest higher levels of doping among Olympians than was ever recognised at the time, meanwhile authorities in the UK were slow to address the problem (Waddington 2005). Chinese sport came under the spotlight when athletes and swimmers were caught with doping substances in the mid-late 1990s. The Australian shot putter Werner Reiterer wrote an account of widespread use of steroids in many sports (Reiterer and Hainline 2000).

If the IOC had failed to prevent doping from casting a huge shadow over the Olympics, then other sports must be viewed in an even more critical way. In the USA details slowly emerged of long traditions of amphetamine, steroid and human growth hormone abuse in professional and college sports (Hunt et al. 2014). Large-scale surveys from the 1980s and 1990s showed this was becoming a major public-health issue, with prevalence rates of steroid use of 4–12 per cent among adolescents (Yesalis and Bahrke 1995). The black market for these drugs was estimated to be worth around $300m in 1990 in the US alone (Hunt et al. 2014).

Professional and strength sports seemed to lack concern about the growing problem. Doping has a long tradition in cycling, and by the late 1980s erythropoietin (EPO) was becoming more widely used. Paul Kimmage's book *Rough Ride* exposed some of the doping within the peloton but professional cycling was a tight-knit community that did not allow details of doping to seep out into the public gaze (Kimmage 2009). It would seem the participants accepted the reasons for drug use, sometimes for recovery or pain management, and at other times to improve their speed. It would take a catch at a border control and the intervention of the French state in 1998 to expose the wide acceptance of drug use among professional cycling teams. During that year's Tour de France several of the leading teams were investigated by police, and the global media coverage put more pressure on sports organisations to respond to the doping crisis.

Despite the attention focused on cycling, the following year saw Lance Armstrong win the first of his seven consecutive Tour de France titles. Doping continued unabated until the Federal Bureau of Investigation (FBI) and United States Anti-Doping Agency (USADA) investigation into US Postal/Lance Armstrong scandal in 2012 (and to an unknown extent still remains a part of the sport). Strength sports like weightlifting and competitive bodybuilding continued the tacit acceptance of doping throughout this time period. There have even been attempts to organise separate events that distinguish between 'controlled', that is with drug testing, and 'uncontrolled'. The normalisation of steroid use in these sports at elite level was replicated among amateur and fitness enthusiasts (Monaghan 1999).

The governing body for football, Fédération Internationale de Football Association (FIFA), did not embrace the global approach to anti-doping in the 1990s (Wagner 2011). In the absence of a coherent policy and regular testing of players, we are left with a great deal of uncertainty as to whether football has had a doping culture. Some less 'lower risk' sports such as golf, cricket and tennis have also been criticised for failing to engage with anti-doping education and testing systems.

The sheer scope of the problem was recognised in texts from this period. John Hoberman's ground-breaking book *Mortal Engines: Science and the Dehumanization of Sport* blew a large hole in the idealistic historical vision of natural drug-free sport to which anti-doping leaders always referred (Hoberman 1992). If sport was about performance rather than health or fun, and if science was embraced in the requirements for success, then it would be inevitable that the most potent substances would be highly attractive to the most ambitious athletes. Hoberman also focuses attention on the internal conflicts of interest that undermined a consistent and strong policy of sanctioning doping athletes. Many of those caught were given short bans or fines and allowed to return quickly to competition. Sports federations did not collectively work towards developing an out-of-competition testing system until the early 2000s. It would seem the avoidance of scandal was more important than catching drug users.

The impotence in efforts to reduce or completely deter doping was more than evident during the 1990s. However, that decade also saw a number of cases in which the harms of a draconian policy system, and the inhumanity of bureaucrats, were becoming more obvious. One case in point was that of the English track and field athlete Diane Modahl. A routine test conducted in Lisbon in 1994 found high levels of testosterone. She professed her shock and innocence and mounted a lengthy, expensive appeal that fully exonerated her (McArdle 1999). It was also an expensive process for the prosecution as it left the British Athletic Federation bankrupt. Two years later another complex testosterone case involving American runner Mary Decker Slaney showed that anti-doping was failing. Her sample also returned high levels of testosterone which she claimed was related to her use of the birth control pill. Professor at Duke University, James E. Coleman, who experienced the case first-hand as part of Slaney's defence team, was stunned by the dubious evidence base for the case against her. This led him to subsequently criticise the anti-doping test system in an article in which he called 'The burden of proof in endogenous substance cases a masking agent for junk science' (Coleman 2011). The jurisdictional conflicts between sports and civil-law bodies was highlighted in the case of Harry 'Butch' Reynolds whose positive test led to a series of courts appeals and debates over jurisdiction (McArdle 2003).

Anti-doping at a crossroads

The late 1990s were a truly historical moment for sport. The IOC was facing pressure. Not just was it failing in the war on drugs, but the bribery scandal relating to the awarding of the Games to Salt Lake City in 2002 cast a shadow of the IOC leadership. The president, Juan Antonio Samaranch, seemed confused about how to respond to doping. Despite public pressure for clean sport, which inherently included an avoidance of artificial forms of performance enhancement, he opined in 1998 that health should be the only consideration when banning drugs and so the Prohibited List should be reduced. He clearly misread public sentiment and faced a considerable backlash in the aftermath of that media interview (Associated Press 1998).

Samaranch's problems show that by the late 1990s the debate was focused on how to respond to the wide use of drugs through increasing the power of anti-doping policy. Given the extent of the crisis at this stage, it might have been rational for sports organisations, leaders and fans to have reflected upon two realistic propositions. First, that the world of science, nutrition, performance technologies and commercialisation had created a context for doping that was much different to the simpler world of the 1960s, when it was believed doping could be controlled. The motivations, conditions and knowledge about doping products had all been revolutionised. Suppliers innovated to find drugs that were not yet detectable and athletes deliberately circumvented the system. Perhaps it would have made sense to open the doors to drug use: informed, consented and managed by experts. Second, doping was impossible to control. Small doses of powerful drugs could be washed out an athlete's body within hours. The cost of conducting tests in all countries and at all times to ensure 'clean sport' was not feasible. This was an unwinnable war, though no one in power (except Samaranch) was prepared to admit to that.

Instead the World Conference on Doping organised by the IOC in Lausanne in November 1999 focused entirely upon the organisational structure of anti-doping, with government representatives insisting that the best way forward would be to establish some form of independent anti-doping agency. In other words, there was no reflection on the rationale for anti-doping or the changing context of modern sport. The objective remained the same, drug-free sport in a vague and anachronistic sense, but it was imagined that taking responsibility away from the IOC would solve the problem. The delegates assumed that doping could be successfully tackled, if only the high-level ambition remained in place and the organisational approach was improved. This was a political decision, not one that realistically reflected the nature of sport at the time. It was a symbolic gesture, a public statement that sport was about health, and that governments wanted drug-free sport. And thus the central flaw at the heart of anti-doping was reasserted: the political demand for sport to have a positive image that would create economic opportunities and national heroes helped to create WADA, an organisation that would increase the harms caused to athletes, while continuing to lose the war on drugs.

Historians of doping and anti-doping are often faced with a lack of consistent evidence of doping cultures and an almost hagiographical official account of anti-doping's development, purpose and ethical righteousness. The ideological power of anti-doping has led to the simplistic and unquestioning repetition of myths and generic claims that 'fit the message'. However, we can point to shifting patterns over the twentieth century, culminating in a revolutionary *fin-de-siècle* event: the formation of WADA. That moment has a material reality, the ever-expanding pharmacopeia of doping. It had a policy reality in which various organisations cooperated and argued over how best to manage the problem given finite resources, the need to avoid scandal, the need for consistency and the delegation of responsibility. There was also a cultural framing to these in which the very notion of clean sport appeared to be so intractability fixed in the minds of sports fans, reporters, administrators, doctors, and (some) athletes, that it curtailed any meaningful discussion and exploration of how anti-doping might adapt to the broader modernisation, medicalisation, and commercialism of sport. Rather than accept that the present and future were different to romanticised amateurism views of sport, the pressure of scandals and the post-Dubin Canadian influence came together to underpin WADA's response. It would be an attempt to address the proliferation of doping, based on idealism, but with an iron fist. Balancing the exercise of power while protecting the rights and dignity of athletes would become an unresolved dilemma that would come to undermine the basic ethics upon which their work is premised. In the course of working out these tensions, many athletes would suffer. There would be a high price to pay as more draconian policies were gradually rolled out internationally.

References

Assael, S. (2007). *Steroid Nation: Juiced Home Run Totals, Anti-Aging Miracles, and a Hercules in Every High School: The Secret History of America's True Drug Addiction*. New York: ESPN Books.

Associated Press (1998). "Cycling: A call for doping changes". *New York Times* 27 July. Retrieved 2 January from http://www.nytimes.com/1998/07/27/sports/cycling-a-call-for-doping-changes.html

Beckett, A., G. Tucker and A. Moffat (1967). "Routine detection and identification in urine of stimulants and other drugs, some of which may be used to modify performance in sport." *Journal of Pharmacy and Pharmacology* 19(5): 273–294.

Bell, S. K., J. C. Lucke and W. D. Hall (2012). "Lessons for enhancement from the history of cocaine and amphetamine use". *AJOB Neuroscience* 3(2): 24–29.

Bøje, O. (1939). "Doping". *Bulletin of the Health Organization of the League of Nations* 8: 439–469.

Chandler, A. D. (2009). *Shaping the Industrial Century: The Remarkable Story of the Evolution of the Modern Chemical and pharmaceutical industries*: New Haven, CT: Harvard University Press.

Coleman, J. E. (2011). "The burden of proof in endogenous substance cases: a masking agent for junk science". In M. McNamee and V. Møller (eds), *Doping and Anti-Doping Policy in Sport: Ethical, Legal and Social Perspectives* (pp. 27–49). London: Routledge.

Conrad, P. (2007). *The Medicalization of Society*. Baltimore, MD: Johns Hopkins University Press.

Day, D. (2013). "Historical perspectives on coaching." In P. Potrac, W. Gilbert and J. Denison (eds), *Routledge Handbook of Sports Coaching* (pp. 5–15). London: Routledge.

De Kruif, P. (1945). *The Male Hormone*. New York: Harcort, Brace and Company.

Dimeo, P. (2007). *A History of Drug Use in Sport: 1876–1976: Beyond Good and Evil*. London: Routledge.

Dimeo, P. (2016). "The myth of clean sport and its unintended consequences". *Performance Enhancement & Health* 4(3): 103–110.

Dimeo, P., T. M. Hunt and M. T. Bowers (2011). "Saint or sinner? A reconsideration of the career of Prince Alexandre de Mérode, Chair of the International Olympic Committee's Medical Commission, 1967–2002". *The International Journal of the History of Sport* 28(6): 925–940.

Dubin, C. (1990) *Commission of Enquiry into the Use of Drugs and Banned Practices Intended to Increase Athletic Performance*. Ottawa: Canadian Goverment Publishing Centre.

Duchaine, D. (1989). *Underground Steroid Handbook II*. Venice, CA: HLR Technical Books.

Francis, C. (1990). *Speed Trap*. New York: St. Martin's Press.

Franke, W. W. and B. Berendonk (1997). "Hormonal doping and androgenization of athletes: a secret program of the German Democratic Republic government". *Clinical Chemistry* 43(7): 1262–1279.

Gilbert, B. (1969). "Drugs in sport: Part 1: problems in a turned-on world". *Sports Illustrated* 23: 64–72.

Gleaves, J. (2015a). "Manufactured dope: How the 1984 US Olympic cycling team rewrote the rules on drugs in sports". *The International Journal of the History of Sport* 32(1): 89–107.

Gleaves, J. (2015b). "The Prohibited List and its implications". In Verner Møller, Ivan Waddington and John Hoberman (eds), *Routledge Handbook of Drugs in Sport*. London: Routledge.

Gleaves, J. and M. Llewellyn (2014). "Sport, drugs and amateurism: Tracing the real cultural origins of anti-doping rules in international sport". *The International Journal of the History of Sport* 31(8): 839–853.

Goldman, B., P. Bush and R. Klatz (1984). *Death in the Locker Room*. London: Century.

Hitler, A. (1942). *The Speeches of Adolf Hitler, 1922–1939*. London: Oxford University Press.

Hoberman, J. (1986). *The Olympic Crisis: Sport, Politics and the Moral Order*. New Rochelle, NY: Caratzas.

Hoberman, J. (1992). *Mortal Engines: The Science of Performance and the Dehumanization of Sport*, New York: Free Press.

Hoberman, J. (2005). *Testosterone Dreams: Rejuvenation, Aphrodisia, Doping*. Berkeley, CA: University of California Press.

Hunt, T. M. (2011). *Drug Games: The International Olympic Committee and the Politics of Doping, 1960–2008*. Austin, TX: University of Texas Press.

Hunt, T. M., P. Dimeo, F. Hemme and A. Mueller (2014). "The health risks of doping during the Cold War: A comparative analysis of the two sides of the Iron Curtain." *The International Journal of the History of Sport* 31(17): 2230–2244.

Kimmage, P. (2009). *Rough Ride*. London: Random House.

Krieger, J. (2016). "Intended. Underrated. Disputed. The IOC Medical Commission's 'Subcommission on Doping and Biochemistry in Sport' between 1980 and 1988." *Performance Enhancement & Health* 4(3): 88–93.

Lucas, C. J. (1905). *The Olympic Games, 1904*. St Louis, MO: Woodward & Tieran Printing Company.

Mangan, J. A. (2013). *The Cultural Bond: Sport, Empire, Society*. London: Routledge.

McArdle, D. (1999). "Elite athletes' perceptions of the use and regulation of performance-enhancing drugs in the United Kingdom". *Journal of Legal Aspects of Sport* 9(1): 43–51.

McArdle, D. (2003). "Reflections on the Harry Reynolds litigation". *The Entertainment and Sports Law Journal* 2(2): 90–97.

Mills, J. H. (2005). *Subaltern Sports: Politics and Sport in South Asia*. London: Anthem Press.

Møller, V. (2004). "The anti-doping campaign: Farewell to the ideals of modernity". In J. Hoberman and V. Møller (eds), *Doping and Public Policy*. Odense: University of Southern Denmark Press.

Møller, V. (2009). *The Ethics of Doping and Anti-doping: Redeeming the Soul of Sport?* London: Routledge.

Monaghan, L. (1999). "Challenging medicine? Bodybuilding, drugs and risk". *Sociology of Health & Illness* 21(6): 707–734.

Porritt, A. (1965). "Doping". *The Journal of Sports Medicine and Physical Fitness* 5(3): 166–168.

Reiterer, W. and B. Hainline (2000). *Positive: An Australian Olympian Reveals the Inside Story of Drugs and Sport*. Sydney: Pan Macmillan Australia.

Ritchie, I. (2013). "The construction of a policy: The World Anti-Doping Code's 'spirit of sport' clause". *Performance Enhancement & Health* 2(4): 194–200.

Ritchie, I. (2015). "Understanding performance-enhancing substances and sanctions against their use from ther perspective of history". In Verner Møller, Ivan Waddington and John Hoberman (eds), *Routledge Handbook of Drugs in Sport*. London: Routledge.

Ritchie, I. and G. Jackson (2014). "Politics and 'shock': reactionary anti-doping policy objectives in Canadian and international sport". *International Journal of Sport Policy and Politics* 6(2): 195–212.

Taylor, W. N. (1991). *Macho Medicine: A History of the Anabolic Steroid Epidemic*. Jefferson, NC: McFarland.

Terney, R. and L. G. McLain (1990). "The use of anabolic steroids in high school students." *American Journal of Diseases of Children* 144(1): 99–103.

Todd, T. (1983). "The steroid predicament". *Sports Illustrated*. 59: 62–78.

Waddington, I. (2005). "Changing patterns of drug use in British sport from the 1960s". *Sport in History* 25(3): 472–496.

Wagner, U. (2011). "Towards the construction of the world anti-doping agency: Analyzing the approaches of FIFA and the IAAF to doping in sport". *European Sport Management Quarterly* 11(5): 445–470.

Wilson, W. and E. Derse (2001). *Doping in Elite Sport: The Politics of Drugs in the Olympic Movement*. Chicago, IL: Human Kinetics.

Woodland, L. (1980). *Dope: The Use of Drugs in Sport*. London: David & Charles.

Yesalis, C. E. and M. S. Bahrke (1995). "Anabolic-androgenic steroids". *Sports Medicine* 19(5): 326–340.

3

THE CREATION OF WADA

Politics, Olympism and the illusion of reform

In Chapter 2 we explained that there is no single point of origin for anti-doping in the broader historical landscape. However, we do have a point of origin for the environment that has emerged since the arguments in Lausanne in November 1999. The scandals of the 1990s created the political platform for a more enhanced and co-ordinated approach to anti-doping policy and planning, including international cooperation, athlete education, evolvement of a more purposeful testing system and clearer processes for sanctions and appeals. It was considered that the IOC alone could not deliver on these objectives.

The Lausanne conference ended with greater resistance than predicted to the IOC's attempt to retain leadership. However, the politicians who argued so vehemently for the end of IOC's leadership of anti-doping did not seem to mind too much that Juan Antonio Samaranch and Dick Pound successfully proposed a solution that would keep the IOC firmly embedded within WADA, and indeed allowed WADA to align much of its work with the Olympic movement. Governmental representatives had come armed with trenchant criticisms of the IOC, but had not prepared a viable alternative vision. They insisted upon a truly independent anti-doping agency. Thus, the pragmatic outcome was that the IOC-proposed Olympic Anti-Doping Agency was overturned in favour of a world agency, but without a blueprint for a new organisation or indeed any option to open up a bidding process to run anti-doping. Dick Pound would later claim that he perceived an opportunity for the IOC to keep a strong position and, in fact, turn the situation to their advantage.

In a move which ostensibly looked like defeat and compromise, Samaranch would agree to a new independent agency. However, in a shrewd political manoeuvre that agreement would be based on Pound (who was an IOC vice-president) being nominated as president of the agency. The IOC would offer 50 per cent of the funding if that was matched by governments. In effect, the realpolitik meant that the IOC now having more authority and support from world leaders, could assert its anti-doping ideology over all sports and all countries, even if the façade of independence and objectivity was promoted through the establishment of WADA. The representative nature of the committee followed the principle of 50:50 ratio of politicians and IOC members. In reality, the politicians are not as familiar with sports organisations and the operational aspects of anti-doping as the IOC and other sports federations, and not very involved with governance matters. Hence the sports leaders of IOC and the federations could dominate the proceedings and influence strategy.

A first question therefore is why those politicians accepted the compromise? Samaranch seemed genuinely surprised and distressed by the scathing attacks from governmental representatives like the British sports minister Tony Banks, the US White House drugs advisor Barry McCafferty and others. These politicians only had a short time to make statements to the conference, which they used to criticise the failed policies of the IOC. Those highly influential statements accusing the IOC of having a vested interest in protecting the image of the Olympics for economic reasons, did not sufficiently lead to a model of reform that was truly focused on independence. It was as if the very act of shifting the leadership of anti-doping from the IOC was enough to satisfy the critics (Hanstad et al. 2008). The politicians did not want to be involved in the minutiae of what a new agency would look like, its funding, its rationales and methods, only that the ambition of drug-free sport remained in place, and the policies not be dictated by the organisers of the largest sports event in the world. The consensus around anti-doping as an ethical ambition in order to protect the health of athletes and the level playing field was reinforced by the wider range of delegates at the Lausanne conference. The delegates agreed with the stated outcomes of anti-doping, but simply wanted another form of governance that had the appearance of independence. There were no other viable solutions, no other organisations with the breadth of experience as the IOC, no other global sports organisation with remit for almost all sports, and few other funding alternatives. The outcome would be that WADA was an extension of the IOC.

The intertwining of the IOC and WADA can be found in a number of places (WADA 2017). The names of committees are quite similar, such as the Executive and Foundation Boards. The IOC is governed by an Executive Board with a president, four vice-presidents and ten other members (IOC 2017b). WADA is governed by an Executive Committee, with a president, one vice-president and ten other members. The IOC has a series of commissions which report to the Board. WADA has a series of working committees which report to the Board. This problem has been recently recognised by the groups of national anti-doping agencies (NADOs), collectively known as Institute of National Anti-Doping Agencies (iNADO group), who described the situation as:

> WADA's governance is based on a representational model involving only those organisations which fund it. By definition then, the organizational

interests of those representatives are meant to impact on the exercise of WADA's anti-doping mandate. In practice WADA's governing body, the WADA Foundation Board, and its executive board, the WADA Executive Committee, have remained subject to substantial influence from sport. The thirty-eight member Foundation Board has nineteen sport representatives. Likewise, the twelve member WADA Executive Committee has six sport representatives. Additionally, WADA's President [Sir Craig Reedie] in his second three-year term is a long-time sport executive and current IOC member. Throughout his first term the WADA President was an IOC Vice President and IOC Executive Board member. This illustrates the structural nature of WADA's independence deficit which raises doubts about the unqualified pursuit of WADA's mandate.

(Institute of National Anti-Doping Organisations 2017)

The chronology of the Olympic cycle has also been important, in that WADA was established just in time to demonstrate commitment to anti-doping ahead of the 2000 Games; the first WADC was published just before the 2004 Games. Recent events regarding Russian doping had a strong emphasis on eligibility for the 2016 Rio Olympics, and a significant proportion of retesting of historical samples has been a joint IOC/WADA effort focusing upon the 2008 and 2012 Olympics.

Beyond the practicalities of committees and testing, the fundamental ideological framework of the WADC refers to the Olympics. The concept of the 'spirit of sport' in the Code is closely related to the ideas of Olympism including 'celebration of the human spirit, body and mind' and emphasises 'ethics, fair play, honesty' and health. Whereas Olympism is identified by the IOC as:

a philosophy of life, exalting and combining in a balanced whole the qualities of body, will and mind. Blending sport with culture and education, Olympism seeks to create a way of life based on the joy found in effort, the educational value of good example and respect for universal fundamental ethical principles.

(IOC 2017a)

The WADC describes the 'spirit of sport' as 'the essence of Olympism', and with echoes of de Baillet-Latour, continues to praise 'the pursuit of human excellence through the dedicated perfection of each person's natural talents' (WADA 2015). The overlap between the IOC and WADA is a cause for concern identified by the iNADO group:

Sports influence within WADA does not stop at the WADA board memberships and executive positions held by sport officials. Sport also has influence upon WADA because the IOC is by far the single largest contributor to WADA. The IOC provides 50% of WADA's annual funding.

Although collectively public authorities provide the other 50% of WADA's annual funding, no other funder contributes more than about 6%. Additionally, while purporting to recognise the importance of the principle of WADA independence, the IOC regularly holds 'Summits' and issues statements regarding how the IOC is implementing reforms to WADA and the global anti-doping system. These announcements are frequently coupled with IOC declarations that additional funding to WADA is tied to WADA's acceptance of IOC demands regarding restructuring the anti-doping system.

(Institute of National Anti-Doping Organisations 2017)

However, the dilemmas inherent in anti-doping – the control of performance enhancement in environments where athletes, coaches and doctors constantly seek to enhance performance – actually reflect the dilemmas inherent in Olympism and elite sport.

Olympism has been a powerful part of world sport since the nineteenth century, as it represents populist notions of why sport is a healthy and beneficial part of society. There are few more powerful messages than health, ethics and honest competitiveness that people from diverse countries and political ideas can relate to. These are ideas that governments can support, even while promoting the 'excellence' of a small minority of their own athletes who can be presented as successful role models to inspire the rest of the population. The implicit contradiction is rarely discussed and politicians tread the line between public health and elite sport using the athlete as role-model paradigm. Yet, of course, elite sports men and women are not 'naturally' talented, they are the products of organised and expensive sports development systems, from which only a small minority have successful careers in sport. The emotional and financial cost for all the athletes, and their families, who fail to make a career in sport is very rarely acknowledged in political idealisation of the benefits of sport. Nor are elite athletes healthy in the sense that the general populace is expected to aim for, which is more related to regular moderate physical activity.

Politicians and sports leaders are also often supportive of investing in sports events and facilities when there is a perceived potential for economic benefit through additional tourism, business opportunities, positive image of a place, or jobs for the local population. Although countries that host the Olympics rarely achieve a net economic gain, the prospect of economic development through hosting events and the management of sponsorship and media coverage has proven to be attractive to many countries. The political support for anti-doping dovetails with the optimistic claims made for the various components of organised sport (Horne and Manzenreiter 2006, Coalter 2007). The outcome is an organisation that needs to negotiate a complex environment of various competing demands (Wagner 2009).

The interweaving of the idealism of the Olympics with WADA's fundamental rationale was manifest in policy through the applied use of the 'spirit of sport' as one of the three criteria for including a substance or method on the Prohibited List. The other two criteria are: the risk or potential risk to the health of the athlete; and the potential for the substance or method to enhance performance. A further aspect of this interweaving is that the concept of the 'spirit of sport' was developed in Canada through the Canadian Centre for Ethics in Sport (CCES), in the aftermath of the Ben Johnson scandal, when the country's sports leaders and politicians sought to recover a sense of purpose to sport that would be the opposite of the over-emphasis on elite sport that created the conditions for organised doping in the 1980s. Prior to WADA's formation, the 'spirit of sport' had been about celebrating and promoting sport as part of health, community, ethics and the investment of public money into mass sport. It has been influenced by the Dubin Commission which proposed sport to be associated closely with health and the traditional ethos of amateurism. Thus, the spirit of sport was a reaction to the Ben Johnson scandal at a national level: it looked backwards to a time when sport was supposedly purer; and forward with optimism to a time when anti-doping would help restore this purity (Ritchie 2013). It reflected implicit notions of clean/dirty, purity/corruption, and promised to identify which athletes could participate in sport on account of their ability to follow the rules and ideas governing 'clean sport' (Henne 2015).

In summary, the core ideals promoted by WADA and laid out in the first version of the WADC are reflective of Olympism, are a legacy of amateur values and reactions to scandals. They constructed a vision simple enough to build a consensus that can be supported by governments and the IOC, their main funders. It means the organisation was never truly independent, and did not provide a realistic assessment of the motivations for, and patterns of, doping behaviours. Doping was presented as the antithesis of sporting integrity. The reform was important in terms of global policy and implications for athletes. It was organisational change rather than philosophical. It built upon Olympic ideas to gain support; and the utopian vision of drug-free sport remained. Moreover, it put the IOC front and centre of the new globalisation and empowerment of anti-doping. The crisis of 1999 had been skilfully manipulated into an opportunity.

Myth and power

The consensus around anti-doping related to the positive messages about sport and society, that athletes could and should be positive role models, and that drug taking is to be absolutely discouraged. However, it would appear that such an amorphous and abstract notion as 'clean sport' needed to be expanded in order to support anti-doping. It was not enough to loosely hope that athletes and their doctors would accept the boundaries of good behaviour and stay within them. Anti-doping leaders sought also to invoke fear in order to enhance power: this was done, and continues to be done, by reinforcement of basic ideas and 'common sense' truths that justify the need for draconian measures of power.

After all, when a system punishes citizens, other citizens need to be assured that the punishment is just, correct and proportionate.

The most foundational myth is that doping is a form of cheating that denies clean competitors a fair shot at winning and thus steals their rightful position in the event. In this sense, doping is considered to be a corruption of sport, reflecting language that has been used since the interwar period to describe doping. This is of course related to the statement in the WADC that doping is 'contrary to the spirit of sport'. This idea is often reinforced in media narratives with references to athletes who believe they have lost out unfairly to doped athletes. It is reinforced by the images of specific situations such as Ben Johnson opening up a gap of several metres over his rivals in the 1988 Olympic 100m final, or Lance Armstrong's seven Tour de France titles, or in general Russian track and field athletes winning Olympic medals after the revelation of systematic doping in Russia prior to the 2016 Olympics. By assuming the cause-and-effect of doping-to-win, anti-doping imagery leads the public to believe in a highly simplistic idea that doping is the reason for success. However, the reality is much more complex.

First, the ingredients of success are vast and varied, such that a substance taken in pill form or injected can best be understood as making a minor contribution to the overall level of performance that an individual can achieve. We cannot assume that two close rivals would have been the same were it not for one using doping products. In Ben Johnson's case, any proposal that he won because of doping assumes that his closest rivals were not doping, and fails to explain why he lost several races in the years prior to the 1988 Olympics. Regarding Lance Armstrong, since we know many of his rivals doped, there must be other factors such as his genetic ability, personality and determination, team strategy or training methods that help explain his success. The evidence of success in the Olympics, specifically Russia's medal winners, ostensibly points towards the benefits of doping. However, those athletes were developed through a highly organised and scientifically advanced sports system, and they did not always win. This situation is even more complex in team sports where tactics and cooperation, and response to the opponent's strategy, are key factors in success. The impact of one or a handful of players in a team being able to run for longer due to doping can only be one among many different aspects in determining the outcome including some which are equally unfair such as financial resources, sports education, access to state of the art facilities and coaching expertise etc. Sports that require mental or physical skills more than strength and endurance are not easily identifiable with doping as a reason for success. And some 'doping' substances do not have a potent performance-enhancing effect, so many cases of apparent cheating are not necessarily linked to any form of competitive advantage.

Second, the negative health effects of doping have long been over-stated in a bid to deter through fear and to help resource policy agencies. The idea that doping can kill has been central to stories about individual athletes from Arthur

Linton in the 1880s, to Knud Enemark Jensen in 1960, Tommy Simpson in 1967, Florence Griffith-Joyner in 1998, as well as the alleged EPO related deaths among European cyclists in the 1980s and early 1990s exposed as a myth by the Spanish scholar Bernat López (López 2011). While each of these cases is far more complicated than would at first appear, they collectively serve a purpose, which is to demonstrate that doping needs to be prevented to save lives. The fact that some of them are based on little or no evidence has not stopped anti-doping campaigners repeating them in order to instil fear of the dangers of doping into potential users.

Third, the promotion of the idea that 'clean' athletes have proven themselves to be embracing the ethics of sport by not cheating, treating everyone fairly, and not artificially enhancing their performance. History shows us that we cannot be certain that athletes who have not been caught by the testing system in place during their career can be guaranteed not to have used doping products. Moreover, 'bending' the rules can, at certain moments, be considered the sign of intelligence and creativity. Many athletes and teams deliberately use all possible means of 'legal' performance enhancement which benefits the wealthy and creates economic disadvantage. Athletes who are 'pure' and successful are hailed as heroes, without stopping to assess the true reasons for that success. As we shall see (Chapter 4), the power of this clean/dirty principle has led to numerous sanctions given out to athletes whose 'doping' violation has not led to any form of increased success; they simply have not followed the rules correctly.

In this respect, we can see that myths are closely related to power. Those who hold power circulate simplistic assertions, vague generalisations and even claims that have been proven to be wrong, in order to enhance their power and demean their critics. They promote a division of clean and dirty, praising the former (despite the ambiguities noted above) while denigrating the latter. As the German lawyer Carl Schmitt explains:

> Only in myth can the criterion be found for deciding whether one nation or a social group has a historical mission and has reached its historical moment. Out of the depths of a genuine life instinct, not out of reason or pragmatism, springs the great enthusiasm, the great moral decision and the great myth. In direct intuition the enthusiastic mass creates a mythical image that pushes its energy forward and gives it the strength for martyrdom as well as the courage to use force. [...] Wherever this is lacking, no social and political power can remain standing.
>
> *(Schmitt 2000 p. 68)*

Scandals, fear and policies: WADA's early initiatives

WADA is the product of scandals and the critical failings of anti-doping in 1990s. This decade shifted the parameters as the Cold War ended, so the political issues that fostered sportive nationalism could no longer justify passively accepting doping. Commercialisation meant that more funds were available for anti-doping. And this addressed a problem that had plagued earlier Olympic Games. Commercialisation also meant that the image of sport needed to be easily marketed and commodified (Dick Pound had previously led the IOC's sponsorship and media strategies). However, the rationale for anti-doping had originally been based upon amateur sports ideologies and thus global sports leaders wanted a modern rationale for anti-doping, one that allowed for professionalism and commercialism, and keeping the focus on ethics and health. They turned anti-doping into a policing force that prevented explicit cheating from ruining the competitive balance of events and the positive healthy image of sport. Perhaps the post-Cold War period ushered in some optimism that the formerly problematic doping cultures of the USSR and GDR could be resolved through international cooperation. Perhaps it was considered easier to engage the USA, West Germany and other Cold War allies and to address doping practices in the Olympics and in non-Olympic professional sports. Nonetheless, WADA and anti-doping more generally required a supportive network of allies, to ensure there was a consensus that doping was wrong and that WADA was on the right track.

The early years of WADA's emergence were characterised by policy inertia. It took over three years to set up the organisation, communicate with stakeholders and develop the first WADC. The headquarters were initially to be in Lausanne, but the decision was made to locate the organisation in Montreal (where Dick Pound was a partner in a law firm). During this period, 2000–2003, media and scholarly debates were increasingly focusing on the dramatic and exploitative nature of doping through the 1970s–1990s. A series of publications described the aforementioned exploitation of young females in East German sport who were given male hormone steroids without their or their parents' consent. Even two decades later, the most often-cited examples from that country are those women who suffered physiological and psychological trauma, and the gender realignment case of Heidi Kruger who became Andreas Kruger. These examples were cited in books in both German and English in the late 1990s and early 2000s (Ungerleider 2001).

As noted already, governments tended to have an arms-length approach and make public statements in support of the ambitions of drug-free sport. Even President George Bush, Jr spoke out against doping in his 2004 State of the Union address. By that year, WADA had developed the first WADC, and set in place a number of highly controversial new strategies such as the strict liability rule and the whereabouts system (Overbye and Wagner 2014). These were designed to reduce the chances of athletes doping out-of-competition, and of athletes circumventing sanctions by claiming inadvertent consumption. It is sufficient for the present to identify the fact that WADA had taken some audacious steps to substantially monitor and disempower athletes, which critics saw as an infringement of their human and civil rights (Houlihan 2004). This might have looked from the outside as a necessary approach in the fight for clean sport, especially given the scandals of the 1990s. The WADC would be the cornerstone of the new approach. Athletes would become subject to the rules and legal processes. With support of the Court of Arbitration in Sport (CAS), the Code thus became a substantial form of legal power designed to be unchallengeable by non-sports judicial bodies. Athletes have no right of appeal beyond CAS, and cannot challenge the substance or the regulations outlined in the WADC (David 2017).

In the space of four years, anti-doping had progressed from a state of disrepair, lacking clear lines of authority and trust, and failing to reduce doping in various sports and countries, to fast becoming the most powerful, omnipotent sports policy. Many media stories backed up the need to reform in order to address cultures of doping. Scientists often joined this movement by highlighting, even if without evidence, the health risks of doping products (López 2011). The examples of corrupt collusion among sports officials and managers, for example in the historical development of a state-led doping programme in East Germany, were used to show that, without some form of surveillance and monitoring, doping would increase. Athletes were increasingly mistrusted, treated as potential dopers, whether or not they had shown any form of risky behaviour or attitudes. All athletes had to be subject to regular testing, in order to demonstrate that the homogenised, global approach was working, and for a stronger deterrence to be in place. Thus, athletes at no risk of doping would become part of the surveillance process as much as those at risk, harmonisation meant that any sport seeking Olympic status and perceived anti-doping legitimacy would have to ensure their athletes were tested. Each country would have to demonstrate they had a NADO covering all signatory sports.

The logic of this approach is clearly to have a blanket, universal, fair means of dealing with potentially all sports in all countries. However, in a world of limited resources, this means a lack of specificity and targeting, although target testing is allegedly a priority as the introduction of registered testing pools bears witness to. The approach taken of focusing resources on athletes with minimal risk of doping, and not only those at high risk, means that consistently fewer than 2 per cent of all tests return an adverse analytical finding. Athletes in sports with no tradition of doping, nor even much utility in building endurance and strength (such as golf or curling) have been under the same testing system as high-risk sports (such as cycling, weightlifting and athletics). Despite this ineffectiveness, the impact of new surveillance systems would be felt by many athletes, and combined with the strict liability rule would lead to many inadvertent cases.

WADA took many controversial decisions and enhanced the anti-doping community of stakeholders on the basis that the critical situations of the 1990s needed to be quickly and demonstrably addressed. A UNESCO convention in 2005 underpinned the WADC (Jedlicka and Hunt 2013), leading to WADA being able to insist that governments follow their guidelines. They had become an international supra-power, able to cross boundaries in order to pursue harmonisation (Houlihan 2014). Athletes had to agree with the Code. This was officially deemed to be a voluntary choice, but of course if they refused the alternative was to quit sport, which for many was not really a choice (Geeraets 2017). Those in the whereabouts system had to provide information for three months on their day-to-day movements. Any athlete could face out-of-competition testers arriving at their house or training facility. As such, the impact of new rules was felt by clean athletes as much as by those who used banned drugs and techniques (Møller 2011a).

The BALCO scandal of 2002 emphasised the need for continued vigilance. Under the leadership of Victor Conte, the laboratory had been supplying legal and illegal performance-enhancing substances for several years. As we saw in Chapter 1, leading US and UK athletes were part of this programme which Conte had developed using a range of drugs including the undetectable designer steroid THG. WADA got a lucky break as a syringe containing some of this drug was sent to USADA by a former coach (Fainaru-Wada and Williams 2006). The exposure of an organised doping network that could not be blamed upon secretive, totalitarian regimes once again demonstrated the need for enhanced policy making. This scandal also impinged upon the image of the Olympics, with the American runner Marion Jones losing her three gold and two bronze medals from the 2000 Games and being imprisoned as a consequence of this and other investigations. It was also linked to the unfolding scandals within baseball that led to a 2005 Congressional hearing.

Doping stories continued to plague the Olympics as well. In the days preceding the start of the 2004 Games in Athens, two leading Greek sprinters, Kostas Kenteris and Ekatarina Thanau staged a motorbike accident in order to avoid an out-of-competition drug test. It emerged they had managed to avoid the testers for several previous months, and once they had been found out were withdrawn from the Games (MacKay 2004).

By the time of the WADC and the UNESCO convention, WADA had increased its resources, set out requirements for all countries and sports and increased testing. They had developed criteria for compliance to the Code, and threatened disqualification from all sports for those who failed to comply. By doing so, it had emerged into a highly powerful, centralised, homogenising force ensuring severe punishments for anyone who failed to accept and respond to the demands. Countries were required to establish independent NADOs, and the standard two-year ban for a violation was forced upon all sports (that signed the Code) regardless of the variations within the career life-cycle of athletes in those sports and variations in the seriousness of the doping incident. However, this appearance of success which focused on tightening up rules and processes, belied various problems relating to athletes' rights, ineffectiveness of the testing system, cases of inadvertent doping and social stigma faced by sanctioned athletes.

Gaining support for a failing project

The launch of the WADC was supported by sports organisations and the media. WADA required 30 countries to ratify the UNESCO convention before it could become adopted by its General Conference (which occurred in October 2005). One of its main strategies was to persuade governments to join and thus support anti-doping by initiating more education, testing and trafficking controls. We can see, therefore, a blend of approaches: cultural and ideological consensus backed up by international agreements; focus on the athlete as the main target of testing, regulation and sanctions; increased testing and scientific developments; accreditation of laboratories; education and social marketing around the clean sport message; and a controversial plan to allow retesting of samples for up to eight years.

The WADA president, Dick Pound, did not allow critics to distract WADA from their mission. At the 2007 Play the Game conference in Reykjavik, Iceland, he declared in a panel discussion that anyone who did not support the strict liability rule 'are people who want the cheaters to prevail', and he furthered his uncompromising attitude as he was quoted in the conference magazine as saying: 'I don't see a moral problem with a lifetime ban for doping. If you do it again, I am sorry there is no excuse: Go somewhere else, don't play with us' (Sparre 2008 p. 9). Athletes who complained about the surveillance and testing processes were given little respect for their experiences or opinions. Three years earlier he had published a book called *Inside the Olympics: A Behind-the-Scenes Look at the Politics, the Scandals and the Glory of the Games* in which he highlighted the worst-case examples of cheating in the Olympics and articulated the need for a stronger fight against current and future doping (Pound 2004).

The dilemmas faced by those trying to control doping in order to avoid scandal was evident in the Olympic Games. During the 1970s–1990s, the IOC seemed to prefer to avoid too many doping scandals. The Ben Johnson incident was an example of how negative impressions followed a high-profile scandal. When Dick Pound and Juan Antonio Samaranch compromised and agreed to support WADA, with the IOC being central to its development, the IOC lost control over scandal management, even if they still had significant influence in terms of funding and governance. A more independent organisation, even if it received half of its funding from the IOC, would be expected to make decisions in the pursuit of clean sport, not for political reasons.

The impact of this new arrangement, the IOC having to work alongside other organisations, was somewhat ambiguous. In the years preceding the Lausanne conference, doping cases at the Olympics did not appear to be too troublesome. There are seven positives associated with the 1996 Games, 15 with the 2000 Games, but by 2004 that had jumped to 37. It is possible to argue that WADA had helped develop better testing methods and so had improved the anti-doping system and it was much harder to dope without being caught. Certainly when the IOC ran anti-doping for the Olympics there appears to have been vested interests and a lack of independence at national level, leading to allegations of cover-ups to reduce the number of scandals (Jones 2005). In that sense, WADA at least seems to have ensured that all positive tests were made public. However, a higher number of positives does not simply mean that anti-doping is more successful; it also means that we know athletes were still turning to banned performance-enhancing drugs to pursue their career ambitions. Having a unified Code, more education and testing, the threat of retesting and working towards harmonisation had not cured the problem of doping.

The biggest test case for WADA's empowerment and creation of a global consensus around the need for anti-doping was professional cycling. The 1998 Tour de France scandal had been a major blow, but by the mid-2000s after the formation of WADA, there was scant evidence to suggest that cycling had reformed to become 'clean'. Certainly, Dick Pound was not convinced as he accused the International Cycling Union (UCI) of not doing enough to combat the problem (BBC 2006a).

When Lance Armstrong announced his retirement in 2005, having won the seventh of his consecutive Tour de France titles, he seemed to have proved his critics wrong and won 'clean'. However, cycling would come under a great deal more pressure in the immediate aftermath of this apparent success. Media coverage of riders' testimonies about doping created something of a scandal. The information provided by David Millar, Jesus Manzano, Matt DiCanio and Christophe Bassons, all pointed towards the continuity of doping within cycling. Academic researchers found further evidence showing a less structured approach as team managers tried to distance themselves from doping cyclists (Christiansen 2005). Spanish police raided the clinic of Fuentes in 2006 and found evidence of blood doping of professional cyclists, some of whom were named. Consequently, the organisers of the Tour de France chose to pre-emptively exclude some of the top contenders from the 2006 event. This, however, did not prevent a doping scandal from happening as it was revealed after the race that the celebrated winner, Floyd Landis, had tested positive for testosterone. High-profile cases like those of Floyd Landis (2006) and Michael Rasmussen (2007) showed that the UCI were struggling to ensure that athletes were not doping for the major races, even if those cases were much more complicated than would first appear. Even after he admitted to other types of doping Landis insisted he did not use testosterone, the substance found in his sample (Landis and Mooney 2007). Rasmussen's exclusion for providing wrong information on his whereabouts was even more controversial. According to the rules the maximum sanction for whereabouts rule violations should be a one year suspension. Had the authorities acted in accordance with the letter of the UCI's anti-doping regulations, Rasmussen's whereabouts failure would not have led to an anti-doping rule violation (Møller 2011b). Nevertheless, the authorities handed him a two-year ban claiming his whereabouts rule violation was in fact tampering with the doping control.

The profile of anti-doping was raised during this time as media representations of doping as scandal influenced political and public opinion on the subject. The more intensive and frequent nature of scandals allowed WADA to enforce their authority on the basis of the simplistic consensus that doping needed to be removed from sport. Cycling and baseball became prime examples of the need for more action towards clean sport. They were also used to demonstrate the need for an independent agency and that the sports federations could not be left to manage their own athletes.

Another significant challenge for WADA during this period was the prospect of doping scandals at the 2008 Beijing Olympics, and lack of commitment to anti-doping within the Chinese sports system. The history of anti-doping in China is not very well documented. There was some evidence of athletes from that country doping in the 1990s (Hong 2006). While there was some support for anti-doping from 1989, when the first Chinese anti-doping laboratory was created, and in 1993 when the Testing Division of the Chinese Olympic Committee Anti-Doping Commission was founded, there was no independent anti-doping agency in the run up to the Olympics. Given that the WADC makes that a requirement, it was a timely occurrence that the Chinese Anti-Doping Agency was established in May 2007.

There were 21 positive tests just before or during the 2008 Games and later evidence suggests a much larger problem which was not detected at the time. Retesting of samples in 2016 led to another 30 positives (and 30 more in a subsequent wave of retesting), and it is not clear if that retesting had a wide enough remit as it was part of a specific investigation into doping in Russian sport. Also, the IAAF had collected blood data from 2001, which was later exposed by the *Sunday Times* (in 2015) to show that of 800 athletes in the sample, on average 14 per cent were identified by experts as having suspicious blood-level data. The authors summarised the key findings:

> A third of all medals in endurance events at the world championships and Olympics, including 55 gold medals, were won by athletes who had given suspicious blood samples at some point in their careers. Ten medals awarded at the London Olympics were won by athletes who have had suspicious blood test results. More than 80% of Russia's Olympic and world championship medals were won by suspicious athletes. Kenya is renowned for producing many of the world's greatest distance runners but 18 of the country's medals were won by athletes judged to have had suspicious blood test results.
>
> (Sunday Times 2015)

In response, the IAAF argued that the scientific protocol for using that information was not fully in place until 2009 when the Athlete Biological Passport was formally introduced. It is therefore quite feasible that the 2008 Olympics included a number of athletes who had manipulated their blood values through

EPO and/or blood transfusions. A study of world level athletes in track and field in 2011 showed that over 40 per cent admitted using a doping product in the previous 12 months (Ulrich *et al.* 2017). There was not a test for EPO until the mid-2000s, and so usage was easy to hide. Even when a test was implemented, a number of scientists had raised concerns that it was flawed and inconsistently applied: their study showed that two WADA-accredited laboratories produced different outcomes (Lundby *et al.* 2008).

WADA had become adept at arguing the case for more resources. The number of worldwide tests has increased every year, yet the percentage of positives has remained much the same. They had some success in encouraging countries to sign up to the UNESCO convention and WADC. Their approach was gathering momentum and cooperative support. Media organisations still presented doping as a scandal, and (auto)biographies and investigative journalism continued to show that it was an ongoing problem. Anti-doping testing was unsuccessful at catching cheats, but WADA was winning the propaganda war by establishing a powerful position in the ideological consensus. It was increasingly difficult to propose alternative models of policy planning and implementation. The WADC has only been reviewed in 2009 and 2015, with the most significant updates being towards the enhancement of regulation, surveillance, control and punishment.

The war on drugs gets tougher

By the late 2000s, many countries had their own independent national anti-doping agency which meant greater human and financial resources dedicated to education, testing, deterrence and sanctions. For example, UK Anti-Doping (UKAD) started in 2009 with a budget of £7.2m per year. WADA's authority was demonstrated when it successfully annulled the lifetime ban imposed by the British Olympic Association (BOA) for sanctioned athletes' inclusion in Olympic squads. Support from CAS was obvious in cases where evidently inadvertent doping situations where the athlete appealed were generally upheld by CAS (Amos 2007). The requirement that countries and organisations follow the WADC had a variety of outcomes. The overruling of the BOA policy seemed to favour the athlete and allow dopers to represent their country in the Olympics. On the other, the ideas behind strict liability were beginning to take effect. Similarly, instances of sanctions imposed for missing tests were upheld. For example, in 2006 the English 400 metre Commonwealth Games champion, Christine Ohuruogu was banned for one year after missing three tests (BBC 2006a). Moreover, there were occasions where WADA appealed to CAS in order to contradict NADO or international federations' (IF) decisions which were seen as too lenient (in regard to imposing the WADC) even if they were cases of inadvertent doping.

The greatest scandal of the twenty-first century however would be the US Postal and Lance Armstrong investigation, led initially by the FBI and subsequently by the United States Anti-Doping Agency (USADA). In some ways, this case illustrates how specific investigative journalists have driven the anti-doping agenda by pursuing suspicious athletes and ignoring the potential problems within anti-doping organisations. Certainly, the role played by French journalist Pierre Ballester and the *Sunday Times* reporter David Walsh was instrumental in piecing together testimonies from Armstrong's teammates and other people that knew him. As Walsh explained, he had long held suspicions about Armstrong and worked hard to gain the trust of people close to the Motorola, Discovery and US Postal teams (Walsh 2013). Once that information had been made public, along with confessions from teammates like Tyler Hamilton and Floyd Landis, the evidence was overwhelming. The interest of the FBI was based on the potential misappropriation of public funds, as sponsorship from the government came indirectly through US Postal mail company.

WADA was a secondary partner in these developments, and it had to rely upon more powerful investigatory bodies. It also highlights the ambivalent relationship between civil and sports-specific legal processes. When the FBI subpoenaed witnesses including Hamilton and George Hincapie, some of the evidence was apparently passed to USADA, or at least helped the anti-doping agency, even after the FBI decided there was no public prosecution case to pursue (Shipley 2012). Thus, national and international anti-doping benefited from the US government resources, similarly to the benefits gained from the French government's attempt to crack down on doping in cycling in 1998. Nonetheless, neither USADA or WADA have the power to threaten imprisonment for perjury so the involvement of the FBI was vital.

The Armstrong scandal was unfolding in the years preceding the 2012 Olympics and indeed came to fruition in October 2012. The pressure on other cycling teams to demonstrate they were clean is shown by the number of teams who publicly declared their clean status and in some cases refused to employ anyone who had a previous sanction for doping. The run-up to the Olympics was an opportunity for WADA to work along the IOC and the London Organising Committee, led by the English ex-athlete Sebastian Coe, to prove how serious and successful anti-doping had become. In the six months prior to the Games, 107 athletes were sanctioned for doping (Grohmann 2012). However, many of the high-profile competitors had previous sanctions such as Alexander Vinokourov, Justin Gatlin, LaShawn Merritt, Dwain Chambers, David Millar, Carl Myerscough and Yohan Blake. The Jamaican anti-doping system was brought into question by former executive director of that country's anti-doping organisation, Renée Anne Shirley. Subsequent investigations led to the conclusion from WADA and the IOC that the Olympics had been 'sabotaged' by cheating Russian athletes, and subsequent retesting focused on medal winners from Russia and a range of other countries, mostly East European and North African. Numerous events have now had the places reallocated to an extent that creates a certain level of absurdity. For example, in the women's 1500 metres the athletes who placed 1, 2, 4, 5, 7 and 9 have all been sanctioned for doping, leaving the medals being allocated those who finished in places 3, 6 and 8 (Huebsch 2016).

Sebastian Coe had presented an image of the 2012 Olympics as clean. He continued to maintain this image until 2015 when the *Sunday Times* and German television ARD published the leaked IAAF blood files not long after he was appointed president of the IAAF. His immediate response was to accuse the journalists, calling their story a 'declaration of war' on athletics (AP 2015). He became increasingly embroiled in scandal, due to his link to the now-disgraced former President Lamine Diack, to the sportswear company Nike, and his failure to address doping during his seven-year period as vice-president of the IAAF. In the meantime, two Russian whistleblowers, who had failed to attract the attention of WADA and the IAAF, took their story to ARD and the *Sunday Times*. These two media outlets made several prominent feature stories detailing the widespread and corrupt doping practices in Russia. From that point onwards, WADA could no longer ignore the issue and instructed its now former president, Dick Pound, to lead an investigation, which reported in November 2015, leaving no credible defence to the accusation that doping was rife and had undermined the 2012 Games. Subsequent investigations were led by Canadian lawyer Richard McLaren, after evidence emerged from the Russian whistleblower Grigory Rodchenkov, leading to partial bans from the 2016 Olympic Games. Moreover, it was not just Russia, but Kenya, Turkey, Ethiopia and Morocco that were under pressure from the new allegations. In summary, doping has continued throughout the period since WADA was established and given the responsibility to reduce the extent and nature of cheating through doping. Various forms of evidence suggest that global sport still has a major challenge in preventing the misuse of drugs, despite the economic and political resources devoted to anti-doping and the high cost for clean athletes, inadvertent dopers and deliberate dopers. The incentives underpinning doping behaviours have not changed, if anything the financial rewards and pressures have increased, while the deterrence factors have evidently not been a success.

The other side of the coin

Media-driven public scandals have served WADA's purpose of requesting more funding. Since Sir Craig Reedie was appointed president in 2013, they hasve raised over $12m to promote scientific research into improved testing systems. Governments continued to commit money to WADA and to establishing their own anti-doping agencies. International sports federations are subject to scrutiny regarding their seriousness in combating the problem. Major international news outlets promote the scandalous aspects, portraying a moral landscape that requires immediate and drastic intervention. We can see a consensus continuing to be built in spite of the apparent flaws and failures. Anti-doping has a powerful ideological underpinning, a strong sense of right and wrong. By associating doping with corruption and focusing on the worst-case examples, the meaning and ramifications of doping are presented as much more serious than simply an athlete trying to find a way to improve his or her performance, relieve pain, or help recovery.

While the initial impression might be that anti-doping has been gradually winning the war on drugs, there are several ways in which the situation is much more complex. It is the case, clearly, that WADA, NADOs and IFs need help from external agencies in order to pursue information and sanctions. The overall effectiveness of testing has not improved since 2002 with less than two per cent of all tests being returned as positive. Yet, WADA seem content to pursue cases where the nature of the substance used and the absence of intention combine to suggest that the athlete has not deliberately cheated or benefited from the doping method.

Moreover, there are cases where athletes have been denied medical use of drugs because they are on the Prohibited List, even in cases where they can present evidence from doctors that their health is at risk if they are not permitted access to the drugs in question. And cases where the TUE system might have been deliberately exploited to access a banned substance for reasons more associated with performance enhancement than genuine medical need. In other words, the public image of success masks some problematic decisions and strategies that do not support the stated objectives of anti-doping: to protect the health of athletes and the level playing field.

Another issue that deserves more attention is the way in which sanctioned athletes are stigmatised and left alone to manage the consequences of their situation. There is an absence of psychological support, rehabilitation or even any form of concern for their well-being.

The system also fails to produce standardisation and fairness consequently there has been inconsistency between sanctions accorded to similar violations. The reason for this rests with the key organisations coming to an agreement on the case in point. The now standard four-year ban can be reduced if the athlete can provide some information in their defence, and/or if they are young athletes who have not been exposed to anti-doping education and testing. However, there is a certain vagueness here which opens up questions of how decisions are made. WADA have some influence as they can appeal against the initial decision through CAS, but that also appears to be an unpredictable process as arbitration is undertaken on a case-by-case basis.

Lastly, a central pillar of WADA's ambitions has always been harmonisation. However, that relies on countries having the same proportion of resources to commit to anti-doping, of being relied upon to deliver independent testing and sanctions, and in fact to have a culture that supports anti-doping. It assumes that the values set out by middle-class Western men in developed countries with a history of amateur sports ideologies can be transferred to the rest of the world.

The developmental history of anti-doping reflects a need to respond to scandals (Ritchie and Jackson 2014; Johnson 2014). The demand for a globalised and consistent approach resulted in the creation of WADA whose leaders did a lot of work to build a model that all countries and all sports could agree with. The support of UNESCO and national governments helped achieve the political foundation for WADA's vision of a tougher policy system. Since then, various scandals have emphasised the importance of anti-doping for the integrity and image of sport. The policies were controversial in that athletes now faced more out-of-competition testing, more rigorous observation of the urine test, and disproportionate sanctions for innocuous breaches of the rules. As previously mentioned, the athletes had no choice but to accept the system if they did not want to quit elite level sport. The use of CAS for appeals that are not satisfied at the national level means that athletes can face large legal costs and a lengthy decision-making process. The apparent high-level consensus around the idea of clean sport does in fact hide a multitude of problems,in relation to the ineffectiveness of the testing system, the excessive and involuntary impositions on athletes, and the undignified treatment of those who face sanctions. Thus, the consequences of anti-doping are problematic, and we turn now to address the evidence of, and reasons for, the failure to prevent doping from continuing in many sports and in many countries.

References

Amos, A. (2007). "Inadvertent doping and the WADA Code". *Bond Law Review*, 19(1): 1–25.

AP (2015). "Lord Coe: allegations against IAAF are declaration of war on my sport". *The Guardian*, 4 August. Retrieved 8 January from https://www.theguardian.com/sport/2015/aug/04/lord-coe-allegations-iaaf-drug-testing

BBC (2006a). "Wada boss slams Armstrong 'farce'" 2 June. Retrieved 4 January 2018 from http://news.bbc.co.uk/sport2/hi/other_sports/cycling/5043260.stm

BBC (2006b). "Ohuruogu is hit by one-year ban" 15 September. Retrieved 4 January 2018 from http://news.bbc.co.uk/sport2/hi/athletics/5328420.stm

Christiansen, A. V. (2005). "The legacy of Festina: patterns of drug use in European cycling since 1998". *Sport in History* 25(3): 497–514.

Coalter, F. (2007). *A Wider Social Role for Sport: Who's Keeping the Score?* London: Routledge.

David, P. (2017). *A Guide to the World Anti-Doping Code* Cambridge: Cambridge University Press.

Fainaru-Wada, M. and L. Williams (2006). *Game of Shadows: Barry Bonds, BALCO, and the Steroids Scandal that Rocked Professional Sports*: Harmondsworth: Penguin.

Geeraets, V. (2017). "Ideology, doping and the spirit of sport". *Sport, Ethics and Philosophy* 1–17. Retrieved 4 January 2018 from http://www.tandfonline.com/doi/full/10.1080/17511321.2017.1351483

Grohmann, K. (2012). "Testers nab more than 100 athletes prior to London –WADA". Reuters, 24 July. Retrieved 4 January 2018 from https://www.reuters.com/article/us-oly-dop-wada-adv3/testers-nab-more-than-100-athletes-prior-to-london-wada-idUSBRE86N16420120724

Hanstad, D. V., A. Smith and I. Waddington (2008). "The establishment of the World Anti-Doping Agency: A study of the management of organizational change and unplanned outcomes". *International Review for the Sociology of Sport* 43(3): 227–249.

Henne, K. E. (2015). *Testing for Athlete Citizenship: Regulating Doping and Sex in Sport*. New Brunswick, NJ: Rutgers University Press.

Hong, F. (2006). "Doping and anti-doping in sport in China: An analysis of recent and present attitudes and actions". *Sport in Society* 9(2): 314–333.

Horne, J. and W. Manzenreiter (2006). "Sports mega-events: social scientific analyses of a global phenomenon". *Sociological Review* 54(Suppl. 2): 1–187.

Houlihan, B. (2004). "Civil rights, doping control and the world anti-doping code". *Sport in Society* 7(3): 420–437.

Houlihan, B. (2014). "Achieving compliance in international anti-doping policy: An analysis of the 2009 World Anti-Doping Code". *Sport Management Review* 17(3): 265-276.

Huebsch, T. (2016). "Nearly half the 2012 Olympic women's 1,500m finalists have been linked to doping", *Canadian Running*, 6 March. Retrieved 4 January from https://runningmagazine.ca/womens-1500m-final-2012-olympic-doping/

Institute of National Anti-Doping Organisations (2017). "Proposals for WADA governance to ensure independence", 7 February. Retrieved 4 January from http://www.inado.org/fileadmin/user_upload/member-docs/iNADO_Resources/WADA_Goverance_Proposals_-_Ensuring_Independence__2017.02.07_.pdf

IOC (2017a). "Promote Olympism in Society". Retrieved 8 January 2018 from https://www.olympic.org/the-ioc/promote-olympism

IOC (2017b). "IOC Executive Board". Retrieved 8 January 2018 from https://www.olympic.org/executive-board

Jedlicka, S. R. and T. M. Hunt (2013). "The international anti-doping movement and UNESCO: A historical case study". *The International Journal of the History of Sport* 30(13): 1523–1535.

Johnson, M. (2016) *Spitting in the Soup: Inside the Dirty Game of Doping in Sports*, Boulder, CO: Velo Press.

Jones, J. (2005). "Exum claims large-scale cover-up of doping positives". *Cycling News* 29 April. Retrieved 4 January from http://www.cyclingnews.com/news/exum-claims-large-scale-cover-up-of-doping-positives/

Landis, F. and L. Mooney (2007). *Positively False: The Real Story of How I Won the Tour de France*. New York: Simon and Schuster.

López, B. (2011). "The invention of a 'drug of mass destruction': Deconstructing the EPO myth". *Sport in History* 31(1): 84–109.

Lundby, C., N. J. Achman-Andersen, J. J. Thomsen, A. M. Norgaard and P. Robach (2008). "Testing for recombinant human erythropoietin in urine: problems associated with current anti-doping testing". *Journal of Applied Physiology* 105(2): 417–419.

MacKay, D. (2004). "The man who pulled a fast one on the Games". *The Guardian*, 15 August. Retrieved 4 January 2018 from https://www.theguardian.com/sport/2004/aug/15/athensolympics2004.olympicgames6

Møller, V. (2011a). "One step too far: About WADA's whereabouts rule". *International Journal of Sport Policy and Politics* 3(2): 177–190.

Møller, V. (2011b). *The Scapegoat*. Copenhagen: Art People.

Overbye, M. and U. Wagner (2014). "Experiences, attitudes and trust: An inquiry into elite athletes' perception of the whereabouts reporting system". *International Journal of Sport Policy and Politics* 6(3): 407–428.

Pound, D. (2004). *Inside the Olympics: A Behind-the-Scenes Look at the Politics, the Scandals and the Glory of the Games* Toronto: John Wiley & Sons.

Ritchie, I. (2013). "The construction of a policy: The World Anti-Doping Code's 'spirit of sport' clause". *Performance Enhancement & Health* 2(4): 194–200.

Ritchie, I. and G. Jackson (2014). "Politics and 'shock': reactionary anti-doping policy objectives in Canadian and international sport". *International Journal of Sport Policy and Politics* 6(2): 195–212.

Schmitt, C. (2000). *The Crisis of Parliamentary Democracy*. Cambridge, MA: The MIT Press.

Shipley, A. (2012) "Lance Armstrong will not face charges as federal doping investigation is shut down", *Washington Post*, 3 February. Retrieved 8 January 2018 from https://www.washingtonpost.com/sports/cycling/lance-armstrong-federal-case-is-closed-as-us-attorneys-office-ends-probe/2012/02/03/gIQARWk5nQ_story.html

Sparre, K. (2008). "This is not a Mr Nice Guy job". *Play The Game Magazine*. Retrieved 4 January 2018 from http://www.playthegame.org/upload/magazine2007/pdf/pages/playthegamemagazine07pg9.pdf

Sunday Times (2015). "The Doping Scandal". Retrieved 4 January 2018 from http://features.thesundaytimes.co.uk/web/public/2015/the-doping-scandal/index.html#/

Ulrich, R., H. G. Pope, L. Cléret, A. Petróczi, T. Nepusz, J. Schaffer, G. Kanayama, R. D. Comstock and P. Simon (2017). "Doping in two elite athletics competitions assessed by randomized-response surveys". *Sports Medicine* 48(1): 211–219.

Ungerleider, S. (2001). *Faust's Gold: Inside the East German Doping Machine* Basingstoke: Macmillan.

WADA (2015). *World Anti-Doping Code*. Retrieved 4 January 2018 from https://www.wada-ama.org/sites/default/files/resources/files/wada-2015-world-anti-doping-code.pdf

WADA (2017). "Executive Committee". Retrieved 8 January 2018 from https://www.wada-ama.org/en/executive-committee

Wagner, U. (2009). "The World Anti-Doping Agency: Constructing a hybrid organisation in permanent stress (dis)order?" *International Journal of Sport Policy* 1(2): 183–201.

Walsh, D. (2013). *Seven Deadly Sins: My Pursuit of Lance Armstrong*. New York: Simon and Schuster.

4

WHY ANTI-DOPING FAILS

In contrast with societal efforts to combat drug misuse, anti-doping harshly punishes users, and defines users in such a way that innocuous and accidental usage can be heavily sanctioned. Users are stigmatised, demonised, held up as bad role models, and offered little opportunity to reintegrate into their professional role. The public are offered salacious tales of doping through media representations over-emphasising the cheating and unethical aspects of drug use. Nonetheless, as will be addressed in this chapter, there are significant questions around the effectiveness of anti-doping.

Anti-doping, or indeed sports culture more broadly, is unique in that it expects its workers (athletes) to behave in accordance with a certain pre-defined set of ideas. Concepts of clean and pure underpin exclusionary notions of 'athlete biological citizenship' (Henne 2015). In order to belong to the global community of athletes, to participate in their profession, to have an income, much less to be successful, every athlete might sign up to, understand and comply with the World Anti-Doping Code (WADC). There can be few other walks of life where membership depends upon conforming to such a strict set of rules, a core document that is over 150 pages long, with some highly complex science and legal elements, that – if not observed – can lead to a period away from employment and social stigma that remains through the athletes' life to disrupt their social capital and earning opportunities during and after their competitive career.

Even more concerning is that those rules are not simply for the athletes' professional working environment. They are not similar to, for example, rules preventing airline pilots from having alcohol in their blood before take-off. It is hard to imagine any form of occupational identity that requires availability to the 'employer' every day of the year, not to mention that the individual could be subject to the strict rules of their workplace when they are in 'non-work' situations. For athletes, the rules apply during their leisure time, family time, holidays – their 'citizenship' is an all-encompassing concept. In order to become an athlete, many personal freedoms are expected to be sacrificed.

This is enshrined in the WADC. Article 5.2 states: 'Any Athlete may be required to provide a Sample at any time and at any place by any Anti-Doping Organisation with Testing authority over him or her' (WADA 2015b p. 37). The definition of 'athlete' is quite complex: 'Any Person who competes in sport at the international level (as defined by each International Federation) or the national level (as defined by each National Anti-Doping Organisation)' (WADA 2015b p. 131). These definitions imply a clear understanding of what constitutes national- and international-level competition. It is left to the NADO to decide which athletes should be tested because literally all athletes who play sport in high or low divisions in a country compete at national level, but it would be impossible and probably also superfluous to test them all. This opens up the scope for diversity across countries. Nonetheless, the point remains that athletes whom the NADO find reason to test must sacrifice their rights to privacy simply by being under the authority of sports organisations. There is no other occupation where the regulator can demand citizens follow rules designed for the workplace in non-work situations. Indeed, the idea that athletes should be allowed a clear separation of work and non-work has simply been neglected by WADA.

In the following, we first review the strictness of anti-doping policy, and the extensive methods of surveillance used to ensure athletes have followed the rules. If the intrusiveness of this system could be positively weighed against its success then perhaps we could accept its legitimacy. However, there is a clear deficit between the number of athletes caught using drugs to cheat and the evidence found elsewhere of prevalence. Thereafter, we consider why the attempt to force all athletes, in all sports and in all countries, to behave according to the 'clean sport' mantra has failed so badly despite increasing policy efforts, government support and financial resources.

Surveillance

Being under surveillance is part of being an athlete. Exposed to public audiences during competitions, many famous athletes also attract media attention as they are celebrities. To some extent, lack of privacy is also normalised through their socialisation as athletes, which entails sacrificing parts of their private life others would have considered sacrosanct. They might, for example, have to share a hotel room with a teammate when travelling for competitions, or take a shower in communal areas. Bodily functions that impact upon their training and performance, possibly including menstruation, will have to be communicated to their coaches and sports doctors, as would any symptoms requiring a medicine. They will be required to have regular examinations by doctors and physiotherapists. This ambivalence over privacy has been exploited by sports organisations in order to enhance specific policy and control systems. Historically, one of the most obvious examples is the introduction of gender verification testing in the 1960s. The loss of privacy is profound at the moment when a woman has her genitalia inspected, by anyone, much more by a stranger or by a man (Heggie 2010).

When anti-doping testing started, also in the 1960s, some athletes protested against the invasion of privacy and their human rights, but major sports organisations did not appear concerned about any resistance. Providing a urine sample was introduced by the IOC and supported by international federations, and at that time the athlete was allowed to take the sample collection bottle into the bathroom by themselves. The fact that their urine could then be analysed in a laboratory to inspect the contents of their bodies, was an issue of privacy. Strangely, there is little evidence of resistance to that particular process, arguably due to a perception that scientific laboratories had protocols that would protect confidential information. However, the power of the authorities to insist on drug testing, directly linked to the ideology of clean sport and the purity of 'athlete citizenship', meant that resistance could be interpreted as immoral, unhelpful or even as a distraction from the athletes' own behaviours. Essentially, speaking up against this intrusive surveillance could lead to accusations that they must be cheating, or want to cheat, or are unsupportive of global efforts to ensure sport is fair and clean.

For three decades, athletes were allowed the privacy of urinating alone. When rumours surfaced of various strategies for swapping samples, the authorities took a view that privacy needed to be sacrificed to ensure the validity of the sample. No longer could an athlete hide a pre-prepared sample in a body cavity in order to dupe the testers. No longer could men use a fake penis that stored another sample (Jendrick 2006).

By the 2000s, WADA had formulated clear procedures and given the observation role to a trained drug control officer (DCO). Athletes under the age of 18 could also be accompanied by a chaperone, to ensure they were protected while left alone by the DCO. As we saw in Chapter 1, there is no stated minimum distance between the DCO and the athletes' genitalia. However, they must be positioned in such a way as to observe the urine leaving the body. As we also saw, evidence from surveys show that some athletes find this process distressing, can cause nervousness which in turns affects their ability to urinate (Elbe and Overbye 2014). Given also that DCOs can visit athletes at their houses any time between 6 am and 11pm and have to remain in the presence of the athlete at all times until they can provide the sample (which could be several hours), WADA has created a set of procedures which trample all over societal ideas of privacy and dignity. As Kathryn Henne explains:

> The current [anti-doping regime] is a global network supported by scientific testing, an array of biomedical surveillance devices, corporatized sports actors, national governments, and international law. The synergies

between these actors yield a unique transnational caste of citizen subjects – that is, elite (or aspiring elite) athletes – who are increasingly subject to expectations of bodily purity that are policed by routine bodily scrutiny, a number of surveillance mechanisms, and binding regulatory codes.

(Henne 2015 pp. 2–3)

Testing system failures

The absolutist and romanticised vision of drug-free sport has never been a reality and is very unlikely to become a reality. The pressure placed upon athletes through monitoring and punishments has not produced an environment which is clean, healthy or fair. Recent scandals demonstrate that organised doping can still occur, and that there are countries and sports were testing is not carried out with an organised sense of purpose. If a system were in place that ensured all athletes were competing on a level playing field, then perhaps the pressure placed on those athletes would seem justifiable. If that system could distinguish between deliberate cheating, borderline but legitimate performance enhancement, and accidental doping, then we would know who are the real cheats. If the health of athletes was of paramount importance then, it could be argued, the entire apparatus of anti-doping would have some rationality. But these ambitions have failed, as should already be apparent from what we have presented so far.

The feeling that anti-doping is an unwinnable war led the pioneering anti-doping scientist Professor Arnold Beckett to reflect, when asked in 1980 if the IOC's Medical Commission was prevailing in their anti-doping campaign: 'No. We can only prevent the more serious aspects of the problem. We win some; we lose some. The war goes on' (Hunt 2011). Arguably, anti-doping testing is inherently destined to fail, because new drugs produced by pharmaceutical companies can only become banned when sports organisations realise they are being abused by athletes. The period since 1980 has witnessed a dramatic expansion of the pharmaceutical opportunities available to athletes. The intrinsic motivations to dope have not changed over the past 60 years. If anything the financial incentives have only increased. The increasing power of anti-doping to test and sanction athletes has not proved a deterrent to the continuity of doping.

In a report compiled for WADA by leading experts in 2013 (Pound *et al.* 2013), it was demonstrated that the system of testing does not perform very well: 'To date, testing has not proven to be particularly effective in detecting dopers/cheats.' (p. 3). The authors of this report, the former WADA president, Dick Pound, the director of the WADA-accredited laboratory in Montreal, Christine Ayotte, the CEO of UK Anti-Doping, Andy Parkinson, and former athlete Adam Pengilly (who has represented athletes on various committees in WADA and the IOC), are among the most knowledgeable experts in this field. Their overview was an honest appraisal of decades in which anti-doping has been consistently defeated by both organised dopers and by passive attitudes.

They contended that the science is not the problem, nor did they reflect critically on WADA's policies, but instead focused on the political and cultural issues:

> The primary reason for the apparent lack of success of the testing programs does not lie with the science involved. While there may well be some drugs or combinations of drugs and methods of which the anti-doping community is unaware, the science now available is both robust and reliable. The real problems are the human and political factors. There is no general appetite to undertake the effort and expense of a successful effort to deliver doping-free sport. This applies (with varying degrees) at the level of athletes, international sport organizations, national Olympic committees, NADOs and governments. It is reflected in low standards of compliance measurement (often postponed), unwillingness to undertake critical analysis of the necessary requirements, unwillingness to follow-up on suspicions and information, unwillingness to share available information and unwillingness to commit the necessary informed intelligence, effective actions and other resources to the fight against doping in sport.
>
> *(Pound* et al. *2013 p. 3)*

How sizeable is this deficit?

The number of athletes sanctioned for doping every year is not very clear. We know that of all the samples collected, tested and the results reported to NADOs and WADA, less that two per cent have an adverse analytical finding (AAF); in 2013 this was 2.31 per cent, in 2014 it had fallen to 1.36 per cent. In 2015 there were 1.26 per cent AAFs and in 2016 this had increased to 1.60 per cent (WADA 2017). This percentage has remained roughly the same since 2003, despite the number of tests being conducted increasing from 130,000 to 300,000 (in 2016). More testing does not mean more effectiveness in catching athletes whi use doping. Moreover, the total AAFs is not an accurate reflection of detection, instead there is a great deal of vagueness for several reasons.

First, the AAFs can include more than one positive for an individual athlete. For example, Russian swimmer Yulia Efimova tested positive for meldonium six times in a period between mid-February and the end of March 2016. She was not banned as the substance had only been banned since 1 January 2016, she appealed against the proposed sanction on the basis that she had stopped using it before then but insufficient scientific information was available on excretion rates so it was possible that it remained in her system for several weeks after use (FINA 2016).

Second, the AAFs can include the use of substances banned only during competition, but were used out-of-competition; and might include substances for which the athlete has a therapeutic use exemption (TUE).

Third, WADA do not publish specific details on how many AAFs lead to a sanction: there may be many cases where a scientific or legal issue derails a formal sanction.

Fourth, many of the cases (potentially 40 per cent) are for substances taken inadvertently, without intention of enhancing performance, or for social reasons (de Hon and van Bottenburg 2017).

And fifth, a number of AAFs will be for non-elite or amateur athletes, or older athletes, whose doping behaviours are varied. Some might be using anti-ageing therapies or medicines which they simply do not know are banned (Henning and Dimeo 2015). As such, the 1–2 per cent is an over-estimation of the numbers of deliberate doping cheats who have been caught: the actual figure probably is closer to 1 per cent. In 2015, David Howman the director-general of WADA commented: 'We acknowledge that analytical studies over the years have suggested that the prevalence of doping is considerably higher than the current 1–2per centadverse analytical findings range typically reported in our annual Testing Figures Report' (WADA 2015a). Indeed, Howman said in 2011 that 'Statistically the numbers of people being caught is between one to two per cent, that's the numbers of positives against the number of tests. But the number of people doping are in the double digits' (Magnay 2011).

The low level of testing success means that world sport is no closer to a level playing field than it was before WADA was established. If we can imagine that 10 per cent of athletes have doped and less than 1 per cent are caught, then 9 per cent have gained the artificial advantage that allegedly makes the difference between winning and losing. However, other evidence suggests that even the 10 per cent figure is an under-estimation.

A number of research papers (de Hon et al. 2015, Dimeo and Taylor 2013) contrast the low percentage of positive tests globally with other evidence of prevalence. The science of prevalence measures is not exact, and there have been different methodologies used to assess patterns of drug use. As noted in Chapter 3, one of the most striking recent sources of information was data collected over the period 2001–2012 using blood samples from international track and field athletes. This information was leaked to investigative journalists in 2015. Of all the athletes that provided samples, 15 per cent had blood levels considered by experts to be 'abnormal'. The highest individual country was Russia, but the following countries had over 15 per cent of their athletes having recorded suspicious levels: Ukraine, Turkey, Greece, Morocco, Bulgaria, Bahrain, Belarus and Slovenia (Sunday Times 2015). This media coverage bears similarity to a scientific analysis of 7,289 blood samples from 2,737 athletes collected between 2001 and 2011. The authors found a remarkable contrast between the country with the highest prevalence of blood doping (48 per cent) and the lowest (1 per cent) suggesting that harmonisation is not effectively working to ensure parity in different contexts. They also found an average prevalence of 14 per cent, which is much higher than the number of AAFs in WADA's testing statistics (Sottas et al. 2011).

Other evidence of prevalence rates points to consistently higher levels of doping. A series of studies show that prevalence of doping is between 14–39 per cent (de Hon *et al.* 2015). Of course, there are methodological problems in establishing non-analytical evidence, not least whether respondents are being honest, and if they understand exactly what constitutes a doping violation. This is why the discussion of blood samples was a highly important contribution to the evidence base. We can contrast these types of evidence with examples from specific countries. In 2013, the US Anti-Doping Agency (USADA) reported 29 violations out of 9,197 tests in 2013. In 2012, Germany's anti-doping authority (NADA) reported only two violations out of 8,567 out-of-competition tests (Brown 2015). While these are selective examples, they serve to demonstrate the ineffectiveness of the testing system. German studies that used the randomised response technique (which has been found more effective because it encourages honesty by ensuring anonymity (Stubbe *et al.* 2014)) found prevalence rates among elite athletes in that country of consistently over 20 per cent in 2005 (Pitsch *et al.* 2007) which was replicated with similar results in 2011 (Pitsch and Emrich 2012). A similar method was used to survey 2,167 athletes at two sporting events: the 13th IAAF World Championships in Athletics (WCA) in Daegu, South Korea in August 2011 and the 12th Quadrennial Pan-Arab Games (PAG) in Doha, Qatar in December 2011. The outcome was an estimated prevalence of doping in the previous 12 months of 44 per cent (Ulrich *et al.* 2017).

It is estimated that over 1,000 athletes were in the Russian doping programme from 2010 to 2016. One of the major challenges facing researchers and policy officials is understanding the extent of drug use and areas of higher use. It would serve sport better if an organised global approach to prevalence studies was taken in order to highlight where the problem is greater, and where the problem is (almost) absent. However, prevalence studies are expensive to conduct and thus far we lack systematic and longitudinal studies. In an ideal world, baseline prevalence would be established so that the impact of specific interventions (education and testing, or increased sanctions) could be evaluated and resources used more effectively. There is a clear absence of evidence-based policy making, and resources are allocated arbitrarily and irrationally. Moreover, there are significant gaps in the homogenised deterrence approach because some sports and countries are not testing their athletes to any significant degree. If the 2013 WADA report is correct, and the problem lies with the lack of commitment from major stakeholders, then a useful response would be a systematic organisation of social science research and policy interventions, which in turn might need a paradigm shift from the current focus on testing and science towards improved understanding of the interplay of sports organisation economics, culture and individual motivations. The competing vested interests need to be mapped out and addressed, not simply ignored in the vain hope that science and excessive surveillance of athletes will solve the doping problem.

Harmonisation problems: the un-level playing field

In order for anti-doping to be successful, the global sports community would need to accept and engage with harmonisation which has been one of the core objectives of WADA since it was founded. Harmonisation essentially means that the WADC rules should be applied in all sports and countries in such a way as to promote the vision of drug-free sport. Education, testing and sanctions should be rigorously applied. Harmonisation relates directly to the concept of a 'level playing field', which might ostensibly refer to all athletes competing 'clean'. Deterrence through education, fear of being caught, and an efficient testing system should all be in place to ensure athletes are not tempted into using performance-enhancing drugs. Harmonisation also has a secondary or implied meaning which is that all athletes should operate under the same kind of anti-doping environment. Two rival athletes might be clean, but if one of them has never been tested then we cannot be assured that they are clean. As Hanstad and colleagues pointed out, if athletes are not functioning under the same conditions then the policy ambition has created an unintended consequence of disadvantaging those who live in a country or are part of sport where anti-doping is taken seriously, is well-funded and well-managed: 'The fact that athletes in different countries are treated differently by their NADOs is' they wrote, 'detrimental to the legitimacy and sense of fairness of anti-doping. … Moreover, lack of harmonization appears to be a severe legitimacy problem for the anti-doping movement' (Hanstad et al. 2010 p. 425). If athletes do not believe that anti-doping is uniformly applied then it can undermine their trust in the fairness of the competitive environment (Overbye 2016).

If harmonisation was a simple matter of economics, then a solution would be achievable: raise more money to deliver more testing. However, harmonisation is based on a naïve assumption that people within the sports system are not corruptible. In other words, it is possible to imagine situations where the trust that WADA place in NADOs and national governing bodies can be abused. The potentially simple act of bribing a drug control officer would be sufficient to undermine the testing system while ensuring the appearance of compliance. Similarly, if a laboratory manager would be prepared to dispose of potentially positive samples then harmonisation is once more undermined. Before WADA was created there was ample evidence of the lengths to which East German officials went in order to avoid doping athletes being caught by external anti-doping testing processes (Franke and Berendonk 1997). Many of the same types of approaches, and others, were used by Russia during the 2010s to give the pretence of taking anti-doping seriously while actually working to subvert the system. Among other methods, Russian officials simply disposed of potentially positive samples, doctored them with salt and coffee granules, swapped them for other samples by removing the seal, and in some cases allowed the positive to emerge, and extorted the athlete for payment to cover it up (McLaren 2016). At the same time, by announcing regular positive tests, mainly of lower-level athletes, the superficial appearance of compliance and integrity could be presented to the global sports community. Ironically,, Russia are one of the most transparent organisations when it comes to management information provided on their website (Martensen and Møller 2017).

Perhaps the Russian situation could be excused as a unique anomaly if we could believe that no similar organised doping system operated in other countries, and that WADA was determined to ensure that such systems could not function. We cannot say anything with any certainty about other countries because only Russia has been the subject of such intensive investigation. We only have information about the Russian context because whistleblowers Yuliya and Vitaly Stepanov were prepared to risk their lives and assume new identities in a secret location as a consequence of providing the information which subsequently underpinned investigations organised by WADA and led by Dick Pound and Richard McLaren. Another important person is the former police investigator Jack Robertson who unearthed some of the evidence by visiting Russia to conduct interviews and review documents. Robertson questioned the extent to which both WADA and the IOC were determined to confront doping in Russia and to protect the whistleblowers, and he said those organisations needed new leaders (BBC 2016b).

There is some other evidence that WADA failed to respond to the initial contact from the Stepanovs (Ford 2016), and it was only when the latter took their information to the German investigative journalist Hajo Seppelt that the publicity led to a response from WADA. It seems quite feasible to believe without the whistleblowers' determination, media interest and Robertson's dogged pursuit of new information that the Russian doping programme would have continued unexposed. At least WADA was in no rush to initiate any form of investigation until it was absolutely necessary. Given all these circumstances there is reason to believe that other countries have similar organised strategies that encourage athletes to dope, use various methods of eluding the testers that have not yet come to the public's attention because they have been successful. Indeed, the entire exposé of the Russian system only began because Yuliya Stepanova was caught using anabolic steroids after abnormalities in her athlete biological passport (Ash 2016). If her coach had been more knowledgeable and careful about the administration, she would not have been caught, and none of the evidence would have emerged.

Even if we can assume that the political corruption of sport, which exists in many other ways, did not affect countries' attitudes towards anti-doping, there is still a matter of economics – affordability. Setting up a national anti-doping organisation is quite an expensive business. For example, UKAD has a budget of around £7m per year. Given that the UK has one of the best elite sports systems in the world for Olympic sports, resulting in a position of third in the 2016 Rio Games, we might imagine that there would be a healthy level of resourcing for sport. The national sports agency UK Sport has around £350m over the four-year cycle between the Olympics to fund athletes and sports organisations likely to win medals. Therefore, we can see that in a country that historically has been at the forefront of anti-doping, whose elite athletes frequently speak publicly in support of clean sport, and recently hosted the Olympics, only a small fraction of the total spend on Olympic sport goes towards anti-doping. UKAD is also responsible for highly resourced professional sports like football, rugby, and cycling. The annual turnover of a major football club dwarfs UKAD's total budget. For example, Chelsea reported a turnover in 2016 of £329m with a profit of £4.7m. Thus, we can clearly see that even in a wealthy sports context, anti-doping has not been given high priority.

Countries facing severe economic depression, political crises, or ongoing humanitarian challenges such as war or famine, are understandably much less likely to fund sports organisations, much less subsidise anti-doping education, testing and the complex sanctioning and appeals procedures. As an example, Ethiopia sent 38 athletes to the 2016 summer Olympics, winning one gold, two silver medals and five bronze medals; by comparison Great Britain had 366 competitors. A simple calculation might lead to the suggestion that Ethiopia spend £700,000 on anti-doping (10 per cent of the UKAD budget). However, Ethiopia recurrently faces tragic situations where persistent droughts leaves millions of people suffering from extreme hunger, thirst and malnutrition (Laing 2016). Should the government have a pot of money equivalent to £700,000 there are clearly much more important ways to spend these resources.

In other contexts, where governments are investing heavily in sport, anti-doping might remain low on the list of priorities. The Brazilian government spent over $12bn, possibly up to $20bn, on hosting the 2016 Olympics (CBS News 2016). Regarding anti-doping specifically, $60m was spent to refit the anti-doping laboratory and train the technical staff. Even though the laboratory was suspended by WADA just before the Games, the decision to invest so much money clearly shows how hosting an event of the scale of the Olympics might prompt spending. Nonetheless, it was revealed that Brazilian athletes had not undergone out-of-competition testing in the months preceding the Games, and that during the Games on-site staff only managed to collect around half of the expected number of urine and blood samples (Rumsby 2016).

There are other reasons why high-level organisations might not wish to doggedly pursue a strategy of rooting out cheats and deterring potential dopers. Regardless of the funding environment, political corruption or other reasons, one of the most obvious barriers to successful harmonisation and dedication to anti-doping is that sports organisations do not want to see their best athletes prevented from participating in the most important events. As the British professional cyclist, Nicole Cooke, wrote in her statement to a parliamentary inquiry:

> Internationally, the conflicts of interest of so many of those charged with defending clean riders are such that they cannot be trusted to carry out

their responsibilities effectively. National and International Federations cannot be allowed to have any part in anti-doping activity. They are compromised at so many levels.

(Cooke 2017)

Arguably, that logic also extends to the public and media, many of whom would prefer the details of how athletes enhance their performance to remain out of sight, while they enjoy the spectacle of exciting events and national successes. Given the cultural and political ways in which anti-doping is fraught with competing interests, alongside the methods which can be used to subvert the system, perhaps it is no surprise that testing catches so few deliberate dopers. The infrastructure is simply not in place.

Beyond harmonisation: implementation at the ground level

Even if a country or a sports federation looks Code-compliant and therefore as if they are implementing the education, testing and sanctions according to the WADA's rules and model guidelines, we cannot be confident that local sports organisations are committed to anti-doping. There are clearly cases, some of them known to WADA, where testing has been so low that it hardly constitutes a deterrence threat. As an example, in the world's most popular sport – football – one of the most successful countries in recent years has been Spain. The Champions League tournament was recently won by Real Madrid (2014, 2016, 2017) and Barcelona (2011, 2015), the Europa League was won by Sevilla (2014, 2015, 2016). The national team won the World Cup (2010) and European Championships (2008, 2012). Yet, there was an absence in testing during the 12 months from March 2016 to February 2017, even after WADA had declared the Spanish NADO non-compliant, thus identifying a major weakness to be addressed:

The World Anti-Doping Agency has described the lack of drug testing in Spanish football during the past 11 months as 'alarming' and 'deeply disappointing'. The National Anti-Doping Organization of Spain (AEPSAD) was declared non-compliant in March 2016, since when no WADA-compliant testing has been conducted across the country's various football levels, including La Liga. 'The lack of testing in a country with one of the leading football leagues worldwide for a period of 12 months is alarming and will do little to instil confidence in clean sport at a time when it is needed most,' read a WADA statement. 'After AEPSAD was declared code non-compliant on 19 March 2016, WADA encouraged an agreement between AEPSAD and International Sport Federations that would ensure testing would be carried out on national-level athletes in Spain during the period of non-compliance. It is deeply disappointing that some International Federations did not sign the agreement, as this has prevented effective anti-doping programs from being run at the national level in Spain in a number of sports [during this period of non-compliance].'

In response, AEPSAD said it expects to be able to resume drug testing once the government approves a global code, possibly by the end of this month.

(The Guardian 2017)

Around this same time, it was revealed that similar problems existed in England, Germany and Scotland.

The example of Spanish football aptly illustrates the point made by the WADA experts in 2013 that the willingness to deter and punish cheats is not always evident. That might be because athletes have been invested in by organisations, sometimes literally in the case of transfer fees, and have a high public profile. The possibility of a long-term ban, or in some cases the loss of corporate funding and sponsorship, means that the vested interests do not always support the cause of anti-doping. This is not a new problem. Nicole Cooke used the example of Manchester United's star player Rio Ferdinand who was banned for eight months after he missed a test in 2004:

> Rio Ferdinand had recently been purchased for £30 million by Manchester United, a fee that was a new record. Were he to be banned, his team would not get economic reward against this investment. At this time both FIFA (President Sepp Blatter) and the UCI (President Hein Verbruggen) were resisting all calls for their sports to sign up to the new WADA protocols which clearly defined missed tests as infractions.
>
> *(Cooke 2017)*

Over a decade later, another example showed the ways in which football clubs occasionally do not proactively support anti-doping. When Manchester City FC failed for a third time to accurately report their players' whereabouts to the anti-doping testing authorities in the UK, it could have been interpreted as a serious Code violation. Those of a more suspicious mindset might have interpreted it as a deliberate strategy to evade the testers. The club were fined just £35,000 because the actual nature of the offence was considered relatively innocuous:

> A first-team player missed a test on 1 September 2016 because the hotel address provided was no longer correct. In addition, City also failed to inform the FA of an extra first-team training session on 12 July 2016, while anti-doping officials were unable to test reserve players on 7 December, 2016 because six of them had been given the day off without the FA being informed.
>
> *(BBC 2017)*

Missing tests is a highly contentious issue for anti-doping, often attracting controversy. Athletes are 'allowed' to miss two tests in 12 months, thus offering some flexibility for genuine reasons. However, it remains quite feasible for an athlete to be doping, and to deliberately avoid the testers by not answering the doorbell, or in fact being in a completely different place. There are numerous cases where missed tests have been allowed to happen because the authorities believe the athlete's explanation. While many might be true, we simply do not know how many are fictions created by the athlete and their entourage in conscious subversion of the anti-doping system. However, if the policy on missed tests is to be a deterrent, it should be taken seriously, and for a wealthy club like Manchester City a £35,000 fine is hardly a punishment to be concerned about.

This lack of determination to ensure sport is clean and the playing field is level can be further illustrated by the problems faced by whistleblowers. During the early 2010s, and especially in the run up to the 2012 Olympic Games, Renée Anne Shirley, realised that the organisation she worked for as executive director, the Jamaican Anti-Doping Commission (JADCO), was not functioning properly. In 2013 she came public and 'disclosed that only a single out-of-competition test had been conducted by JADCO between March and July before the London Olympics' (Scott-Elliot 2014).

Rather than being embraced by WADA and the IOC, she has faced serious personal issues, including being 'branded a "Judas" and a "traitor" to her country, and forced to relocate because of the backlash against her … she has been "blacklisted" because of her actions, saying she is "ostracised in the eyes of the entirety of Jamaica".'(Scott-Elliot 2014). There appears to have been no attempt from the IOC, WADA, JADCO or governments to support her in the course of making the allegations and having to cope with the emotional stress of the aftermath.

In regard to the passive nature of investigating doping cases, there have been the series of high-profile stories which have yet to be brought to conclusion in spite of the widespread public interest. As mentioned in previous chapters, the Spanish blood doping clinic run by the Spanish doctor Eufemiano Fuentes in the 2000s was raided by police in 2006. Over ten years later the outcome has not been resolved and the identities of the athletes involved have not been revealed. One of the problems has been the legal system and decision making:

> The sentence emitted from a Madrid lower criminal court on April 29, 2013 considered to have found proof that since the year 2002, there was a pattern of blood extractions and the administration of drugs such as EPO, IGF-I, testosterone, insulin, etc. to athletes – at a price, and with risks for their own health. But these proven facts were then taken to the Madrid Provincial Court, whose ruling went the opposite way and acquitted all of those who had been found guilty in the first case. The Provincial Court

considered that the blood was not a medication and as such there was no crime. And that was in spite of the abundant jurisprudence that the sentence itself included finding the opposite. Whereas the lower court had decided not to hand over samples of the blood bags that were seized, the Provincial Court authorised them to be handed over to the AMA, the International Cycling Union, the Italian National Olympic Committee and the Spanish Royal Cycling Federation.

(Bastida 2017)

As the author of the above summary, Enrique Bastida, noted in conclusion to his article: 'The problem is not discovering that there is corruption; the problem is not responding to that corruption in a firm and a determined manner'.

If the legal complexities around Operación Puerto were the only case where WADA has been frustrated by an inability to uncover the truth of the matter, we might consider the situation to be anomalous rather than indicative. However, media investigations into the supply of doping products to elite-level athletes in Kenya did not lead to a full-scale investigation or any serious sanctions against the governing bodies (Roan 2016).

Similarly, the English doctor Mark Bonar, whose story appeared on the front page of the *Sunday Times* after he boasted of supplying performance-enhancing drugs to around 150 athletes not knowing that he was talking to an undercover reporter. The chief executive of UKAD had to admit to a parliamentary inquiry that his organisation had been lapse in not following up on the initial information provided about Dr Bonar by a whistleblower, Dan Stevens (BBC 2016a).

Another whistleblower is Steve Magness, who first took evidence of malpractice in American athletics to USADA in December 2012. He showed the BBC Panorama programme photographic evidence that appeared to suggest that the British runner Mo Farah's training partner Galen Rupp was taking testosterone as a 16-year-old. However, a lack of follow-up activity led Magness to criticise UK Athletics (UKA) for its approach since the allegations first surfaced in June 2015:

'I think we all need to realise that as the national governing body you send the message of what the entire sport stands for in your country,' he said. 'They set the standard from the elites to our youth. Simply looking at the admitted behaviours, it's clear UKA is sending a message that performance is all we care about, everything else be damned. And if I'm a UK athlete, that's quite concerning.'

(Ingle 2015)

It was later discovered that a doctor working for athletics coach Alberto Salazar had altered Magness' medical records (Daly and Epstein 2017). It has taken over four years for any decision to be reached, despite official investigations and extensive media coverage of the accusations made against Salazar.

The British government's inquiry into the misuse of medicines at British Cycling and Team Sky has also taken a long time to come to a conclusion. The allegations surfaced in summer 2016, and various riders in the two organisations revealed details of such practices as overusing painkillers and asthma inhalers, and requesting TUEs that might not have been necessary. UKAD had failed to thoroughly investigate, so this responsibility was taken up by the Minister for Culture, Media and Sport, Damian Collins. A series of parliamentary committee meetings included interviews with senior managers and team members, leading to publicity that significantly undermined the reputation developed within British Cycling as being proactively anti-doping. What we have seen recently is evidence of athletes and teams trying to find an edge in ways which are up to the limit of legal.

One of the greatest challenges faced by anti-doping agencies, and indeed by sports organisations in a broader sense, is in persuading athletes, coaches, doctors, even parents, that sport is indeed about honesty and integrity. The concept of the 'spirit of sport' has been defended by some sports philosophers as reflective of a socially valuable meaning of sport (McNamee 2012). By contrast, elite athletes have a way of thinking about the world which is focused primarily on their own success. Steve Magness explained in 2013:

> When I left Nike last year, I often thought back to my interactions with a known drug cheat like Lance [Armstrong]. I saw the extreme competiveness and manipulative tendencies that fuel the psychology of a doper. The desire to be great and the willingness to do anything to win is a trait that many great endurance athletes possess. In the past, it meant Emil Zatopek doing forty 400m repeats in army boots. Now, for some it means crossing the grey line into cheating.
>
> *(Magness 2013)*

It is evidently the case that most athletes understand the 'grey line' and avoid crossing it due to a range of reasons from the fear of being caught to personal morality (Jalleh *et al.* 2014). However, it is also true to say of the past, present and future of sport that a certain percentage of athletes will deliberately cross that line; and that the interaction of incentives and barriers to doping are complex (Overbye *et al.* 2013). Some athletes, like Dwain Chambers, are not completely sure they are crossing it. Others, like David Millar, were gradually brought there and encouraged to participate in the accepted doping practices. Yet there is a wide variety of doping situations, and the apparently compulsory nature of doping in Russian sport forces us to concede that while users of performance-enhancing drugs are cheats, they might not always be willing cheats.

The working conditions of athletes are often insecure. They might easily feel that under-performance can lead directly to redundancy and no alternative career path. They might be motivated by the prospect of a huge professional salary and sponsorship endorsement contracts. Their working conditions are also structured by sports scientists, psychologists, nutritionists, coaches, doctors and various forms of technology, all of which aim to optimise the athletes' mind and body towards improved performance. In other words, the context within which they are socialised is geared much more towards success and performance outcomes than towards ethics, values, fair play and other such idealised notions of sporting cultures.

Anti-doping has developed to ensure athletes 'consent' to the WADC. By doing so, they become subjected to a system that intrudes upon their privacy in many ways. Aspects of this system have become more successful, in the sense that a stricter and more consistent environment has been promoted through a single Prohibited List, strict liability, clear sanctions, more rigorous accreditation and monitoring of laboratories, and an appeals process that is highly structured and avoids external courts from having jurisdiction.

However, these have not led to an improved anti-doping policy, in the sense that doping continues to occur and many dopers are not caught. There are many inconsistencies in the testing of athletes, and the delegation of power to localised organisations leaves open the opportunity for 'street-level' actors to disrupt the ambitions of WADA. It is an incomplete 'top-down' policy, made complicated by those who aim to undermine it, or ignore it, or can't afford to pay for it. The science is incomplete, and doping doctors work out new methods ahead of the testers. Therefore, the ambition of anti-doping to protect the level playing field has not succeeded.

References

Ash, L. (2016). "100 Women 2016: Russian doping whistleblower gives rare interview" 9 December. Retrieved 8 January 2018 from http://www.bbc.co.uk/news/world-europe-38253541

Bastida, E. G. (2017). "Spain must seek the truth behind the Operation Puerto doping scandal". *El País*, 23 May. Retrieved 8 January 2018 from https://elpais.com/elpais/2017/05/23/inenglish/1495534655_473113.html

BBC (2016a). "Dr Mark Bonar: UKAD 'missed opportunities' over doping allegations" 11 July. Retrieved 8 January 2018 from http://www.bbc.co.uk/sport/36761908

BBC (2016b). "Russian doping: Ex-investigator Jack Robertson criticises WADA and IOC". 4 August. Retrieved 6 November 2017 from http://www.bbc.com/sport/olympics/36972964

BBC (2017). "Manchester City broke anti-doping rules three times in less than five months" 24 March. Retrieved 8 January 2018 from http://www.bbc.co.uk/sport/football/39383967

Brown, A. (2015). "Prevalence of doping in elite sport likely to be between 14% and 39%". Sporting Integrity Initiative. Retrieved 8 January 2018 from http://www.sportsintegrityinitiative.com/prevalence-doping-elite-sport-likely-14-39/

CBS News (2016). "Why hosting the Olympics is a 'terrible idea'" 3 August. Retrieved 8 January 2018 from https://www.cbsnews.com/news/rio-2016-olympics-problems-cost-worth-hosting-games/

Cooke, N. (2017). Written evidence submitted by Nicole Cooke MBE (BDA0012), Department of Culture, Media and Sport, Blood Doping in Athletics Inquiry.

Daly, M. and D. Epstein. (2017). "Drug probe doctor 'altered athlete medical records'". 3 Retrieved 5 November 2017 from http://www.bbc.com/sport/athletics/40096586

de Hon, O. and M. van Bottenburg (2017). "True dopers or negligent athletes? An analysis of anti-doping rule violations reported to the World Anti-Doping Agency 2010–2012." *Substance Use & Misuse* 52(14): 1932–1936.

de Hon, O., H. Kuipers and M. van Bottenburg (2015). "Prevalence of doping use in elite sports: a review of numbers and methods". *Sports Medicine* 45(1): 57–69.

Dimeo, P. and J. Taylor(2013) "Monitoring drug use in sport: The contrast between official statistics and other evidence." *Drugs: Education, Prevention, and Policy* 20(1): 40–47.

Elbe, A.-M. and M. Overbye (2014). "Urine doping controls: The athletes' perspective." *International Journal of Sport Policy and Politics* 6(2): 227–240.

FINA (2016). "Statement on Yulia Efimova (RUS)" 15 July. Retrieved 8 January 2018 from http://www.fina.org/news/statement-yulia-efimova-rus

Ford, B. (2016). "McLaren Report further exposes inaction, Russian corruption" 10 December. Retrieved 8 January 2018 from http://www.espn.co.uk/skiing/story/_/id/18244371/mclaren-report-latest-unravels-even-more-russian-doping-corruption

Franke, W. W. and B. Berendonk (1997). "Hormonal doping and androgenization of athletes: a secret program of the German Democratic Republic government." *Clinical Chemistry* 43(7): 1262–1279.

Guardian (2017). "WADA describes lack of drug testing in Spanish football as 'alarming'" 10 February. Retrieved 8 January 2018 from https://www.theguardian.com/sport/2017/feb/10/wada-describes-lack-of-drug-testing-in-spanish-football-as-alarming

Hanstad, D. V., E. Å. Skille and S. Loland (2010). "Harmonization of anti-doping work: Myth or reality?" *Sport in Society* 13(3): 418–430.

Heggie, V. (2010). "Testing sex and gender in sports: Reinventing, reimagining and reconstructing histories." *Endeavour* 34(4): 157–163.

Henne, K. E. (2015). *Testing for Athlete Citizenship: Regulating Doping and Sex in Sport.* New Brunswick, NJ: Rutgers University Press.

Henning, A. D. and P. Dimeo (2015). "Questions of fairness and anti-doping in US cycling: The contrasting experiences of professionals and amateurs". *Drugs: Education, Prevention and Policy* 22(5): 400–409.

Hunt, T. M. (2011). *Drug Games: The International Olympic Committee and the Politics of Doping, 1960–2008.* Austin, TX: University of Texas Press.

Ingle, S. (2015). "Alberto Salazar whistleblower unhappy at UK Athletics clearance" 18 September. Retrieved 8 January 2018 from https://www.theguardian.com/sport/2015/sep/18/alberto-salazar-uk-athletics-oregon-project

Jalleh, G., R. J. Donovan and I. Jobling (2014). "Predicting attitude towards performance enhancing substance use: a comprehensive test of the Sport Drug Control Model with elite Australian athletes." *Journal of Science and Medicine in Sport* 17(6): 574–579.

Jendrick, N. (2006). *Dunks, Doubles, Doping: How Steroids are killing American Athletics.* Gulford, CT: Lyons Press.

Laing, A. (2016). "Ethiopia struggles with worst drought for 50 years leaving 18 million people in need of aid". *Daily Telegraph* 23 April. Retrieved 8 January 2018 from http://www.telegraph.co.uk/news/2016/04/23/ethiopia-struggles-with-worst-drought-for-50-years-leaving-18-mi/

Magnay, J. (2011) "London 2012 Olympics: one in 10 athletes are drugs cheats, says anti-doping chief executive", *The Telegraph*, 18 August. Retrieved 8 January 2018 from http://www.telegraph.co.uk/sport/olympics/london-2012/8710041/London-2012-Olympics-one-in-10-athletes-are-drugs-cheats-says-anti-doping-chief-executive.html

Magness, S. (2013). "My Interactions With Lance Armstrong" 18 Jan. Retrieved 8 January 2018 from http://running.competitor.com/2013/01/news/magness-my-interactions-with-lance-armstrong_64596.

Martensen, C. K. and V. Møller (2017). "More money: Better anti-doping?" *Drugs: Education, Prevention and Policy* 24(3): 286–294.

McLaren, R. (2016). *Independent Person Report*. Montreal: World Anti-Doping Agency.

McNamee, M. J. (2012). "The spirit of sport and the medicalisation of anti-doping: Empirical and normative ethics". *Asian Bioethics Review* 4(4): 374–392.

Overbye, M. (2016). "Doping control in sport: An investigation of how elite athletes perceive and trust the functioning of the doping testing system in their sport." *Sport Management Review* 19(1): 6–22.

Overbye, M., M. L. Knudsen and G. Pfister (2013). "To dope or not to dope: Elite athletes' perceptions of doping deterrents and incentives". *Performance Enhancement & Health* 2(3): 119–134.

Pitsch, W. and E. Emrich (2012). "The frequency of doping in elite sport: Results of a replication study". *International Review for the Sociology of Sport* 47(5): 559–580.

Pitsch, W., E. Emrich and M. Klein (2007). "Doping in elite sports in Germany: Results of a www survey". *European Journal for Sport and Society* 4(2): 89–102.

Pound, R., C. Ayotte, A. Parkinson, A. Pengilly and A. Ryan (2013). *Report to WADA Executive Committee on lack of effectiveness of testing programs*. Montreal: World Anti-Doping Agency.

Roan, D. (2016). "Doping commonplace in Kenyan athletics" 11 February. Retrieved 8 January 2018 from http://www.bbc.co.uk/sport/35553195

Rumsby, B. (2016). "Rio 2016 Olympics: Anti-doping branded 'worst' in Games history". *Daily Telegraph* 17 August. Retrieved 8 January 2018 from http://www.telegraph.co.uk/olympics/2016/08/17/rio-2016-olympics-anti-doping-branded-worst-in-games-history/

Scott-Elliot, R. (2014). "I had to go into hiding, says drug test whistle-blower Renee-Anne Shirley". *The Independent*, 19 March. Retrieved 8 January 2018 from http://www.independent.co.uk/sport/general/athletics/i-had-to-go-into-hiding-says-drug-test-whistle-blower-renee-anne-shirley-9203734.html

Sottas, P.-E., N. Robinson, G. Fischetto, G. Dollé, J. M. Alonso and M. Saugy (2011). "Prevalence of blood doping in samples collected from elite track and field athletes." *Clinical Chemistry* 57(5): 762–769.

Stubbe, J. H., A. M. Chorus, L. E. Frank, O. Hon and P. G. Heijden (2014). "Prevalence of use of performance enhancing drugs by fitness centre members." *Drug Testing and Analysis* 6(5): 434–438.

Sunday Times (2015). "The Doping Scandal". Retrieved 8 January 2018 from http://features.thesundaytimes.co.uk/web/public/2015/the-doping-scandal/index.html#/

Ulrich, R., H. G. Pope, L. Cléret, A. Petróczi, T. Nepusz, J. Schaffer, G. Kanayama, R. D. Comstock and P. Simon (2017). "Doping in two elite athletics competitions assessed by randomized-response surveys." *Sports Medicine* 48(1): 211–219.

WADA (2015a). "WADA Director General: 'Organizations must carry out quality anti-doping programs if true reflection of doping prevalence is to be known'". Retrieved

8 January 2018 from https://www.wada-ama.org/en/media/news/2015-02/wada-director-general-organizations-must-carry-out-quality-anti-doping-programs

WADA (2015b). *The World Anti-Doping Code*. Montreal: World Anti-Doping Agency.

WADA (2017) "WADA publishes 2016 Testing Figures Report", 25 October Retrieved 8 January 2018 from https://www.wada-ama.org/en/media/news/2017-10/wada-publishes-2016-testing-figures-report

5

COLLATERAL DAMAGE

While various scandals were both catalyst and fuel injector to the development of the WADC, the longer-term background had been concerns that athletes could easily beat the system, and that certain sports federations were more lenient than others. And indeed, that some countries did not have a positive approach to clean sport. The national level problems were to be addressed by insisting that every country or region create an independent anti-doping organisation, that would essentially be answerable to WADA and not engrained within the elite sports system of the specific place. The sports federations' problems were to be addressed through standardisation: any positive test would lead to a two-year ban (increased to four years in 2015), unless some exceptional circumstances could be demonstrated, in which case the athlete could appeal to their national or regional anti-doping organisation (NADO/ RADO) or to the CAS. The WADC would undermine sports federations' power to decide on what would be the most appropriate sanctions for their athletes.

These higher-level political moves firmed up WADA's position. The power structure was pushed forward quickly, so that WADA, at least formally, soon had more authority than the IOC, and could make cross-national decisions without requiring legal power from any government or court. As such, we focus upon how WADA chose to address the problem of athletes beating the system. The introduction of more out-of-competition testing, and its associated whereabouts systems, was a manifestation of a strategy towards enhanced deterrence. The foundational stone of anti-doping would become the application of the principle of strict liability (as mentioned in Chapter 1): without this the entire edifice would soon crumble. While ostensibly this principle aimed to prevent athletes and their lawyers exploiting loopholes, it has had some profound and disastrous effects on the athletic community.

The nature of strict liability

Strict liability is defined in the WADC as:

> 2.1.1 It is each Athlete's personal duty to ensure that no Prohibited Substance enters his or her body. Athletes are responsible for any Prohibited Substance or its Metabolites or Markers found to be present in their bodily Specimens. Accordingly, it is not necessary that intent, fault, negligence or knowing Use on the Athlete's part be demonstrated in order to establish an anti-doping violation under Article 2.1.
>
> *(WADA 2003 p. 8)*

Supporters of anti-doping imagined this position to be necessary, to encourage athletes' vigilance against consuming a banned substance, and to ensure they cannot invent excuses for that substances being in their body. Vanessa McDermott points out that this rule: 'implies all athletes are potentially "cheats" or "folk devils", and this automatic presumption of guilt has been controversial' (McDermott 2015 p. 85). She goes on to briefly explain several cases of accidental consumption of a banned drug, before concluding that the 'severe sanctions ... the personal costs for athletes, including to their health and well-being, heighten the importance of anti-doping information and education' (McDermott 2015 p. 86).

While McDermott appears initially critical of the strict liability consequences, she simply reasserts the anti-doping dogma that the solution lies, not with a revision of the rules, but with increased pressure upon sports organisations and athletes to pre-emptively learn about all the different ways in which a doping sanction might occur (accidentally or otherwise). This position is reflected in other research studies where the emphasis is placed upon educational programmes to deter deliberate doping and try to prevent accidental doping (Backhouse *et al.* 2012). This leads us into the muddy waters of intention, fault and negligence. The overarching purpose of the policy is to protect athletes' health, the level playing field and the spirit of sport. Yet, it is possible to fall foul of the rules without any health risks, any performance-enhancing benefit, or indeed any sense that the spirit of sport has been violated. Athletes can find themselves sanctioned for a whole raft of reasons far beyond their control, or beyond any predictability. They are considered fully responsible for any substance in their body, even if they do not fully understand the Prohibited List or the complex ways that contamination can occur (Geyer *et al.* 2008).

A more critical position has been outlined by Geeraets. Among a number of criticisms, he focuses upon the fact that athletes are compelled to consent to this system:

> The fiction of voluntary consent is useful from a rhetorical point of view because it makes athletes' complaints against the imposition of sanctions

seem suspect from the start. An athlete seeking to appeal can always be put back in his place by being told that he agreed with the Code in the first place. More importantly, claiming that the Code is based on voluntary consent enables the doping authorities to characterise the Code as contract law. This means that the athlete cannot call in safeguards typically related to criminal law.

(Geeraets 2017 p. 10)

Of course, strict liability is not a new concept and has been applied in criminal law. Perhaps the most suitable comparable situation where it would be applied is for drink driving incidents. Any person who takes a breathalyser test is assumed to have known that they have alcohol in their body. However, there are a number of pre-emptive steps which can justify this outcome. First, is that to pass a driving test to be allowed to drive involves answering questions on the legal limit of alcohol consumption. Second, that drivers are of a minimum age. In the vast majority of the world's nations one has to be 18 years old to get a full driver's license. This is because one is supposed to be mature enough to make reasoned decisions. In combination with national educational campaigns and the threat of being suspended from driving or even imprisoned, there are many countries where tougher rules and policing have led to reduced drink-driving incidents.

Can the same be said of anti-doping? In this case, there are over 300 drugs that might be consumed to lead to a sanction, some of which appear in everyday medicines or supplements, most of which are (in a criminal law sense) legal for personal consumption. There is no formal test that athletes take in order to prove they fully understand the rules. There is no minimum age for anti-doping testing, so young people whose abilities to digest important and complex information are not fully matured can be sanctioned. The person supplying the 'drug' might be doing so in good intention, not aware that they are potentially risking the athletes' career with a contaminated substance. Unlike alcohol, the potential routes of ingestion are varied, diverse and sometimes invisible. And unlike the simple breathalyser test, there is a complex laboratory procedure to be undertaken that might not always be as accurate, efficient and transparent as we would like it to be, if we are interested in protecting the rights of athletes.

It is worth taking some cognisance of the justification proposed by WADA for the use of strict liability. In the first WADC (2003) the CAS judgment on the case of *Quigley* v *UIT* is quoted in length. That case had involved an athlete consuming a banned substance in a cough medicine, as a result of poor labelling on the bottle and faulty advice given to him by a doctor (Anderson 2010). CAS upheld a sanction despite the panel admitting the outcome to be 'unfair' on the individual athlete. The arbitrators contended that 'it appears to be a laudable objective not to repair an accidental unfairness to an individual by creating an intentional unfairness to the whole body of other competitors' (WADA 2003 p. 9). In other words, the lack of intention is not important if there might have been a performance-enhancing effect. It is therefore assumed that, having accidentally consumed a performance-enhancing substance, the individual athlete has achieved an artificial advantage over their rivals. As we shall explain through examples below, this is a highly questionable assumption. The arbitrators further their support for strict liability by claiming that 'it is likely that even intentional abuse would in many cases escape sanction for lack of proof of guilty intent' (WADA 2003 p. 9). This is an articulation of the wider anxieties of deliberate exploitation of loopholes by those who planned and organised their performance-enhancing doping programme. A final point made by CAS regarded the legal process, and their desire to simplify it to the cost of the individual athlete: 'it is certain that a requirement [to prove] intent would invite costly litigation that may well cripple federations – particularly those run on modest budgets – in their fight against doping' (WADA 2003 p. 9). No specific case is referred to, however, cases throughout the 1990s proved to be highly expensive and complex legal processes which it seems CAS and WADA were keen to avoid in the new structure of the WADC.

In discussing this approach, Jack Anderson identifies a number of criticisms. He argued that it was 'unnecessarily and unreasonably dogmatic' as it did not allow a defence to be made that the athlete had no 'moral fault' since the doping violation was unintentional (Anderson 2010 p. 125). Thus, a variety of ways in which athletes could accidentally consume a banned substance would not be considered relevant for any appeal. Anderson lists such situations as: 'a prescription error by a medical adviser; a dispensing error by a pharmacist; an honest and reasonable belief that the substance was not prohibited; or, even, the malicious act of a third party who might have "spiked" the drink or food of an opponent' (Anderson 2010 p. 125). The consequences for athletes are severe, including financial, psychological, upon their reputation and time away from their sport (in some cases the end of their career). Given the imbalance between the outcomes and the intentionality, Anderson contends that 'it appeared unconscionable, even uncivilised, to promote a system that could lead the lengthy disqualification of an athlete in the absence of any moral fault' (Anderson 2010 p. 125). This is a clear critique from an expert in sports law about the imbalances of strict liability. Describing the policy as uncivilised is striking, as it shows that some ethical fault might lie with the policy makers and not all the blame should be directed at athletes.

In later versions of the WADC the rules were slightly adapted to allow a reduction or even no sanction. This would lead to more confusion as decisions were made on a case-by-case basis rather than through a consistent framework of comparative examples that are used to set a precedent. It would remain very difficult for athletes to prove their innocence, and the decision-making would still emphasise that the responsibility lies with the athletes to check every substance that enters their body.

As another sports law expert David McArdle shows, the modified approach still offers 'very little comfort' to athletes who have not deliberately used a banned substance (McArdle 2015 p. 294). Strict liability means an assumption of guilt, even if that guilt is the result of negligence rather than intention. The WADC (Article 10.5.1.2) describes the situation of 'contaminated products' in such a way that offers flexibility of the sanction imposed of zero to two years, but emphasises that this depends upon establishing the degree of fault, which opens the possibility of disputed interpretations of the athletes' actions:

> in cases where the *athlete* or other *Person* can establish *no Significant fault or negligence* and that the detected *Prohibited Substance* came from a *Contaminated Product*, then the period of *Ineligibility* shall be, at a minimum, a reprimand and no period of *Ineligibility*, and at a maximum, two years *Ineligibility*, depending on the *athlete's* or other *Person's* degree of *fault*.
>
> *(WADA 2015 p. 64)*

The procedures after a positive test call for an immediate suspension, with the athlete able to request that their B sample be tested as well (their urine sample is divided into two which are known as the A and B samples). A final decision can take months to be formally announced, and an appeals process can take years. As we shall see, the rules and the processes are heavily weighed against the athlete.

Depending on the nature and complexity of the case, an athlete could have their appeal heard at a NADO tribunal, and if not satisfied with the outcome, can appeal through CAS. However, there is an arbitration fee to pay, three arbitrators need to be appointed, the case is heard 'de novo', and so cases can take 6–12 months and in some instances even longer. Athletes often need to pay for their own legal representation, which can be (unpredictably) expensive. The outcome is also hard to predict given that key legal concepts like fault and intent are open to interpretation. Even if athletes are exonerated, they will have lost significant time from their training, and a burdensome anxiety about the outcome. Given the challenges in mounting an appeal, it is understandable if some athletes decide to accept the sanction.

Before the World Anti-Doping Code

From the perspective of 'cleaning up' world sport, there was a need for a tougher approach. Since the 1950s, athletes had managed to dope with impunity, the authorities were in effect powerless to stop them. Those who were caught could invent reasons through stories about how they accidentally had drugs in their body. Some of these were more fantastic than others.

Ben Johnson has always denied taking the stanozolol that was found in his urine sample after the 100 metres Olympic final in 1988. He claims to have had his post-race beer spiked by an associate of arch-rival Carl Lewis (McRae 2010). Of course, it did not help Johnson's argument that he and his coach, Charlie Francis, would admit that the sprinter had been using a plethora of doping drugs for around seven years prior to the 1988 race. Francis did claim to be surprised by the presence of stanozolol as this was one drug Johnson was not taking (Francis 1990). Thus, it remains a possibility that the positive test was either due to spiking or a false positive.

There have been a diverse range of other explanations. In 1996, the race walker Daniel Plaza tested positive for nandrolone. His initial ban of two years was overturned after he claimed that he must have ingested it from giving his pregnant wife oral sex. The American sprinter Denis Mitchell said that his high testosterone levels were the result of having sex four times (Steinberg 2013).

These are only a sample of the strange reasons cited by athletes for a positive test. In the absence of a global regulatory body, some cases prompted inconsistent decisions and years of appeals and counter-appeals, mounting up huge legal costs and difficult decisions about jurisdiction. For example, when Mary Decker Slaney tested positive for testosterone in 1996, she was banned by the IAAF for two years (decided in 1997). In September 1999, a USA Track and Field (USATF) panel reinstated her. This led to an IAAF appeal which was upheld in arbitration. She lost her silver medal from the 1997 World Championships. However, her legal team argued strongly that there was a lack of good science and that it remains possible that long-term use of the birth-control pill could lead to this outcome (Rowbottom 1999).

Another influential case during the 1990s was that of the American sprinter Harry 'Butch' Reynolds. After testing positive in 1990 he undertook a series of appeals that challenged the sports law decision-making system as much of the debate surrounded jurisdiction. Reynolds was in the end defeated by the IAAF and sanctioned for two years. The case took four years to be resolved and as Mack (1994) argues highlighted the need for a new arbitration process.

These cases suggest that a more efficient appeals process in which athletes had little chance to win a case due to strict liability would serve the interests of clean sport. During this time period there had been cases to suggest that, in fact, a stringent policy based on strict liability and reduced athletes' rights, would not be able to protect athletes against being falsely accused or disproportionately punished for relatively minor offences.

An early case involved 16-year old swimmer, Rick De Mont, who represented the USA in the 1972 Olympics. He was advised to use an inhaler in order to reduce the symptoms of asthma. His doctor had the assurance from the US Olympic Committee (USOC) that De Mont was allowed to use this medicine, which led to ephedrine being identified in his urine sample. He had won gold in the 4200 metres freestyle but was disqualified. His positive test meant he could not compete in any other event, thus losing the opportunity for further success. De Mont's appeal was ignored until the USOC finally admitted that it had mishandled the medical information but the IOC refused to return his gold medal. The incident had a profound effect on De Mont, who told a reporter in 1979:

> After Munich I felt like a total loser. I was afraid to face my friends, and all
> I could think of was, why did this happen to me? I was afraid that every
> time I got on the starting block people were thinking of me as some kind
> of speed freak, and I'm sure that's one reason my swimming went bad. I
> was just sort of going through the motions in swimming; my heart wasn't
> in it. I was praying that God would bless me with a gold medal at Montreal
> to make up for the one I lost at Munich.
>
> *(Kirshenbaum 1979)*

Unfortunately, he never recovered success in swimming. Despite President
Nixon having said in 1973 that De Mont was innocent, a national poll
showed 76 per cent of Americans agreed, and even the Chair of the IOC
Medical Commission, Prince Alexandre de Mérode, said that De Mont was
being punished for other people's mistakes, he did not get his medal back
(Kirshenbaum 1979).

Taking a medication without full awareness that the product contains a banned
substance would be a common problem, as we will outline below. However,
by the time WADA was formed there had been many other types of incidents
showing that other flaws in anti-doping processes could lead to a great deal of
suffering for individual athletes. For example, Diane Modahl was shocked to
hear that her urine sample had tested positive for elevated testosterone in 1994.
She was so determined to prove her innocence that a two-year legal battle, in
which she proved the drug-control personnel had left her sample in the high
temperature of the Portuguese summer until it had degraded, left her financially
bankrupt and very depressed. In her autobiographical account (Modahl 1995),
she describes moments in which she seriously contemplated taking her own
life. The sense of being abandoned by the sports community is a common
theme where an anti-doping violation has occurred. The stigma is profound,
and the loss of identity, alienation, of being drastically cut off from all forms of
group support. Modahl's husband and trainer revealed 'that she tried to commit
suicide after failing the 1994 test' (BBC 2000). One of the other consequences
was that the financial expenses borne by the British Athletic Federation led to its
bankruptcy and demise.

Returning to the case of Daniel Plaza is revealing in many ways. He might
have had a good defence since none of his further tests showed nandrolone
use even though the drug can remain in the body for up to three months.
For reasons which are unclear, it took the Spanish Supreme Court ten years
to overturn this ban, and he had not competed since it was imposed in 1996
(BBC 2006). So, one explanation is that he never used nandrolone and his test
result was a false positive. Or he consumed a small amount accidentally that
only breached the threshold on the occasion of his test. Nonetheless, he was
sanctioned for two years and did not race again. It is hard to imagine what ten
years wait to prove ones innocence does to a person. To add to the injustice,
his oral sex explanation is regularly mocked on website stories of the worst

doping excuses. A problematic test has ruined his sporting career and publicly humiliated him.

Had Plaza been an exceptional case it could be explained away as a most unfortunate consequence of an otherwise solid and well-functioning system. But it is not, there are disturbingly many controversial cases. Tellingly, two further incidents occurred during the first Summer and Winter Olympics Games of the new millennium, just as the WADC was being prepared.

The first of these involved 16-year-old Romanian gymnast, Andreea Răducan. She won a gold medal during the 2000 Games in Sydney. Much like Rick De Mont in 1972, her young age could have been taken into account. She was provided with tablets to counter symptoms of a common cold by the team physician. These turned out to contain the banned substance pseudoephedrine. She subsequently took her appeal to the CAS, which concluded that the decision was correct: 'The Panel is aware of the impact its decision will have on a fine, young, elite athlete. It finds, in balancing the interests of Miss Raducan with the commitment of the Olympic Movement to drug-free sport, the Anti-Doping Code must be enforced without compromise.' (Wong 2002 Note 5.3.9). A second case, already mentioned in Chapter 1, is that of the Scottish skier Alain Baxter during the 2002 Winter Olympics.

Thus, we see two corresponding developments which appear to serve the ambitions of clean sport but also discriminate against athletes. Strict liability was introduced to prevent dopers from making excuses to reduce their sanctions. Centralised appeals process supported by CAS was introduced to avoid jurisdictional conflicts, prolonged decisions and legal authorities, external to sport, having an influence. However, the outcome was that athletes who had a genuine reason for testing positive unintentionally had almost no way to avoid a sanction.

Contamination

As we described in Chapter 1, the Spanish cyclist Alberto Contador proposed in his own defence that he might have eaten some clenbuterol-contaminated meat. In 2010 the successful English hurdler, Callum Priestley, tested positive for the same substance while on a training camp with the UK team in South Africa. He was 22 years old and aspired to represent his country at the London Olympics.

There is evidence to support Priestley's claim that he also was the victim of contamination. During that same period a number of other athletes fell sick with apparent food poisoning, a fact confirmed by the team doctor. WADA had already accepted that clenbuterol could be in the food chain in high-risk countries such as Mexico and China. Yet, Priestley was offered no support. His father explained: "'They [UK Athletics] said Callum was wholly responsible for what he ate which on the UK Athletics training camp. This is shameful. The UKA took him to the hotel and fed him. Then he failed a drugs test'" (ESPN 2011). He also referred to the emotional toll: "'Callum has been hurt really quite badly. He's moving on with in life and he doesn't want to expose himself to anything like that anymore'". A combination of a two-year ban, lack of support and unwillingness to mount an expensive legal battle, cost Priestley his sporting career. As the former head of the UK Sport Anti-Doping Directorate and sports integrity consultant, Michelle Verroken said, "'Something needs to be done to protect athletes. When you don't think you've done something, it's incredible to think that you could go through the process and lose your whole career over it'" (ESPN 2011).

Another form of contamination has been through dietary supplements, taken for a variety of reasons. In 2003, the American cyclist, Amber Neben, tested positive for 19-norandrosterone after the Montreal World Cup race. She appealed her case, and during the arbitration process it became clear that there was little education or information provided by them for athletes using supplements. The written arbitration decision included the comment: 'There appears to be little to no attempt at communicating the dangers of contaminated supplements to the thousands of USA cyclists' (North American Court of Arbitration for Sport 2003). This despite expert witnesses agreeing that supplements were a normal part of sports nutrition. Moreover, the panel agreed that Neben's use was not intentional and decided to reduce her sanction to six months.

Around this same time period, several other US athletes tested positive for low amounts of banned substances. The swimmer Kicker Vencill was banned for two years after his urine sample showed traces of 19-norandrosterone. Initially, USADA imposed a ban of four years, but that was reduced after an appeal to CAS. As a result of the ban, he missed the 2003 Pan-American Games and the trials for the 2004 Olympics. Unusually in such cases, Vencill managed to demonstrate that the source of the banned substance was a sports nutrition supplement and that he was not at fault. The multivitamins he used were contaminated. However, this evidence merely served his civil law suit against the supplier, Ultimate Nutrition, and while he was awarded $578,635 he did not have his ban annulled. In the aftermath of which he described the impact of this incident on his life:

> "I deserve every penny of (the jury's award), though I would much rather have swum for my country at the Pan-Am Games in 2003 and had my shot at making the US Olympic team last year. Through its contaminated product, Ultimate Nutrition took two years out of my life – probably the best two years of my competitive career. I can never have that back."
>
> (Swimming World 2005)

The rule of strict liability meant that there would be no recompense for his loss of career opportunity, or indeed any reduction in his period of suspension. His lawyer did not try to blame WADA, USADA or CAS, but instead shifted the direction of attack towards the wider supplement industry and its regulation by the government:

Supplement companies need to make sure that they have real quality control procedures in place, to prevent this type of contamination. They cannot be allowed to continue to put our Olympic and professional athletes at risk. It is time for Congress to re-examine the lack of regulation of the supplement industry.

(Swimming World *2005*)

By contrast, Vencill was more scathing about the sports organisations involved: 'They can say I was careless, but I cared 100 percent. Was I cheating? No. Can they make an example of me? Yes.' (*Swimming World* 2005). Nonetheless, he was in a stronger position than other athletes in that he could afford to pay for a top defence lawyer and for scientific testing on the supplements he used (McMullen 2004).

The Australian triathlete Rebekah Keat was also the victim of a contaminated supplement in 2004, supplied by Hammer Nutrition. She would join forces with Amber Neben, and the Canadian Mike Vine to sue the company in 2008. There is no official record of the outcome of that suit, it was led again by lawyer Howard Jacobs, who explained the context and aims:

'The raw materials can be contaminated to start with. Or, they are making a product with norandrostenedione and don't clean the encapsulation machine. Or, it's intentionally spiked. The purpose is to reimburse the athlete for lost income, but it's the damage to the reputation that is often the bigger part of the puzzle,' the athlete's lawyer told *Triathlete*. 'You can't ever turn back the clock, but to some degree, it helps athletes have closure on the event. Right now, if you Google Rebekah Keat, the first thing you find is that she tested positive. It was the same with Olympic swimmer Kicker Vencill. But if you do it now, you're likely to find stories about how he sued a supplement company and the jury awarded him about $600,000.'

(*Abrams Landau 2008*)

Jessica Hardy tested positive for clenbuterol at the 2008 US Olympic trials. Although it was agreed by the American Arbitration Association that this positive came from a contaminated supplement, Advocare Arginine Extreme, she was still banned for a year. It transpired that Hardy had been offered 'personal assurances' from the manufacturer that it contained no banned substance. In response AdvoCare challenged the evidence. The company claimed that they were not represented at the arbitration process, and threatened a law suit against Hardy. It was clear that the athlete had been through some intense emotional turmoil and missed a significant career opportunity, she said:

I am extremely happy that the Arbitration Panel was persuaded by my scientific proof of supplement contamination, and that they believed me when I told them that I never have and never will use performance enhancing drugs. I look forward to returning to competition as soon as possible and proving that my prior successes, including at the Olympic Trials, were achieved solely through hard work and discipline, with no shortcuts. The past year, including missing the 2008 Olympic Games, has been heartbreaking, the most difficult year of my life. It was made more tolerable by the numerous expressions of support I received from teammates, competitors, and fans all over the world, for which I will always be grateful.

(Swimming World *2009*)

Sadly, her recovery was far from simple. She felt under scrutiny when she returned to competitive swimming. An article in the *New York Times* summed this up:

Although Hardy has served her sentence and essentially cleared her name, she recognises that her punishment may never end. 'It is my identity,' she said Indeed, she describes being ostracised by other athletes, and that she's had to 'toughen up'.

(Crouse *2010*)

The reporter aptly summarised the effects:

The close-knit American swimming community is divided in its assessment of Hardy. She is seen as having been victimised by an imperfect drug-testing system or having deftly manipulated that system. Her critics talk as if Hardy was treated leniently for cheating – though not on the record, because they do not want to be labelled poor sports.

(Crouse *2010*)

And in the same article, Kicker Vencill explained the paranoia and stigmatisation:

I would step on the deck and I would feel people were boring holes through me [...] I'd imagine everybody was whispering in everybody's ear about me. I'd be talking to people and I'd be thinking, "What if they have bad thoughts about me?" [...] When you're suspended for doping, it's like a brand. You have to have the courage to wear that, as stupid as it sounds.

(Crouse *2010*)

While the examples above serve to highlight the trauma of an inadvertent case caused by contamination, they also show how arbitrary and varied the end results are. This is a system in which the authorities come to blame the athlete for negligence, even if they can demonstrate no fault, no intent and no awareness of the contamination risk. In some cases, the amount of the banned substance digested is so low that it would not produce any form of performance enhancement. It is highly unlikely it would contravene the WADC principle of being a risk to their health. Those cases from the mid-2000s appeared soon after the WADC was beginning to take effect. There was no indication that the policy should be reconsidered. However, there were some indications that it would not be consistent. In 2004, a number of tennis players, including several leading British players, were not banned despite having tested positive for nandrolone, because the Association of Professional Tennis (ATP) conceded that the pills containing the banned substances was inadvertently handed out by trainers employed by the ATP (Coleman 2011). As noted in Chapter 1, the clenbuterol cases at the youth World Cup in Mexico were accepted as contamination. If strict liability seems unfair or unreasonable when imposed in a case of clear unintentional usage; another dimension of unfairness is that some athletes are 'let off' while others are punished.

An even more critical case involved Polish kart driver Igor Walilko, who consumed nikethamide, probably from an energy bar. He was 12 years old at the time. His initial two-year ban was reduced to 18 months by CAS, on the basis that the original sanction was 'excessive and disproportionate'. The treatment of minors within the anti-doping world is rarely discussed as requiring any specifically different treatment, despite the fact that civil and criminal law does recognise the level of responsibility changes with age. So when Walilko's lawyers raised the question of whether he was too young to be punished for inadvertent doping, the CAS panel dismissed their argument as 'utterly irrelevant' (Associated Press 2011).

Recreational drug use

The WADC clarified and standardised the global sports community's position on the use of narcotics for social purposes by athletes. There had been some testing for drugs like cocaine prior to 2003, but this had been sporadic. Some high-profile athletes had a reputation for over-indulging in both social drug use and alcohol, and while they might have been criticised for being poor role models they were not banned from participating in sport. WADA's approach was much more puritanical and some even argued that since cannabis does not have a performance-enhancing effect there was no reason for it to be banned in sport. Moreover, some confusion has emerged because stimulants and narcotics are only banned in-competition: athletes are free to consume as much as they wish, within the laws of their country, during out-of-competition periods.

Before WADA established the rules, there was some inconsistency and ambiguity. For example, Ross Rebagliati tested positive for tetrahydrocannabinol (THC) after winning the gold in snowboarding at the 1998 Winter Olympics. The positive test led to an initial decision to strip him of his medal, but it was soon established that THC was not a banned substance.

   The arguments for banning athletes for using cannabis or marijuana usually assume they have deliberately consumed it, and have clearly broken the 'in-competition' rule since out-of-competition use is allowable. But when WADA set out a ban that had to be imposed on all sports and athletes who signed the WADC, they established a low threshold level. The difficulty of the athletes' position is underlined by the fact that some athletes may have been banned for either accidental consumption – through passive smoking – or because their deliberate consumption outside of the competition time frame left traces of metabolites which were still detectable and above the threshold level. The unfairness of such an outcome must have been known to the WADA Scientific Committee when it set the threshold and maintained it for over a decade. In 2003 the threshold was 15 ng/ml. When this was changed to 150 ng/ml, a spokesman for WADA said: 'Our information suggests that many cases do not involve game or event-day consumption. The new threshold level is an attempt to ensure that in-competition use is detected and not use during the days and weeks before competition.' (Drier 2013). In other words, WADA knew that athletes could easily be sanctioned for social drug use, even when it was passively inhaled or used in a time period unrelated to competition. They were content to punish athletes unnecessarily.

   Cases involving the use of cocaine have also been varied and complex. This drug is classified as a stimulant, suggesting that athletes could be tempted to use it during competitions in order to gain a performance-enhancing effect. As noted already, there is no provision in the WADC to prevent athletes from using it out of competition, yet if sports organisations were focused upon protecting the health of athletes then it is more likely addictive, unhealthy patterns of usage would emerge in their leisure time than in preparation for a race or match. In contrast to cannabis, cocaine washes out of the body in a short period of time, usually just a few days.

   There have been a handful of cases in which athletes appealed to CAS to explain their positive test for cocaine on the basis of contamination through kissing. Marian Cilic, Shawn Barber and Richard Gasquet all demonstrated that they did not know that the woman they had kissed had used cocaine and thus transferred it to them. Ostensibly this might look like a reasonable outcome, however it does seem somewhat inconsistent that strict liability is not imposed when another person is involved, as compared to a situation where an athlete has consumed a supplement or medicine which almost always lead to a sanction. The underpinning rationale appears to be that athletes should be careful about energy bars, powders pills and drinks, and read the labels carefully, but do not need the same level of vigilance when it comes to possible contamination from another human being.

   The cocaine kissing situation does open up two other issues. First, would it be possible that other substances can be transferred through kissing? If so, there is scope for other appeals to be made on this basis. Second, as contamination through kissing is accepted as a plausible explanation, why don't deliberate cheats or cocaine addicts use this as a defence argument? Either way, the system has created situations which appear inconsistent. Moreover, some athletes who cannot afford to pay for the arbitration process might have simply accepted a ban despite the kissing contamination being a reason for their positive test. And as shown above, even those who have won their arbitration case have potentially had their career prospects undermined by losing a significant period of competitive playing time, damage to their reputation, and may feel somewhat embarrassed by the media coverage.

There are other examples showing the inconsistent approach to cocaine use. Tennis player Martina Hingis was banned for two years in 2007 for cocaine use, even though the amount in her system was very low. Footballers Adrian Mutu and Mark Bosnich were banned and sacked by their club. Mutu was banned for nine months in 2009, and was forced to repay his transfer fee of £14.6m to Chelsea (while this decision was upheld by CAS, it is far from clear how much, if any, has been repaid) (Scott 2009). Bosnich was banned for nine months, lost his contract with Chelsea, sank into a further addiction problems and his career never fully recovered. Even lower-ranking athletes have been severely punished. Scottish football player Jordan MacMillan was banned for 23 months, despite making the case that he had accidentally consumed cocaine that was put into a drink at a house party by another person who admitted to doing so, and that the drink was intended for another of the guests (BBC 2016). The Welsh amateur rugby player Shaun Cleary was treated differently. He used the drug while socialising on a Friday evening, and tested positive after a match three days later on the Monday evening. His case is rather more controversial in that he had not received any anti-doping education, and since his club was non-elite there had never been any testing. The Monday evening match was a friendly against another local Welsh team, which was a late change of plan as usually matches are on the weekends and Mondays are training sessions. Cleary was banned for two years and felt obliged to make statements in the local newspaper of apology to his club and its supporters. However, UKAD were unsympathetic to his situation, saying that athletes are responsible for what is in their system regardless of whether or not there is an intention to cheat (Parfitt 2016).

Yet in some cases a more humane and supportive approach is taken by clubs, federations, and anti-doping authorities. When Hull player Jack Livermore tested positive he was not banned, due to his explanation that he was using the drug to help cope with a family bereavement. It would seem as if, for some drugs in some contexts, the athlete can make a case that contradicts the strict liability rule; but for reasons that are incomprehensible other athletes are sanctioned, sometimes even when an arbitration panel finds little or no reason to believe they had deliberately broken the rules.

The use of medicines

A number of sanctions have involved athletes seeking to use substances for medicinal purposes. The De Mont, Baxter and Răducan cases are examples. It does seem quite feasible for mistakes to be made either accidentally or because of faulty advice.

In 2005, the Argentinian tennis player Mariano Puerta was banned for eight years for a second offence after etilefrine was found in his sample (his first case led to a nine month ban after clenbuterol was found in his sample). When he appealed to CAS, the panel agreed that his explanation was plausible. He said that his wife was taking a medicine in tablet form which she would drink after it was dissolved in water. Once dissolved, it was odourless and colourless. During dinner he visited the bathroom, during which time (confirmed by the guests) his wife put the tablets into her glass. She stood up from the table for a few minutes during which the athlete mistakenly drank the water from her glass (Amos 2007). In response, the then WADA President, Dick Pound, had no sympathy:

> 'Somebody who has tested positive twice in less than two years is someone who clearly doesn't think the rules apply to them,' he said. 'I know that the ITF have been working for a number of years in the interests of the sport and the process is now more transparent. The testing regimes will get better over time and the deterrent effect of these kind of sanctions where positive cases are discovered will I hope persuade players who might otherwise consider using these drugs not to do so. It is a big, big step forward. We're very pleased with [the Puerta verdict] and we will keep working with the ITF to help them make their sport even cleaner.'
>
> *(BBC 2005)*

A more recent case involved the Italian tennis player Sara Errani who ingested her mother's breast cancer tablet by accident. It was apparently mixed in with other food when a meal was being prepared. The two-month sanction recognised the legitimacy of that explanation. Yet the athlete was still found guilty of negligence, labelled a doper and potentially faces a lifetime ban should a second violation occur.

There have been cases of athletes being sanctioned for using hair restorer products that, unknown to them, contained banned substances such as finasteride that are diuretics and therefore potentially could be used to mask the presence of steroids. The American international skeleton slider, Zach Lund, tested positive for a baldness cure he had been using for over five years. The regulation to ban finasteride (but not all baldness medicines) came into force in 2004. This resulted in a one year ban meaning he missed the 2006 Olympics. The initial response to his positive seemed to be a reasonable one, but unfortunately for the athlete, WADA wanted to enforce its new Code:

Lund's lawyer, Howard Jacobs, had successfully argued Lund's case in front of the United States Anti-Doping Agency, which gave Lund only a public warning in January after deciding that information about masking agents was misleading on the Web site of the international federation for skeleton and bobsled. But the World Anti-Doping Agency appealed and the case went to a panel of the Court of Arbitration for Sport, which attends every Olympics so that cases are handled quickly. 'We felt USADA made the proper ruling,' Jacobs said. 'It seems to me the anti-doping rules are lacking any notion of common sense.'

(Zinser 2006)

To add to the sense of injustice surrounding this outcome, finasteride was removed from the Prohibited List in 2009 as testing methods for commonly used anabolic steroids have improved.

The Norwegian skier Therese Johaug was banned for 18 months when it was discovered that the lip balm-cream she had been given by the team doctor contained small amounts of clostebol acetate, an anabolic agent. While the packaging did list this, the panel at CAS agreed that even though it was her doctor who purchased the cream, she was negligent for not checking the contents. In order for the athlete to completely avoid negligence they would have to: mistrust the medical advice; have memorised the Prohibited List; and/ or type every ingredient into the Global Drug Reference Online (Global DRO) database search. The practicalities of doing so are impossible, even for an elite athlete much less an amateur or youth athlete.

A final case to illustrate this point is that of Danish curler Helle Simonsen who tested positive for androstane. She has a hormonal disease or irregularity (called PCOS) and she had taken the herbal medicine to get her hormone levels right in order to get pregnant. She was handed a 15-month ban by the World Curling Federation (WCF) with effect from 12 February 2016 when she was suspended, and she accepted the sanction when she learned about the ruling in May. The WCF announced that the organisation was aware that Simonsen did not intend to use a performance-enhancing substance but still she had violated the anti-doping regulations and therefore should be punished.

The implementation of the strict liability principle has brought many cases under the spotlight, in particular those which have been appealed and therefore examined at CAS. Due to the nature of the evidence, it is not always possible to determine if a sanction has been awarded due to genuinely inadvertent and unintentional consumption of banned substance. We would argue that such a system works to punish the wrong people, while failing (as detailed in the previous chapter) to catch the organised, sophisticated doping cheats.

By outlining some cases in this chapter, we aimed to demonstrate the damaging impact that this policy has upon athletes who do not deserve this disproportionate outcome. We also described how the cases involving recreational drug use are not consistently or fairly managed. Issues around thresholds and excretion rates mean that the difference between in- and out-of-competition usage is sometimes blurred, meaning that the testing system is not fit for purpose as it only shows presence of the substance in the body and cannot distinguish between the times in which it was used legally or illegally. Lastly, the use of medicines in various circumstances can lead to a positive test, which effectively punishes the athlete for seeking medical advice and support. In some cases, the athlete consulted a doctor before using the substance. However, these precautions do not protect athletes from contamination of bottles or equipment that can lead to a positive test and sanction.

If the anti-doping policy consistently ruins athletes' careers and reputations through unreasonable decisions based on a stringent use of the strict liability principle, then the consequences are not as intended: the health of the athlete becomes damaged; the level playing field is not protected; the spirit of sport is not upheld. The significant but largely unrecognised outcome is that the institutions supporting anti-doping increasingly are guilty of punishing the innocent. Their ethics are questionable, and they have a tendency to blame the victim rather than offer any form of empathy or support to the victimised athlete. As Geeraets noted:

> The most important organisations devoted to doping-free sport – WADA and CAS – have committed themselves to ideological arguments when seeking to justifying anti-doping regulation. This suggests that these organisations value notions of fairness not because these notions really mean something in the context of anti-doping regulation, but primarily because of the rhetorical dividend that lip service pays. The organisations' interest is in creating a façade of justice, not in serving justice itself.
>
> *(Geeraets 2017 p. 13)*

References

Amos, A. (2007). "Inadvertent doping and the WADA code." *Bond Law Review*, 19(1): 1-25.

Anderson, J. (2010). *Modern Sports Law: A Textbook*. London: Bloomsbury Publishing.

Associated Press (2011). "Igor Walilko's doping ban reduced". ESPN, 15 September. Retrieved 12 January 2018 from http://www.espn.co.uk/racing/story/_/id/6972514/teenage-kart-driver-igor-walilko-doping-ban-cut-cas

Abrams Landau (2008). "Rebekah Keat lawsuit joined by other pro athletes who allege tainted supplements caused positive drug tests.". Retrieved 20 December 2017 from http://landauinjurylaw.com/theathleteslawyer/2008/10/25/rebekah-keat-lawsuit-joined-by-other-pro-athletes-who-allege-tainted-supplements-caused-positive-drug-tests/

Backhouse, S. H., L. Patterson and J. McKenna (2012). "Achieving the Olympic ideal: Preventing doping in sport." *Performance Enhancement & Health* 1(2): 83–85.

BBC. (2000). "Modahl vows to fight on", 14 December. Retrieved 6 November 2017 from http://news.bbc.co.uk/sport2/hi/athletics/1070719.stm

BBC (2005). "Puerta gets eight-year doping ban". 21 December. Retrieved 12 January 2018 from http://news.bbc.co.uk/sport1/hi/tennis/4549544.stm

BBC (2006). "Plaza overturns 10-year-old ban".10 July. Retrieved 12 January 2018 from http://news.bbc.co.uk/sport1/hi/athletics/5165930.stm

BBC (2016). "Jordan McMillan seeks return to football after cocaine ban". 18 August. Retrieved 12 January 2018 from http://www.bbc.co.uk/sport/football/36907073

Bull, A., S. Burnton, and J. Steinberg (2013). "The joy of six: doping denials". *Guardian*, 25 January. Retrieved 12 January 2018 from https://www.theguardian.com/sport/blog/2013/jan/25/joy-of-six-worst-doping-excuses

Coleman, J. E. (2011). "The burden of proof in endogenous substance cases: a masking agent for junk science". In M. McNamee and V. Møller (eds), *Doping and Anti-Doping Policy in Sport: Ethical, Legal and Social Perspectives*. London: Routledge.

Crouse, K. (2010). "For swimmer, ban ends, but burden could last". *The New York Times*, 7 August. Retrieved 12 January 2018 from http://www.nytimes.com/2010/08/08/sports/08hardy.html

Drier, F. (2013). "Rules change on Olympic marijuana testing". *USA Today*, 17 July.

ESPN (2011). "Hurdler Priestley abandons Olympic dream". ESPN, 26 October.

Francis, C. (1990). *Speed Trap*. New York: St. Martin's Press.

Geeraets, V. (2017). "Ideology, doping and the spirit of sport". *Sport, Ethics and Philosophy* 1–17. Retrieved 12 January 2018 from http://www.tandfonline.com/doi/full/10.1080/17511321.2017.1351483

Geyer, H., M. K. Parr, K. Koehler, U. Mareck, W. Schänzer and M. Thevis (2008). "Nutritional supplements cross contaminated and faked with doping substances". *Journal of Mass Spectrometry* 43(7): 892–902.

Kirshenbaum, J. (1979). "The Golden Moment". *Sports Illustrated*, 20 August. Retrieved 12 January 2018 from https://www.si.com/vault/1979/08/20/823888/the-golden-moment-swimmer-rick-demont-left-with-bronze-medalist-steve-genter-exulted-after-winning-at-the-72-olympics-but-his-medal-was-taken-away-and-his-life-was-never-the-same

Mack, D. B. (1994). "Reynolds v. International Amateur Athletic Federation: The need for an independent tribunal in international athletic disputes." *Conneticut Journal of Internationall Law*. 10: 653.

McArdle, D. (2015). "'Strict liability' and legal rights: nutrititional supplements, 'intent' and 'risk' in the parallel world of WADA". In Verner Møller, Ivan Waddington, John M. Hoberman (eds), *Routledge Handbook of Drugs and Sport*. London: Routledge.

McDermott, V. (2015). *The War on Drugs in Sport: Moral Panics and Organizational Legitimacy*. London: Routledge.

McMullen, P. (2004). "Two who were cheated of opportunity to shine". *Baltimore Sun*, 19 April. Retrieved 12 January 2018 from http://articles.baltimoresun.com/2004-04-19/sports/0404190276_1_multivitamins-swimming-olympic-gold

McRae, D. (2010). "Ben Johnson: 'My revelations will shock the sporting world'". *Guardian*, 5 October. Retrieved 12 January 2018 from https://www.theguardian.com/sport/2010/oct/05/ben-johnson-drugs-olympics

Modahl, D. (1995). *The Diane Modahl Story: Going the Distance The Heartbreaking Truth Behind the Headlines*. London: Hodder & Stoughton.

North American Court of Arbitration for Sport (2003). *USADA v Neben*.

Parfitt, D. (2016). "Eleventh Welsh rugby player handed doping ban after positive test for cocaine". WalesOnline, 27 January. Retrieved 12 January 2018 from http://www.walesonline.co.uk/sport/rugby/rugby-news/eleventh-welsh-rugby-player-handed-10795914

Rowbottom, M. (1999). "Athletics: Slaney doping ban upheld at IAAF hearing". *Independent*, 26 April.

Scott, M. (2009). "Adrian Mutu ordered to pay Chelsea £14.7m for breach of contract". *Guardian*, 31 July. Retrieved 12 January 2018 from https://www.theguardian.com/football/2009/jul/31/cas-chelsea-adrian-mutu

Swimming World (2005). "Kicker Vencill wins suit against nutrition company, awarded almost $600K. 13 May. Retrieved 12 January 2018 from https://www.swimmingworldmagazine.com/news/flash-kicker-vencill-wins-suit-against-nutrition-company-awarded-almost-600k/

Swimming World (2009). "Jessica Hardy suspension reduced to one year, supplement ruled as contaminated; USA Swimming releases statement; USADA press release; AdvoCare disputes findings" updated 4 May.

WADA (2003). *World Anti-Doping Code*. Montreal: World Anti-Doping Agency.

WADA (2015). *World Anti-Doping Code*. Montreal: World Anti-Doping Agency. Retrieved 12 January 2018 from https://www.wada-ama.org/sites/default/files/resources/files/wada-2015-world-anti-doping-code.pdf

Wong, G. M. (2002). *Essentials of Sports Law*. Westport, CT: Praeger.

Zinser, L. (2006). "Lund 'not a cheat,' but panel bars him". *New York Times*, 11 February. Retrieved 12 January 2018 from http://www.nytimes.com/2006/02/11/sports/olympics/lund-not-a-cheat-but-panel-bars-him.html

6

PROBLEMS WITH MEDICINE AND SCIENCE

In earlier chapters we have seen how the strict liability principle can lead to punishment of athletes despite their lack of intention to cheat. These unfortunate outcomes are consequences of a deliberate rigidity that leaves no room for level-headed interpretation of the individual cases.

The intended outcome of anti-doping is to catch cheats. In this respect, cheating is defined as the use of substances or methods which are designed to enhance performance and which could be unhealthy. As such, anti-doping rests upon an implied understanding about these substances and methods. This understanding might include research on the performance-enhancing effects of a substance or method, or the ability of a substance to act as a masking agent. These two aspects might cover such drugs as steroids in which the idea would be to ban the drug and the (potential) masking agent. Other issues that can lead to a substance being banned would be related to the abuse of medicines. Certain painkillers or recovery medicines are not allowed as they might be abused to enhance performance by healthy athletes or overused by those in recovery as an artificial method. These issues raise challenging questions when athletes request medicines through the therapeutic use exemption (TUE) system.

It might be expected that the characteristics of these drugs and methods are understood before they are placed on the Prohibited List. Moreover, where a substance is allowed out of competition but not in competition we would expect the authorities to understand metabolism and excretion rates such that they could establish how far in advance of the in-competition period that the athlete consumed the substance.

These questions will be considered in the first sections of this chapter. Thereafter, we focus upon issues relating to the science of testing. Again, given that athletes' reputations and livelihoods are at stake, it might be expected that the analytical laboratory process is accurate. If athletes have to take full responsibility for any substance in their body, and potentially suffer serious consequences even if they consumed something unintentionally, then surely the powerful organisations that test, analyse and sanction athletes have a responsibility to ensure their decisions are based on sound procedures and science. These procedures should ideally be externally assessed and validated, and if there are any doubts, the athlete should be fully exonerated, as would be the case in criminal law.

Legal medicines and health

Caffeine is an effective performance-enhancing substance. Numerous research studies demonstrate that, so long as the optimal dose for the mode of activity is understood, the increase in performance could be as much as 10 per cent. Thus, the difference between winning and losing could boil down to the advice obtained by a sports nutritionist. Through the 1990s there was some concern about caffeine, sufficient to warrant its place on the IOC Prohibited List until it was removed in 2004. During this time caffeine was banned above a certain threshold some athletes were sanctioned due to exceeding the allowable levels of the stimulant. Yet, caffeinated drinks were increasingly common, and companies like Coca-Cola and Red Bull that produce such drinks have sponsored major sports events.

Caffeine is a good substance for sports performance, so athletes want to use it. There are no health issues, unless seriously abused. Caffeine is also profitable. The commercialisation of sport, including the Olympics, has been supported by businesses interested in promoting caffeinated drinks. Sports scientists have produced research studies on how to optimise caffeine consumption for performance-enhancing effects. The athletes who were sanctioned prior to 2004 must feel especially aggrieved, not simply at the changes in rules, but in the contingent and unclear methods by which WADA, the IOC and others set about defining what is legal and what is not. We might also ask whether the sports authorities should be more concerned in the caffeine-liberalisation period whether there is a risk that some athletes could abuse the substance to an extent that could damage their health. The ambiguities over caffeine demonstrate the sometimes paradoxical and confused nature of anti-doping policy (Pielke 2016).

If athletes' health was the main concern of anti-doping legislators, then we might expect regulation of powerful painkillers. This issue was addressed by sports sociologist Ivan Waddington (2000) in his analysis of the overuse of non-steroidal anti-inflammatories by football and cricket players in the UK. There has been much discussion about corticosteroid injections being used to speed up recovery from injury, sometimes even to get important players back on to the field of play. Without such medicines being available, there may be occasions where the top athletes would not have been able to participate in the most vital matches or events. Another substance that could be questioned is tramadol, which has been associated with cycling for several years. British professional cyclist Jonathan Tiernan-Locke exposed the overuse of the painkiller by coaches determined to help the riders mitigate the pain of excessive training in order to improve their performance (Slater 2017). Yet outside sport many experts have raised concerns about the short- and long-term health consequences of regular consumption of tramadol, as it is an opiate which could be addictive and have serious health side effects (Fretz 2017).

It was reported in 2017 that professional American football clubs have been giving their players extensive medications. Powerful painkillers such as Toradol and Vikoden were regularly used, and a case brought before criminal laws included accusations that club doctors had:

> violated federal laws governing prescription drugs, disregarded guidance from the Drug Enforcement Administration on how to store, track, transport and distribute controlled substances, and plied their players with powerful painkillers and anti-inflammatories each season ... In the calendar year of 2012, for example, the average team prescribed nearly 5,777 doses of nonsteroidal anti-inflammatory drugs and 2,213 doses of controlled medications to its players.
>
> *(Maese 2017)*

This reflects increasing concern among public health experts in the USA that doctors are overprescribing opioid-based pain relief leading to overuse, addiction and fatalities (Kolodny *et al.* 2015).

The use of painkillers in sport is a cause for concern in and of itself. Pain, as inconvenient as it feels, is a protective mechanism. It is the body's way to protect itself against injury and, where the body has been injured, aggravation of the injury by carrying on. Painkillers work to suppress the body's warning signals. Danish football player Daniel Agger, who played as a centre-back for Liverpool from 2006 to 2014, explained the detrimental effect the use of painkillers had had on his body that eventually led to his career ending at the age of only 31, two years after he had returned to Denmark to play for his boyhood club Brøndby in the much less demanding Danish Super League. Throughout his Liverpool career he had a number of niggling injuries and, in 2007, developed back problems. An unlucky fall during the 2008 pre-season led to a discus prolapse and leg pain. After a lengthy lay-off, he returned to the first team. In order to be able to play he took anti-inflammatory drugs beyond the recommended dosages. The medication took away the pain but also made him lethargic. So, in order to get ready to play he took caffeine shots and energy drinks. He did not realise what he had done to his body until he collapsed after having come off the pitch 29 minutes into the derby against local rivals FC Copenhagen. A week before the game Agger had a minor injury to his foot but he was determined to play the derby. So he popped two more of these pills during the pre-match meeting, and fell asleep on the team bus. This time, however, the caffeine and energy drinks did not help. Instead he felt unwell and this did not change when he started playing. He could not focus, and was not himself so he had to come off. Sitting on the bench he collapsed and was helped to the physio room. During his career, he had taken so much medicine just to keep standing and his body could not cope with it anymore he explained:

> The maximum dose should be taken for only three days. The body reacts to what is put into it and it was my body's way to tell me that it had had enough. When the head can't work it out, then the body had to do it.
>
> *(Christenson 2016)*

Therapeutic use exemptions

Given the above discussion on the ambivalence surrounding medications, we should take into consideration the proposed method of solving at least some of the problems – the TUE system. The principle is that any athlete who genuinely requires some medicine that has been banned can request a TUE if a doctor provides evidence of their health problem. This approach might, for example, allow an athlete who suffers from asthma to use an inhaler containing salbutamol as this substance is classified as a stimulant and thus banned during competition.

As the TUE process only applies to those substances on the Prohibited List, it does nothing to address the issue of medicines which are allowed even if they have health and addiction risks due to overuse. The policy, it could be argued, would make more sense if all medicines required a TUE: this could potentially alleviate problems of abuse (either by the athlete acting alone, or a member of their support personnel advising them). So when an athlete applies for a TUE, in many cases it is because the drug they wish to use has properties which, in normal circumstances, would be performance enhancing. As most medicines are developed to improve health, we might assume that it is the stimulant qualities of drugs that are of concern. The potential abuse of this system is shown in a survey of elite athletes which found that while 19 per cent had been granted a TUE, just over half believed that other athletes in their sport were receiving TUEs without a clear medical need (Overbye and Wagner 2013).

Since early 2016 we have become much more familiar with the consequences of the TUE system due to the publicity generated by the Fancy Bears hack of WADA's database, which exposed many high-profile athletes' use of medicines in order to compete. In some cases, we might speculate about whether it is wise to continue doing competitive sport if someone is so ill that they require medical drugs. A high-profile case in point is that of Bradley Wiggins who continued to race in the Grand Tours when suffering from asthma and pollen allergies. He was given permission to use the prohibited anti-inflammatory drug, the corticosteroid triamcinolone. He defended the decision, by saying that the drug was needed to 'level the playing field' (BBC 2016). However, medical experts cast doubt on whether it was the most appropriate way to treat the symptoms from which he was suffering (Cary 2016). A slightly different situation occurred in 2017, when Team Sky cyclist Chris Froome was found to have used too much salbutamol from his asthma inhaler, without a TUE.

Moreover, the extensive requests for asthma medications suggest that either large numbers of athletes are brave enough to pursue their sporting ambitions in spite of a breathing deficiency, or that sport is causing athletes to have asthma; provoking some debate in the scientific community (Backer *et al.* 2007). Either way, if the protection of athletes' health is paramount then the best strategy might be to disqualify them from competition due to illness; not to allow them to carry on by using drugs to mask the symptoms (we return to this in Chapter 9). Of course, another explanation is that doctors write fake prescriptions to obtain stimulants or blood-boosting drugs in order to help athletes become more successful. If that does occur, anti-doping policy leads both to a less even playing field and to some very unethical and unhealthy behaviours by creating the opportunity for the most unscrupulous to gain an advantage.

Medical requirement for banned drugs: hormonal therapies

There have been cases where athletes genuinely needed banned substances for the sake of their health and the restriction caused them to face stark choices about their involvement in sport.

Once again, there was a case to illustrate the problems WADA would face around the very time of its formation. The cyclist Chris Boardman suffered from low testosterone, with a blood test in 1997 revealing that his levels were similar to an eight-year old boy. In early 1998, he was diagnosed with a bone condition similar to osteoporosis. The Union Cycliste Internationale (UCI) had verbally agreed to his use of testosterone, but then refused after the publicity shone on the sport in the aftermath of the 1998 Tour de France scandal. Boardman was left with no option but to end his career in order to have the medical treatment he required. At the time of his last race, he expressed concern about his future:

> 'I have mixed feelings about stopping. I'm a bit melancholic as I'm still around people doing things that I used to do and that I don't need any more. I'm sad about leaving it all behind. I'm scared that what has been the huge centre of my life for seven years will stop when I cross the [finish] line.'
>
> *(Fotheringham 2000)*

Boardman has had a successful career in cycling, creating a brand of bikes and commentating on cycling for British television. Nonetheless, his choice was an avoidable one as his doctors provided sufficient evidence for a medical use allowance to be permitted. It was the potential exploitation of that process by unscrupulous athletes and doctors that led to the UCI denying Boardman that opportunity.

A much more complex and challenging case is that of Kristen Worley, a Canadian cyclist who transitioned from male and female during her sporting career. The science of hormonal balance is complex, and sports organisations have struggled to define and impose some protocol of what constitutes 'normal'. Scholars have shown that they have tended to have problematic and highly restrictive notions of femininity and masculinity, so that athletes are badly affected if their bodies transcend predefined notions of normal (Amy-Chinn 2012). Worley required testosterone for purely therapeutic reasons. Her request was originally denied and when it was accepted did not allow her sufficient levels to protect her health. As journalist Andy Brown explained:

> Kristen met the protocols outlined in the Stockholm consensus, and received a Therapeutic Use Exemption (TUE) to use synthetic androgens. However, the amount of androgens permitted by her TUE were set below the average range for females at 0.5nmol/L, even though the normal androgen range for non-athletic females is 0.52nmol/L to 5.6nmol/L. This induced 'complete hormone deprivation' in Worley. The impact of 'complete hormone deprivation' removes the body's day to day ability to regulate itself, but especially in the amount of androgens needed to respond to exercise. As the body has no androgens, cell synthesis ceases, causing a number of serious health issues including the induction of an immediate extreme post-menopausal state; a non-natural and aggressive ageing process; complete muscle atrophy (i.e. failure of muscle development and recovery, making sport impossible); anaemia; a large drop in haematocrit levels and more.
>
> *(Brown 2015)*

From the perspective of the fight against doping, perhaps it is rational to ensure that individual athletes do not benefit from increased levels of essential hormones. However, from the perspective of protecting the health of athletes and their right to compete on a level playing field, the way in which Worley was treated is problematic. When she first requested a TUE, it took over four years for a decision to be made. During a meeting with the Head of the IOC Medical Commission Patrick Schamasch in 2006, Worley and another athlete in a similar situation, the Danish golfer Mianne Bagger, were confronted by a dismissive attitude. As she explained:

> 'Mianne and I told Schamasch our experiences and what happens to the female physiology, and it got to the point where he couldn't answer our questions … I argued that the IOC is putting out a policy as the biggest sports leader in the world, about issues involving gender that affect some of the most vulnerable people participating. This has then been transferred to all sport, based on the thinking that the IOC has done the research. We now know that they didn't do that research, and this is what is transpiring.

He told me that he doesn't care – the IOC is all about the Games.' Worley
alleges that she and Bagger were told: 'If you want to come to the Games,
you play by my rules'.

(Brown 2015)

Worley has been determined to fight her case on the basis that her human
rights were contravened, and that she was forced into an unhealthy situation
for two years while not being allowed sufficient access to medicines. However,
there is no clear appeals process. The CAS functions to ensure the rules of
sports organisations have been followed correctly. In order to challenge those
very rules, Worley has developed her case on wider human rights issues. A
landmark ruling in July 2017 forced sports organisations to accept that the
gender policy and related issues on hormone therapy were in fact breaching
her human rights:

On 18 July, the Human Rights Tribunal of Ontario recognised that
policies originating from the International Olympic Committee (IOC)
had infringed the human rights of Canadian cyclist Kristen Worley.
Whilst the agreement recognises that sport's unsubstantiated policies have
needlessly harmed XY female athletes, its real significance is that it could
allow other athletes whose human rights have been infringed to stake
their claim before a court of law.

(Brown 2017)

Unfortunately, there are many more cases where women have been subjugated
to the gender verification rules in tragic and abusive ways (Henne 2015). While
our concern here is upon the critical outcomes of anti-doping policy, the
overlap between gender, hormonal therapy and doping, means in effect that the
suspicions and fears that have created a draconian anti-doping system have an
additional consequence for individuals whose gender has become questioned in
an environment that seeks binary classifications of male/female and has a long
history of unethical gender verification strategies (Heggie 2010).

There have also been a series of cases in which male athletes have required
supplemental testosterone in response to genuine and documented medical
needs, much like Chris Boardman did in 1998.

One such influential figure in this field is Dr Sloan Teeple, whose interest
in the subject is professional as well as personal. He was diagnosed with low
testosterone levels at the age of 33 years. He was a medical doctor, and become
a Board-certified urologist. He was not an elite athlete, and therefore did not
have the access to anti-doping education and advice. Around the age of 40 he
started taking sport more seriously and wanted to compete in his first Iron
Man triathlon event. Knowing that testosterone was on the Prohibited List
he submitted a TUE request, which was flatly rejected, despite him providing
supporting medical documentation. He was surprised by this:

Being a physician and something of an expert in the field at the time, I think I was still a little naive in terms of the regulations and how much the sporting authorities were determined that nobody should use testosterone. So I applied for my TUE and when I was denied, I was a little bit shocked, then frustrated, then a little bit angry. Realisation set in almost immediately when I saw the documentation and the reasons why they denied my TUE. I realised that this was going to be a long battle, but one worth fighting and one I have to do for all other men out there suffering from similar conditions to myself, as well as the patient athletes that I treat. I knew I had to be patient, and it was going to be a long, slow process.

(Brown 2016)

Teeple tested positive and was banned for 18 months. However, he was determined to prove that the anti-doping approach to this matter was simplistic and discriminatory. After a four-year struggle, and at a high personal cost for legal fees of $15,000–30,000, Dr Teeple managed to force USADA to create a 'recreational TUE' category. This is highly restricted to ensure it cannot be exploited by elite athletes: it is really only available to older athletes who have never competed at a higher level. However, it does set an interesting precedent in that previously the WADC had been applied in the same way to all athletes. The recreational TUE subtly contradicts the WADC by allowing differentiation of types of athletes, implicitly accepting that the rules designed for elite athletes are not always appropriate for non-elite athletes.

Teeple's victory at forcing USADA to accept that some athletes have genuine medical requirements supported other athletes in similar situations. Jeff Hammond, who was never sanctioned by USADA but was in the same position as suffering the ill-effects of low testosterone when getting older. He was a cyclist who never competed at a high level, and indeed was motivated primarily by a desire to maintain good health, enjoying his sport and socialise with members of local bike clubs. He was 58 years old when, struggling from general fatigue symptoms, he consulted a doctor who diagnosed hypogonadism and low bone density, for which he was prescribed supplemental testosterone. Aware of the rules on anti-doping, Hammond submitted a TUE application supported by evidence of his ill-health. By his own admission, he was a low-level cyclist, category 4, who had come the sport late in life without any desire for material reward or expectation of success. He decided to stop competing in races after the TUE application was rejected, suffering a real sense of loss as a result:

It was heartbreaking. It really was. But that was the right thing to do. If I wanted to, I could have just not told anyone. I could have continued to race, and truth be told I probably never would have been tested. But there was a chance.

(Beaudin 2013)

The rules which were designed for high-performance, elite athletes who might cheat to gain an advantage, probably with the support of a doping doctor, were being applied in a situation which was materially and conceptually different. USADA wrote to Hammond explaining their concerns that 'Testosterone is an anabolic steroid and has been shown scientifically and medically to improve muscle strength, recovery, and performance. As such it is included on the WADA Prohibited List as a substance prohibited at all times' (Beaudin 2013). Yet, Hammond's argument was that he was only seeking to maintain normal health for a man of his age. The Director of Science at USADA, Matthew Fedoruk, articulated the reasons for his organisation's stringent approach, despite their awareness that competitive sport was increasingly popular among older people and that in wider society age-related therapies were more common:

> There's not an ability to do age-graded evaluations, or [to consider] specific competition criteria. The rules are, fortunately or unfortunately, depending on what side of the fence you're on, applied equally. There has to be more than just generalised symptoms, or a single low blood test, a single low value. They have to be able to show a diagnosis and pinpoint a reason for why they have hypogonadism. So without that, it's impossible for us to grant a TUE. Then you would be opening up, essentially, a Pandora's box if you lowered the bar on the TUE criteria.
>
> *(Beaudin 2013)*

Hammond's frustration with the medical issues is that low testosterone is a symptom, there is not always a clear explanation or cause. However, Fedoruk referred back to the inherent sense of fear that drives the tougher and at times irrational approach to anti-doping whereby individual cases cannot be accommodated because, as he said above, it opens up a Pandora's box of cheating:

> What may be acceptable outside the realm of sport is different, because these substances are performance-enhancing. They build muscle. They increase hematocrit and hemoglobin, which allow an athlete to work harder. And so there's a potential for these athletes to go beyond what may be bringing them back to a normal state of health and go into that realm of performance enhancement.
>
> *(Beaudin 2013)*

The logic underpinning this statement both assumes that therapeutic doses might be performance-enhancing, and that athletes should be pre-emptively regulated on the basis of a potential violation, rather than any controls being based on actual violations, as would normally be the case. And in response to USADA's stance, Hammond makes a perfect logical response that the rules should not be applied in the same way for all athletes

'They're treating us the same as they treat 20-year-old Olympians,' he said. 'Something that's considered a performance-enhancing drug for an 18-year-old may be a necessary ... life-saving medication for a senior athlete. I think it's very unfair. I think they probably do more good than bad. I don't think they're bad people ... I'm sure their intentions are noble. I just think that in some ways they have tunnel vision, and they paint every athlete and every substance with the same broad brush.'

(Beaudin 2013)

Hammond was left to make a choice between his sport and his health. While he felt aggrieved by their decision, he took an ethical decision not to continue racing even though he would be unlikely to get tested at the lower levels events he took part in. He would eventually gain a TUE through the recreational athlete scheme that Sloan Teeple lobbied for. This was granted in October 2015, over two years after his initial application, by which time he had missed out on competitive sport during the years 2013 and 2014 and was aged over 60.

A final example of this category of testosterone requirements is that of Roger Wenzel, which is even more tragic as he died of cancer unable to challenge the two-year ban imposed upon him by USADA. Wenzel was aged 64 when he tested positive for modafinil and an exogenous steroid in August 2012 (United States Anti-Doping Agency 2013).

Wenzel was taking those medicines to combat Parkinson's disease and had been identified as having levels of testosterone around half of what would be expected for a man of his age. He competed in hammer throwing, having started this sport only a few years previously. He had no designs on competitive success, but thoroughly enjoyed the social environment and health benefits. USADA's statement on his sanction highlights some confusion over the TUE application process that led to the positive test:

> Mr. Wenzel advised USADA that he was taking the substances under a doctor's care, but despite being aware of the rules regarding the requirement to apply for a therapeutic use exemption (TUE) prior to competition, he did not seek to obtain a TUE to use either Modafinil or Anabolic Androgenic Steroids in advance of the competition.
>
> *(United States Anti-Doping Agency 2013)*

Thus, it would appear that Wenzel had made some effort to explain his medical situation, but since he had never been an elite athlete was probably unsure how the system worked. It seems also feasible that he was target tested due to having provided USADA with this information but not having completed the TUE application. Media accounts of the context and outcome seems to confirm this:

> He knew that USA Track and Field did drug testing, and since he took so many prescriptions, he wanted to make sure he was doing everything by

the rules. 'I didn't think anybody really cared about what a 64-year-old person was taking,' he said. But just to make sure, he contacted USA Track and Field and told them about his meds. USA Track and Field replied with a notification that his inquiry had been turned over to the U.S. Anti-Doping Agency. There was no indication that anything was wrong, just that USADA would better be able to help him. Wenzel went to the nationals, and to his surprise, he finished third in the weight throw and fourth in the hammer. But after the weight throw competition, he was pulled aside for random drug testing.

(Carlson 2013)

Despite being an amateur athlete, Wenzel did pay for legal support and applied for a TUE on the basis of Parkinson's with hypogonadism. This was rejected. Wenzel died knowing that was wrongly labelled a doper, but had no means to clear his name and restore his reputation. Much like the cases of Teeple and Hammond, we can critically review the claimed outcomes of anti-doping against the unfortunate impact it has on individual athletes. The WADC is designed to protect the health of the athlete, in which case athletes with low testosterone should be allowed to treat their illness with hormonal supplements. It is designed to protect the level playing field, but if these athletes are only using the drug for recovery, and they are unlikely to win a significant competition, then that rationale is unclear. Lastly, the WADC is designed to protect the spirit of sport, which is characterised as being about the intrinsic pleasures of taking part. As Wenzel said:

There is no reason for these people to be out regulating old guys who are out having fun, he said. 'We're doing it for fun.' Wenzel says senior events are like a Friday bowling league. 'It's the greatest time I've ever had as an athlete because it's so friendly and fun. You're competing against yourself. You're trying to get a personal best. You may be doing something wrong, and the guy you're competing against may say, 'Do you know you're releasing a little early?' And they're not screwin' with you.

(Carlson 2013)

Echoing these sentiments, Jeff Hammond said:

When I get out on my bike, I don't have a mortgage payment. I don't have bills. I don't have career worries. It's that kind of freeing — and I think I'm not really a religious person at all — but I think it's the most spiritual thing that I do. In fact, I remember the first time I ever rode up Lookout Mountain [in Colorado] without stopping. I'm sure it was painfully slow, but it was one of the greatest memories that I ever had.

(Beaudin 2013)

These individual examples highlight the human cost of anti-doping, the consequences of applying an absolutist policy founded on anxiety that cheating athletes will exploit loopholes and cracks in the legal process. They do not recognise the complex variety of situations in which athletes take a banned substance (Henning and Dimeo 2014) or the challenges inherent in applying rules to amateur sport (Henning 2017). If these were the only cases, some might argue that a policing system that occasionally catches the wrong person is unfortunate but necessary. However, if it were also possible that the science of anti-doping had problems that ruined athletes' lives, then the complexion of the policy changes once again.

Disputed lab cases

The imposition of a strict liability principle implicitly depends upon having a secure process through which the initial analysis of the athletes' sample can be confidently made. If we reconsider the drink-driving comparison in the previous chapter, cases can only be prosecuted on the assumption that the breathalyser equipment functions properly. Were there to be any questions in that respect the defendant's lawyer might be able to make a strong case for their acquittal. Yet, problems in the process of analysing samples persist, and these can have drastic impacts upon athletes. A recent example is that of 22-year-old Mexican fencer, Paola Pliego, who was forced to miss the 2016 Olympics because her A sample tested positive but it transpired the scientific process was flawed:

> The 22-year-old sabre specialist failed a test for banned stimulant modafinil after competing at the Pan American Fencing Championships in Panama in June. The Mexican National Physical Culture and Sports Commission (CONADE) claimed that her sample had registered 540 nanograms of the substance – usually used to treat narcolepsy. Pliego repeatedly denied any wrongdoing but was banned from competing at Rio 2016. A second test subsequently conducted by German doctor Hans Geyer in Cologne returned a negative result. Geyer claimed that a different method was needed to test for the substance from what had been used by CONADE, who were ordered to send the original urine sample to the German lab by the World Anti-Doping Agency. This led to her being cleared of wrongdoing.
>
> *(Butler 2016)*

Unfortunately, in many cases, there is no route of appeal against problems in the analytical processes. The mid-1990s situation that Diane Modahl found herself in shows that mistakes can be made, and that they are very difficult to rectify. Modahl was fortunate that independent experts were willing to experiment with samples that had been exposed to hot conditions to assess the

though in Colvert's case there is no suggestion of manipulation or distortion of the ways in which they are presented. Instead, Boye *et al.* focus on the fact that the laboratory analysis rests upon a slight tailing or spreading of the bulk of the EPO detected in their analysis of Colvert's urine was caused by EPO which they argue 'is not at all obvious and not much different from that observed in parallel lanes where the urine of athletes deemed to be free of rEPO had been used' (Boye *et al.* 2017). Therefore, this is a matter of importance in procedural terms because, as they note, CAS ruled in 2001 that interpretations should not be based one person's expertise, no matter how experienced they might be. Rather CAS declared that it is 'imperative that the laboratory applies reliable and verifiable criteria, making it possible for third parties to objectively understand the conclusions reached' which is precisely what the scientists say did not happen in the Colvert case (Boye *et al.* 2017).

These examples of problems in the laboratory are only the ones which are known about. The number of sanctions imposed on athletes due to errors are unknown, as it is almost impossible to investigate the analytical process. We can, however, point to studies that demonstrate the likelihood of regular false positives and false negatives, which logically becomes more of a problem as anti-doping testing agencies undertake a higher number of annual tests (Pitsch 2009). Also, WADA regularly report that their own auditing of anti-doping laboratories finds sufficient problems on occasion to warrant a particular facility to lose its accreditation until the problems are resolved. In recent years, even such important laboratories such as in Beijing, Los Angeles, Rio de Janeiro and Moscow have faced such sanctions. While WADA offer reassurances that no athletes have been affected, these situations demonstrate that even the most advanced laboratories can make mistakes.

In this chapter, we have reviewed some of the scientific and medical issues relating to anti-doping, though we could only provide a small selection of the details and themes. A highly public and recent demonstration of the need for more accuracy has been the way in which the drug meldonium was monitored, researched, prohibited and then produced a series of sanctions. The inconsistent applications of sanctions, from no ban to two years, is a result of confusion regarding excretion rates: it was not always certain when an athlete might have stopped using the drug. The complexity of the drugs and hormones involved in health and performance mean that the idea of drug-free sport is a mirage. What is considered acceptable is sometimes based upon societal norms, but also upon testing procedures, and sometimes there is a lack of underpinning research. The lack of rationality is exposed in a recent article by Bernat López in which he shows that the cultural foundation of anti-doping might in fact be inspired by needle-phobia rather than objective science (López 2017).

We have also seen numerous instances in which the politics of anti-doping do not serve either transparency or human rights. We have noted several cases of injustice and inhumanity, including in relation to athletes with medical requirements for hormonal therapies. We do not have quantitative data on how many athletes have suffered due to the flaws in anti-doping systems. However, the individuals have suffered at the hands of a problematic set of policies, scientific processes and legal procedures; their experiences need to be recognised. The only reason for ignoring their plight is to prop up a system that employs people to fight an unwinnable war based on romantic and anachronistic idealism. The situation was poignantly explained by the scientists involved:

> A dependable and robust court system should provide checks and balances that make sure that controversial and erroneous decisions can be revised. In the anti-doping system, there is, in practice, no such mechanism. After a decision by the CAS in Switzerland, the only further possibility is the Swiss legal system which, with very few exceptions, has shown little interest in participating in sports jurisprudence and the chances of receiving a fair and objective treatment in this system are small. The prospects of successfully bringing anti-doping conflicts into the civilian court system appear to be absent. We would argue that this is an unworthy, awkward and untenable situation in which to place an athlete. Importantly, it dramatically reduces the athletes' recourse to a fair trial. It is, of course, regrettable if an athlete who is guilty of doping can avoid punishment, but it is much worse when an innocent athlete is convicted without realistic chances of having the case over-turned.
>
> *(Boye* et al. *2017 p. 3)*

References

Amy-Chinn, D. (2012). "The taxonomy and ontology of sexual difference: implications for sport." *Sport in Society* 15(9): 1291–1305.

Backer, V., T. Lund and L. Pedersen (2007). "Pharmaceutical treatment of asthma symptoms in elite athletes: Doping or therapy?" *Scandinavian Journal of Medicine & Science in Sports* 17(6): 615–622.

BBC (2016). "Sir Bradley Wiggins: No unfair advantage from drug". 25 September. Retrieved 12 January 2018 from http://www.bbc.co.uk/news/uk-37462540

Beaudin, M. (2013). "Is it medicine or dope? A cat. 4 vs. the USADA". *VéloNews*, 21 October. Retrieved 12 January 2018 from http://www.velonews.com/2013/10/news/is-this-man-a-doper_306150

Boye, E., T. Skotland, B. Østerud and J. Nissen-Meyer (2017). "Doping and drug testing." *EMBO reports* e201643540. Retrieved 20 Decmber 2017 from http://embor.embopress.org/content/18/3/351

Brown, A. (2015). "Sport's gender policies: An affront to human rights". Sporting Integrity Initiative, 12 June. Retrieved 6 November, 2017 from http://www.sportsintegrityinitiative.com/sports-gender-policies-an-affront-to-human-rights/

Brown, A. (2016). "TUE inequality: Sloan Teeple's testosterone story." Sporting Integrity Initiative, 20 September. Retrieved 6 November, 2017, from http://www.sportsintegrityinitiative.com/tue-inequality-sloan-teeples-testosterone-story/

Brown, A. (2017). "Worley's case opens the courts to athlete human rights cases." Sporting Integrity Initiative, 7 August. Retrieved 6 November 2017, from http://www.sportsintegrityinitiative.com/worleys-case-opens-courts-athlete-human-rights-cases/

Butler, N. (2016). "Mexican fencer cleared of wrongdoing after re-analysis of 'positive' drug test". Inside the Games, 18 October. Retrieved 12 January 2018 from https://www.insidethegames.biz/articles/1042778/mexican-fencer-cleared-of-wrongdoing-after-re-analysis-of-positive-drug-test

Carlson, J. (2013). "Life-saving meds cheat Roger Wenzel out of competing". NewsOK, 4 March. Retrieved 12 January 2018 from http://newsok.com/article/3761242

Cary, T. (2016). "Sir Bradley Wiggins's last-resort drug was 'utterly bonkers', say medical experts". *The Telegraph*, 21 January. Retrieved 12 January 2018 from http://www.telegraph.co.uk/cycling/2016/09/20/sir-bradley-wigginss-last-resort-drug-was-utterly-bonkers-say-me/

Christenson, M. (2016). "Daniel Agger: 'Maybe my story will make other athletes take fewer pills'" *The Guardian*, 20 July. Retrieved 12 January 2018 from https://www.theguardian.com/football/blog/2016/jul/20/daniel-agger-liverpool-story-athletes-pills

Fotheringham, W. (2000). "Boardman quitting to take drug". *The Guardian*, 12 October. Retrieved 12 January 2018 from https://www.theguardian.com/sport/story/0,3604,380917,00.html

Fretz, C. (2017). "Painkillers and cycling: Tramadol's dark danger". *VeloNews*, 7 February. Retrieved 12 January 2018 from http://www.velonews.com/2017/02/feature/painkillers-and-cycling-tramadols-dark-danger_430306

Heggie, V. (2010). "Testing sex and gender in sports; reinventing, reimagining and reconstructing histories". *Endeavour* 34(4): 157–163.

Henne, K. E. (2015). *Testing for Athlete Citizenship: Regulating Doping and Sex in Sport*: New Brunswick, NJ: Rutgers University Press.

Henning, A. (2017) "Challenges to promoting health for amateur athletes through anti-doping policy." *Drugs: Education, Prevention and Policy* 24(3): 306–313.

Henning, A. D. and P. Dimeo (2014). "The complexities of anti-doping violations: A case study of sanctioned cases in all performance levels of USA cycling." *Performance Enhancement & Health* 3(3): 159–166.

Kolodny, A., D. T. Courtwright, C. S. Hwang, P. Kreiner, J. L. Eadie, T. W. Clark and G. C. Alexander (2015). "The prescription opioid and heroin crisis: A public health approach to an epidemic of addiction." *Annual Review of Public Health* 36: 559–574.

López, B. (2017). "From needle phobia to doping phobia: Can the fear of injections help us understand anti-dopism?" *Drugs: Education, Prevention and Policy* 24(3): 314–320.

Lundby, C., N. J. Achman-Andersen, J. J. Thomsen, A. M. Norgaard and P. Robach (2008). "Testing for recombinant human erythropoietin in urine: Problems associated with current anti-doping testing." *Journal of Applied Physiology* 105(2): 417–419.

Maese, R. (2017). "NFL abuse of painkillers and other drugs described in court filings". *Washington Post*, 9 March. Retrieved 12 January 2018 from https://www.washingtonpost.com/sports/redskins/nfl-abuse-of-painkillers-and-other-drugs-described-in-court-filings/2017/03/09/be1a71d8-035a-11e7-ad5b-d22680e18d10_story.html

Modahl, D. (1995). *The Diane Modahl Story: Going the Distance The Heartbreaking Truth Behind the Headlines*. London: Hodder & Stoughton.

Overbye, M. and U. Wagner (2013). "Between medical treatment and performance enhancement: An investigation of how elite athletes experience therapeutic use exemptions." *International Journal of Drug Policy* 24(6): 579–588.

Pielke, R. (2016). *The Edge: The War against Cheating and Corruption in the Cutthroat World of Elite Sports*: Berkeley, CA: Roaring Forties Press.

Pitsch, W. (2009). "'The science of doping' revisited: Fallacies of the current anti-doping regime". *European Journal of Sport Science* 9(2): 87–95.

Slater, M. (2017). "Jonathan Tiernan-Locke ready to tell British Cycling he WAS offered the controversial painkiller Tramadol while riding for Great Britain in 2012". *Daily Mail*, 17 February. Retrieved 12 January 2018 from http://www.dailymail.co.uk/sport/othersports/article-4236418/Tiernan-Locke-tell-British-Cycling-Tramadol-offered.html

Straubel, M. S. (2009). "Lessons from *USADA* v. *Jenkins*: You can't win when you beat a monopoly". *Pepperdine Dispute Resolution Law Journal* 10(1): 119–156

United States Anti-Doping Agency (2013). "U.S. track and field athlete, Wenzel, receives sanction for anti-doping rule violation", 8 March. Retrieved 12 January 2018 from https://www.usada.org/u-s-track-field-athlete-wenzel-receives-sanction-for-anti-doping-rule-violation/

Waddington, I. (2000). *Sport, Health and Drugs: A Critical Sociological Perspective*. London: Taylor & Francis.

7

SOCIAL STIGMA AND DEHUMANISATION

We have so far explored the various failings and unintended negative consequences of anti-doping. In this chapter, we consider an issue we have sporadically touched upon in previous chapters but which deserves more focused attention as it is largely overlooked in the campaign for drug-free sport, namely the oftentimes devastating consequences a positive test and sanction can have in the short term and in the long term not only for the athlete, their support personnel, and their teammates, but also for families and their broader social network. It seems to us ethically unacceptable to justify these wider consequences with reference to the deterrence effect of WADA's anti-doping strategy. Some might say that such cases are so few that they are a reasonable 'collateral damage' in an otherwise virtuous war on drugs. In response, we would argue that any policy that damages the careers, health and reputation of athletes in an unfair way needs to be critically assessed and reformed.

There is a difference between those who are innocent whose career and lifestyle are so badly affected, and those who have sought to deliberately cheat and risk their own health, or (in the case of suppliers) the health of other athletes. It seems easier to feel some sympathy for the former, even if there is often no route for compensation. However, there is rarely any sympathy or much public discussion about how a deliberate cheat has to deal with the situation caused by their fall from grace. The social stigma associated with doping is so powerful that athletes might understandably see little option than to bear all the responsibility, offer statements demonstrating their shame and regret, offer apologies to people they have 'let down', and serve their sanction without any resistance or indeed much social support.

The emphasis on individual responsibility that has been promulgated by WADA, enforced through the strict liability principle, means that athletes are treated with scepticism if their accounts serve to divert blame on to specific factors such as poverty, the use of doping by their rivals, the influence of their coach, the trust they placed in their doctor, or that they cannot explain how the positive test emerged. Even if they have a plausible reason to deny deliberate attempts to cheat, there is so much suspicion of elite athletes that many people would not entertain the possibility of a false accusation. For example, the Russian swimmer Yulia Efimova faced two sanctions ahead of the 2016 Rio Olympics. The first had been served and was for a contaminated supplement. The second was for meldonium which, she claimed, she had stopped using before it was placed on the Prohibited List in January 2016. The positive tests were for trace amounts still lingering in her body. She was cleared by WADA and the IOC to compete in the Olympics. However, she was treated as if she had been deliberately doping: jeered by the crowds, and publicly called a cheat by her American rival Lilly King (Bull 2016). Tennis player Maria Sharapova was treated in similar fashion when she tested positive for the same substance. An example of the critical response she faced, is a tweet by former elite tennis player, Jennifer Capriati, who had been world number one before she retired due to injuries in 2004:

> I'm extremely angry and disappointed. I had to lose my career and never opted to cheat no matter what. I had to throw in the towel and suffer ... I didn't have the high-priced team of doctors that found a way for me to cheat and get around the system and wait for science to catch up.
>
> *(de Menezes 2016)*

Efimova and Shaparova's experiences highlight the suspicion and stigma that those accused of doping can face. In both cases, the confusion arose because of the complexities related to the substances involved; specifically, in the case of meldonium it has been established that some fault lies with WADA for banning the drug without full scientific research into excretion rates. Even though Sharapova confessed to using it after the ban was in force, there is some inconsistency in the decisions of sanctions awarded to athletes who tested positive. Some athletes, such as the Swedish Abeba Aregawi missed the Rio Games despite being cleared of doping, having tested positive for meldonium only to be cleared after scientists agreed they could not tell if she had used if after the date it had been banned (1 January 2016). This confusion shows that innocent athletes can be treated unfairly as a result of poor policy decisions (Brown 2016).

More broadly, if we also take into account that sanctioned athletes lose their income, are often shunned by fans and teammates, are criticised in the media, and struggle to find a way back into sport, then we can recognise that the challenges facing athletes following a doping violation can be devastating. The lack of concern for an individual's basic human needs and sufferings lead us to propose that the policy has a dehumanising effect on athletes (in respect of the way they are treated) and upon anti-doping leaders, workers and commentators (in that they lose empathy for athletes). The dehumanisation inherent in anti-doping might help explain why the global sports community has come to tolerate the collateral damage incurred in pursuit of the idealistic and unattainable vision of clean sport.

Suicides

While there might not be a large number of athletes who have taken their own lives after a doping sanction, it would be irresponsible to ignore the fact that one consequence of anti-doping has been suicides and suicide attempts. Not least given that anti-doping policy is designed to protect athletes' health, promote fair play and healthy social virtues.

Antonio Pettigrew was an American track and field athlete. He reached stardom at the 1991 World Championship when he won the gold medal in the 400 metres and silver in the 4 × 400 metres. Nine years later he won Olympic gold in Sydney in the 4 × 400 metres. Unfortunately for him, he was called to testify in a criminal trial against his coach Trevor Graham who faced perjury charges in 2008, after he had been implicated by Mexican drug dealer and prosecution witness, Angel Heredia, who claimed that Pettigrew among others had received drugs from him through Graham. Pettigrew admitted having used EPO and human growth hormone from 1997 to 2003. Immediately after his confession he returned his Olympic gold medal although the IAAF did not alter results retroactively. Afterwards he struggled with depression and in 2010 he committed suicide. As an indication of the labelling process, when a major international newspaper announced the news of his suicide, there was little humanity in the headline 'Drug cheat Antonio Pettigrew found dead in car' (*Telegraph* 2010).

Terry Newton was an English rugby league player. While playing for Wakefield Trinity Wildcats, he started using human growth hormone as part of his injury recovery programme. He realised that other players were using this substance without being caught, that it was easy to buy, and he believed that there was no test yet developed to detect usage. He was therefore surprised when UKAD informed him that a sample he had provided returned positive, and that he would be banned for two years (he was the first professional sportsperson in the world to test positive for human growth hormone). Like many other athletes who find themselves facing a sanction, he felt guilt, remorse and shame, and the pressure of social disapproval. He wrote an autobiography in 2010, concluding that he had to face up to his mistakes 'like a man' (Newton 2010). Not long after the publication of that book he committed suicide by hanging (Wilson 2010).

It is probable that in both of these cases the athletes had other challenges in their lives which they came to see as insurmountable. Suicide can be the consequence of a multitude of factors. Being taken out of their sport, their job, and facing public humiliation would be a difficult situation to be in. Other athletes have openly spoken about their love of sport as a panacea for depression relating to other aspects of their lives. Moreover, personal issues such as loneliness, financial problems, and relationship problems, can exacerbate feelings of anxiety and depression that culminate in suicide attempts. An anti-doping violation brings together a number of risk factors: loss of career, isolation, stigma and shame, and real uncertainties about future employment and relationships. For these to be played out in public – especially including abuse from fellow players and fans – must only exacerbate these risk factors. While the research into suicide behaviours and risk factors is complex due to the various circumstances that might increase risk, several rigorous, longitudinal studies demonstrated that feelings of hopelessness, depression and pessimism were indicators of long-term suicidal risk (Kovacs and Garrison 1985). A recent systematic review also showed that males were at higher risk than females, and those who abuse alcohol or drugs were at higher risk (Hawton *et al.* 2013). The tragedies of Pettigrew and Newton's deaths highlight the need for pre-emptive support and counselling measures. Yet, none have been developed by WADA or any other sports organisation.

The Belgian cyclist Jonathan Breyne attempted suicide by taking pills, an hour after discovering he had tested positive for clenbuterol. He was discovered, taken to hospital and had his stomach pumped out. He said:

> The comments from the fans [on social media] drove me to act out [sic]. I could not stand being called a cheater when I'm not. I took my car, I parked in a parking lot near where my girlfriend works. I took pills.
>
> *(Cyclingnews 2014a)*

He had been at a race in China shortly before the positive test, so there is a strong possibility that he was a victim of contamination. In early 2014 he was facing a two-year ban, which led him to express feelings of anxiety at his loss of earnings. He was threatened with having to repay a year of his salary and was moving on to unemployment benefits. His future looked bleak:

> While Breyne has recovered physically from the suicide attempt, he is still struggling mentally with the collapse of his career. 'I'm still broken, I want to cry … Since I learned of my positive control, I haven't been back on the bike. It is not the rain that bothers me, but I do not want anything.'
>
> *(Cyclingnews 2014a)*

A much less clear-cut connection between drugs, anti-doping and death is the tragedy of Marco Pantani in 2004. The successful Italian rider had been accused of using EPO after a high level during the 1999 Giro d'Italia, and the allegations persisted during the intervening years. He died in a hotel room where investigators discovered tranquiliser drugs. It was reported that he suffered from depression and his death 'has prompted calls in Italy for athletes suspected of doping offences to be dealt with more sensitively' (BBC

2004). It was quite widely known that professional cyclists who used doping drugs quite often used painkillers, sleeping pills and recreational stimulants (Voet 2011). A doping ban might be indicative of the need for support, rather than removal from sport. In response to Pantani's death, Gianni Petrucci, president of the Italian Olympic Committee said: "'We all have to believe that we could have done something for Pantani'" (BBC 2004). And the Italian sports minister, Mario Pescante, said that the cyclist was being investigated by at least seven state prosecutors. In a comment that stands in contrast to demands for anti-doping criminalisation (see Chapter 8), Pescante continued: "'To me that seems frankly too many. The penal responsibility of athletes is absurd. Sports sanctions would be enough'" (BBC 2004). While there has been much subsequent discussion about Pantani's career and death, including several books and a documentary film, it is not completely clear how the series of events unfolded. We do see, however, a complicated and tragic interplay of drugs and anti-doping accusations that could have been more humanely dealt with by sports organisations.

Such a conclusion might also be reached when considering the recent experiences of James Hird, the head coach with Essendon Australian Rules Football Club when the entire team and support staff were sanctioned for use of a nutritional supplement that contained a banned substance. This was a lengthy, highly public and controversial case, which involved the club giving players a supplement which was, after some disagreement between the various organisations involved, concluded to contain a banned substance. Thirty-four players were banned for two years (Dadds 2016). In January 2017, Hird was hospitalised after a deliberate drug overdose. He had been at the centre of the media and public attention for around four years. The team manager, Danny Corcoran, described the pressure Hird had faced, not least facing the threat of never working in the sport again:

> Two years ago I said to James, 'No one in the history of Australian sport has ever suffered as much humiliation or persecution and that is going to take its toll on you' … I started to notice little things about him being erratic and angry. He couldn't see anything positive about life after his treatment…. I said, 'You need some help and you should get professional advice'. But like a lot of men, help was offered and rejected … He is a victim and is suffering from post-traumatic stress disorder, I've got no doubt about it. He endured four years of harassment and eventually he just snapped.
>
> (The Age 2017)

This analysis also reminds us that sport can be a highly competitive cultural environment in which athletes are at times discouraged from showing signs of dependence or looking for help, or anything that might be considered a weakness.

Depression

Many athletes have suffered from mental health issues in the period following news of their positive test and sanction. We have noted in earlier chapters the descriptions provided by Rick De Mont, Kicker Vencill, Kristen Worley, Roger Wenzel and others regarding the challenges they have faced.

Diane Modahl wrote her own account of being falsely accused of doping. The news of the positive sent her into a state of acute physical trauma: she fainted several times. She has no memories of that moment but was told by those present that:

> at one point I lay quite still with my eyes wide open and the pupils large and unmoving. Even when Sue [team manager] passed her hand across my eyes they didn't flicker. She was scared. My hands felt cold and she said to herself, 'My goodness, she's dead'.
>
> *(Modahl 1995 p. 96)*

The course of mounting an appeal, and dealing the legal and scientific issues, as well as the personal financial cost, left her feeling isolated, alone and questioning her Christian faith. The first verdict upheld her sanction, leading her to feel:

> It was my life they were playing with, my innocent life … My life as an athlete was ruined, my love for athletics had died, the reason to wake up in the morning had gone, I was half way in the grave.
>
> *(Modahl 1995 p. 169)*

During the months between that initial decision and pursuing the eventually successful appeal, her sense of despair heightened. Her reflections upon that period are poignant:

> Regardless of whether we eventually won the fight for my innocence, we had already lost. We could never go back to what we had … Over and over I have asked myself and asked God why it happened. Why should I have been the victim of an injustice so cruel and relentless that it has robbed me of almost everything?
>
> *(Modahl 1995 p. 182)*

Modahl was cleared of wrongdoing but still had to pay her legal costs. Towards the end of her autobiography she admits frankly that: 'During the eleven months of my ordeal I'd contemplated suicide more than once'. Her family life and religion had supported her, but 'if the verdict went against me once more, I felt I had nothing left to live for and no will to go on' (Modahl 1995 p. 190). The moments of crisis were profound. A final point to make regarding her experiences returns to the laboratory issues discussed in the previous chapter. It was almost impossible to get the authorities to admit that a mistake might have been made, even though her testosterone readings were extremely high. As she wrote: 'Athletes on occasions make mistakes, so why could the IAAF not admit that laboratories are also run by human beings who are not infallible?' (Modahl 1995 pp. 191–192)

Another example is that of Werner Reiterer who aadmitted using steroids in preparation for the 2000 Olympics (he was never tested positive). He explains in his autobiographical account how he was affected:

> Doubtless, it will hurt people, cause me heartache, cost me friends, and will tarnish my name … No words will ever describe the pain of throwing away a sport that has been such a quintessential part of my existence. It will take a long time for the emptiness to pass.
>
> *(Reiterer and Hainline 2000 p. 281)*

In his 2009 autobiography, the English sprinter Dwain Chambers offers a vivid account of the pressure he was under when his 2003 violation was announced:

> The day before the news was due to hit the papers, I was encouraged to leave town as the press would most definitely be outside my door … The next day Dwain Chambers was all over the newspapers and my neighbours informed me reporters were camped outside my door, just like rock fans queuing for tickets for the Rolling Stones last-ever gig. It would be three weeks before the press moved away from my house. I worried about returning home, facing my friends and family … The headlines were scathing … The press were like a pack of hungry hyenas determined to get their teeth into me.
>
> *(Chambers 2010 pp. 122–123)*

That level of intense scrutiny is usually only afforded to those in the public eye for the most scandalous behaviours of politicians, celebrities or athletes. Chambers proceeded to spend £60,000 on legal fees to appeal the two-year ban (Chambers 2010 p. 124). When that was denied, he confessed to using other drugs and offered to provide new knowledge to UKAD and WADA (which he says was ignored). Having served his ban, he realised that other British athletes and sports organisation leaders would continue to publicly criticise him, and that the loss of income and sponsorship put him on the 'breadline'. The full impact of the ban became clearer:

> with no money and no offers of money, no sponsorship or funding, it was going to be tough. It was in June 2006 that the awful truth dawned on me

that perhaps a two-year ban didn't mean two years after all. Here I was out of the ban and yet I still felt I was being penalised.

(Chambers 2010 p. 134)

Later he writes that six years after his ban he still felt ostracised and victimised, including from previous supporters like Sebastian Coe and former minister of sport, Colin Moynihan (Chambers 2010 p. 141).

Chambers found other ways to gain an income and made a return to athletics. He has not though been integrated back into the world of British sport, rarely appearing on sports coverage or being invited to commentate or having a coaching or leadership role. Indeed, when he first returned after the two-year ban, he was shunned by teammate Darren Campbell who refused to shake Chamber's hand after competing together in a relay race (Mackay 2006).

By contrast, the Scottish cyclist David Millar has recovered his reputation after being banned in 2004 for two years. Millar would have his apology accepted, and returned to sport so successfully that he captained the Scottish team at the 2014 Commonwealth Games in Glasgow and became a television commentator. Millar's autobiography detailed both his emotional turmoil before and during doping, then his struggles in the aftermath of his sanction, specifically the loss of income, employment and career purpose. He managed to regain a position in professional cycling and publicly campaigned to support anti-doping (Millar 2011).

In some cases, mental health issues might have preceded the choice to dope; as such, the interweaving of depression, drugs and the punishment of a sanction can be hard to untangle. For some athletes, this is because doping is a response to injury or lower than expected performance; in other words, the pressure of competitive sport can create anxiety which in turn can be the precursor for drug use. However, there might be many other causes of psychological problems.

The American professional cyclist and teammate of Lance Armstrong, Tyler Hamilton, suffered episodes of depression before and during the times in which he doped. In 2009, he decided to retire after a second doping offence, and he explained that he needed to focus on his 'struggle with depression' (Fontecchio 2009). Ironically, the second positive was for dehydroepiandrosterone (DHEA), found in a herbal medicine Hamilton had bought as a natural antidepressant (Hamilton and Coyle 2012 p. 238). In fact, he describes feeling 'desperate for help' and thus the violation prompted him to seek counselling (Hamilton and Coyle 2012 p. 238). Other cyclists, including the Danes Bjarne Riis and Michael Rasmussen, have described suffering serious depression after admitting to doping. In Rasmussen's experience, the sudden loss of a highly successful career, earnings and demonisation after being expelled from the 2007 Tour de France and subsequently confessing to years of doping left feelings of anomie, despair and isolation. In his biography he explains how, when he was driven away to a hotel in a secret location after he had been expelled from the race, it crossed his mind how easy it would be to grab the wheel and crash into an oncoming lorry. And his dark thoughts did not leave him when he was alone in the hotel room:

> If there had been a long thick rope in the room I would probably have hung myself. I searched the room for a solution. If the curtains had been hanging on a string rather than a pole it is likely that the outcome would have been fatal.
>
> *(Rasmussen 2013 p. 266)*

Riis was different in that, having won the Tour in 1996, his doping was not exposed until almost two decades later: at which point he suffered from depression (Cyclingnews 2014b).

It is not just high-profile male athletes for whom anti-doping issues can be bound up with depression. When Chinese swimmer, Ye Shiwen, competed in the 2012 Olympics she was just 16 years old. On the opening day, she broke a four-year-old world record to win the 400m individual medley gold, much to the incredulity of many people in the sport. In light of veiled accusations, Ye later said 'I was very depressed and angry after London' and felt 'hurt' at the implied suggestions she had been doping (Scott-Elliot 2013).

Even in cases where a mistake has been made and the athlete exonerated, the accusation leaves a stain on their career and reputation that can be very hard to recover from. French football player Mamadou Sakho tested positive for a fat-burner supplement while playing for Liverpool. It took around two months to establish that this substance was not actually banned, but he was suspended for one month during that time (BBC 2016). He missed Liverpool's Europa League Cup final and the chance to represent his country at the 2016 European Championships. He failed to re-establish his position for both club and country; he played for Liverpool reserves until January 2017 when he was loaned out to Crystal Palace who signed him in August of that year. So, in effect, he was a victim of a mistake on the part of anti-doping authorities.

Recovering and rebuilding

While it is clear that athletes face emotional turmoil related to doping sanctions, there are few routes for recovery even if they are convinced of their innocence: examples include Callum Priestley and Steven Colvert. Others try to deny that doping was intentional, in which case they have the right to a NADO tribunal, and if still unsatisfied they could appeal to CAS. The latter can prove to be a highly expensive route. The CAS was originally established to support the IOC's policies. Once WADA was up and running, the policy was developed to use CAS to arbitrate anti-doping appeals. This is another instance of organisational overlap between WADA and IOC (see Chapter 3) illustrated by Australian John Coates who simultaneously held the roles of president of the Council of CAS and vice-president of the IOC. The athlete must pay a fee to CAS, but also employ their own legal representative. The arbitration process mirrors other forms of Swiss arbitration, meaning that disputes are essentially private and between two parties: case law is not used and not all decisions are published, leading to potential inconsistencies. The costs are difficult to estimate because of the unknown length of time involved; cases are presented 'de novo' which means a reiteration of the arguments and evidence presented at the NADO tribunal. Established lawyers can charge anything between 200 and 500 Swiss francs per hour (although pro bono lawyers are available). They will also require travel and hotel expenses which could add substantially to the overall costs. The more complex the case, the more time-consuming it will be, the more costly it will be, and these costs are hard to predict in advance which means that athletes are committing themselves to a process they are unlikely to win at an unknown expense. It was estimated that the Floyd Landis appeal cost the athlete around $2m and cost WADA around $1.3m (Stokes 2008).

Arbitration can be a long process, depending upon the issues involved, such that a resolution might not actually emerge until the athlete has already served a substantial part of their ban or missed a major event. If they are not very well paid, or nearing the end of their career, a rational choice might be to avoid the stress of a legal case. Of course, the other intangible cost to the athlete is to their public reputation as every detail of their doping could be exposed. Certainly, there are cases where the full details would be embarrassing. Any athlete caught for recreational drug use might decide to avoid publicity, even if they do not choose to appeal through arbitration, due to the stigma attached to such drugs as ecstasy, cocaine and marijuana (Wivel 2010). A more humane approach to this issue is taken in the sport of American football where athletes are treated differently as the National Football League (NFL) is not a signatory to the WADC so therefore can manage social drug use in a more appropriate way: shorter bans and counselling support.

Sanctioned dopers live with that stigma for the rest of their life. Ben Johnson was one of the world's greatest sprinters, but is largely only remembered for his 1988 Olympics scandal. He has been unable to develop a sports-related career. Lance Armstrong has described his lack of rehabilitation options within sport as a 'death penalty' (Sanchez 2013). Marion Jones disappeared from public life. Even Diane Modahl faced many challenges in developing a new career, despite being proven innocent, and it would take over 10 years for her to establish a new career running a sports charitable foundation. Alain Baxter has a ski equipment shop in Scotland, but will always be associated with the Vicks inhaler incident, not as a hugely successful skier. The players who played for Essendon during the supplements scandal have found it very difficult to re-establish their careers.

A final example in this respect is that of Canadian wheelchair athlete Jeff Adams, whose successful career included six Paralympics and 13 medals. He tested positive for cocaine in May 2006, leading to a two-year ban. He challenged the ruling first at the Sport Dispute Resolution Center of Canada and then at CAS. The latter agreed there was no intention to cheat, no fault or negligence, but he remained guilty of a doping offence under strict liability even though paradoxically his original sanction was reduced to no sanction. The process took two years, being finalised in May 2008 at a personal cost of Canadian $1.2 million. He has had to endure loss of funding, a hugely significant career break, and damage to his reputation. His reflections many years later highlight the gulf between ideal governance and practice:

> I filed a civil suit for damages against the CCES [Canadian Centre for Ethics in Sport], Sport Canada and Athletics Canada because of the improprieties in my case – the A sample not matching the B sample, the CCES withholding evidence of a case prior to mine with identical circumstances of contamination of the sample, CCES witnesses giving false testimony and other pretty egregious things that happened.
>
> *(Kelsall 2016)*

It was also clear that the legacy of this false test has continued to haunt him:

> It's amazing though, even though it happened over a decade ago, no matter that even the CCES conceded that there was no cheating or attempt to cheat in my case, notwithstanding that I was exonerated by the CAS, if someone wants to score cheap shots on me, it's the first thing that comes up. They have to ignore all of the facts to do it, and end up looking foolish, but it is what it is – as an athlete, even when you're completely innocent, any anti-doping accusation has a lifelong potential to continue to harm you.
>
> *(Kelsall 2016)*

It is even more of a tragedy for Adams that the circumstances were similar to other cases where the athlete was exonerated. According to his version of events, he was speaking with a woman in a nightclub when she put a finger in his mouth. There was a strange taste. He did not know what it was but might have been cocaine. As a wheelchair user, he uses a catheter. So unfortunately, when the doping control testers came soon afterwards, and did not offer him a new catheter, he used the one possibly contaminated with cocaine. For that reason, he lost two years of his career, was dropped by many sponsors, and spent a huge sum of money on appealing the case. Yet, the nightclub cocaine contamination reason could have led to a no sanction decision if compared with the cases of Gasquet, Cilic and Barber (see Chapter 5). And if the anti-doping control officers had brought a new catheter with them, to reduce the risk of any form of contamination, Adams would not have faced so many problems.

Inhumanity and dehumanisation

Would it be inappropriate and unreasonable to describe the current anti-doping regime as inhumane? The perception of anti-doping is generally that it is a worthwhile project aimed at reducing the harmful effects of doping and maintaining the purity of sports competition. Surveys of attitudes towards anti-doping among the general public inform us that WADA and NADOs enjoy high levels of support (Engelberg *et al.* 2012). Athletes are also supportive (Overbye 2016), even if certain issues like the whereabouts system are not universally popular (Overbye and Wagner 2014) .

However, there is a lack of scholarship exploring whether the human costs are an unfortunate by-product of policy – an unintended consequence – or if the human costs are in fact an endemic, inherent and necessary part of the overall ambition: clean sport. It might be hard for those working within, or helping to support, the industry of anti-doping to allow themselves to imagine that their work is unethical. If they focus squarely on tasks to improve deterrence and detection, then perhaps they are convinced that their motivations are pure. They are working to prevent doping. If the accused athlete can be blamed for their negligence then there is no reason to believe that any of the decisions made by scientists, NADOs, WADA or CAS arbitrators, are anything other than the methodology for clean sport. Thus, the individual athlete who is sanctioned is stigmatised, marginalised and ignored. It seems as if protecting the system is deemed more urgent than recognising any form of suffering that results from a sanction.

A more person-centred analysis would bring to the forefront of the discussion those cases where athletes (and coaches) have had their careers ruined, had their income-generation potential taken away, had to live with the accusations and stigma for the rest of their lives, and expose the policy as inhumane. Within that category, we can point to cases along a spectrum from the genuinely innocent, to the should-have-known better, to the genuinely guilty. However, it would be unnecessarily critical and callous to propose that we should have more empathy for the innocent than the guilty. Even those people who have been tempted by doping are still human beings who have the right to be treated with dignity and respect. They have families to support and a future to navigate. They have skills and experiences which could be usefully applied to sports and to business. If society can tolerate rehabilitation of criminals and murderers, why should we be opposed to the rehabilitation of dopers? After all, they have simply taken the logic of competitive sport one step too far. Sometimes by their own volition, but at other times by their coach or doctor's instructions.

What explains the promotion and acceptance of an inhumane policy, that also treats clean athletes with methods of surveillance only reserved for convicted criminals? A starting point would be to remember that anti-doping is a system – a series of parts interlinked towards a vague, unrealisable objective. It has not been designed by an individual or a committee; it has gradually emerged in response to scandals and on the basis of developments in drug consumption and drug testing. It is supported by governments and sports organisations, backed up by sections of the media who promote a simplistic scandal-driven version of doping stories. There is, of course, a bureaucracy and a highly detailed set of regulations that make the ideology real in a material sense. Anti-doping is best understood as a system that encompasses education, psychology, testing, laboratories, national and international organisations, and a highly complex set of legal processes. The system has economic and legal power to enforce the regulations: the focal point of the myriad forms of power is the athlete. They are held responsible, they are mostly the people who face punishment.

As we have now established that anti-doping is a system with inhumane consequences, we can introduce the concept of dehumanisation. This has been applied in vast array of historical and contemporary situations, however a useful framework can be found in Haque and Waytz's (2012) exploration of dehumanisation in medicine. First, they explain that the term refers to diminished empathy:

> the central feature of all accounts of dehumanisation is a diminished attribution and consideration of others' mental states ... in virtually all cases, dehumanisation allows people to experience fewer moral concerns for their actions towards dehumanised others, and can justify acts that would otherwise be considered harmful.
>
> *(Haque and Waytz 2012 p. 177)*

In other words, dehumanisation refers to both parties. Doctors and other medical staff can become dehumanised in that they learn to reduce empathy, sometimes for the practical reasons of being effective doctors. Studies show that this process increases after Year 2 of medical school. They treat patients according to the disease and in groups, instead of as individuals. In anti-doping, athletes are treated as a group of people who might be tempted to dope. But dehumanisation also refers to the patients whose suffering is increased due to lack of feelings of support and empathy. The cases outlined above, and other examples such as the German athlete who struggled to provide a urine sample (Chapter 1) highlight this process. Haque and Waytz also explain that patient's self-determination and agency is diminished regarding making choices about their healthcare. Clearly athletes' choices about anti-doping are practically non-existent.

One possible cause outlined by Haque and Waytz is de-individuation where 'an individual becomes immersed in a group or otherwise anonymised' (Haque and Waytz 2012 p. 177). Studies show, for example, that de-individuation can increase aggressive behaviours towards others and antisocial behaviour. This is arguably what social-identity theorists refer to as 'them and us' or 'in and out groups', whereby labelling individuals within groups leads to stereotyping and suspicion. With respect to anti-doping, there is a clear distinction between the representatives of the policy (educators, testers, scientists, NADO staff) and those who are potential dopers (athletes). There is an element of anonymity – the urine or blood sample has personal details removed, the laboratory scientists do not get named in the analysis process. In fact, the very act of obtaining a sample, anonymising it, and sending it for analysis, is depersonalising. The scientists and decision makers do not have to feel personal responsibility or empathy because they are dealing with a sample, not with a person with whom they might come to empathise. Thus, they are dehumanised by the system so they can maintain objectivity and distance in the name of science and fairness. Even when mistakes are made that impact upon individuals there have been no attempt to redress the consequences for the individuals affected.

A second cause is dissimilarity: in medicine, this would be the distinction between doctor and patient. This is manifest through the definition of illness and patient, the labelling of a patient by their illness rather than as a person who has an illness, and the power asymmetries where the power lies with the doctor. Within the anti-doping system, the athlete becomes labelled as clean or as a doper. Once the violation is announced they lose the right to anonymity; a right which is afforded to the laboratory scientists who processed their sample. However, upon that announcement the athlete is characterised primarily by the doping violation, and much less as a 'normal' person. The official statements are so sparse that it seems we are being discouraged from relating to the athlete as a person. Haque and Waytz note that 'such labelling encourages perceptions of the patient as the disease itself rather than as a fundamentally human entity stricken by the disease' (Haque and Waytz 2012 p.178). Anti-doping focuses on the act of doping, not upon the person – their achievements, skills, personality, context for doping, possibility that it was not intentional, or that they were in desperate straits (poverty, injury etc). It is little surprise that sports fans and the media so easily describe sanctioned athletes as dopers, even though there is such a wide range of contexts and reasons for sanctions.

The question of power is also important. The athlete is the focus of hard and soft forms of power, as well as intensive surveillance (Hardie 2014). Haque and Waytz state that 'the experience of power leads people to treat people as means to an end rather than ends in themselves' (Haque and Waytz 2012 p.178). We can say that the process by which athletes are sanctioned is seen as means to an end (clean sport), and in the same way athletes being tested or under the whereabouts conditions are a means to an end. The experiences and responses of athletes are de-individualised, and in fact their agency is reduced to such an extent that they are compelled to consent to the WADC, to out-of-competition testing and the indignity of the testing procedures without having the opportunity to comment or to resist. Such is the power of anti-doping that any resistance can be punished: refusal to take a test can lead directly to a sanction; and as we have said any public comments of disapproval with the anti-doping system can lead to the athlete being suspected of doping or at least of not supporting clean sport.

Anti-doping leaders and managers remain distant from the experiences of the sanctioned athlete. We could draw parallels with the moral disengagement that characterises doctors when they are compelled to use painful medical techniques. This disengagement, 'serves to justify past or prospective harm ... the need to minimise the guilt of inflicting pain (even pain necessary for treatment) likely increases dehumanisation'(Haque and Waytz 2012 p.179).

It could therefore be argued that the idealistic demand for drug-free sport has created an occupational culture among anti-doping leaders and workers that displays the main characteristics of dehumanisation: de-individuation (caused by the scientific approach and distrust of athletes), mechanisation (not holistic) due to analytic procedures, empathy reduction (acceptance of human costs in the wider ambition/vision), empathy reduction (need to follow through on sanctions despite impact on the athlete).

Anti-doping is a highly punitive policy. There is no escape from a positive test. Even in those cases where contamination or laboratory mistakes have been proven and accepted, the athlete suffers personal loss. Yet, WADA and other powerful stakeholder organisations have been on a single track since 1999: to create a system that deters dopers, is tough on those who are caught, and relentless in its pursuit of the amorphous and unrealistic goal of 'clean sport'. It has created an environment where those on the side of 'good' seem to lack any form of empathy or sympathy for those deemed to be on the side of 'evil'. It seems deeply ironic that a policy designed for athletes pays so little attention to the voices and experiences of athletes. It seems tragic that a policy that aims to protect health has no supporting procedures for athletes who are isolated from their career due to anti-doping decisions.

The inhumanity is related to processes of dehumanisation, which serve to emphasise following the rules over basic justice and dignity. Even when arbitrators agree there is no fault or negligence, the athlete might still face the stigma attached to any perception of doping. And, of course, there are the challenges faced by those who want to understand the science behind a doping violation. The ways in which policy and science are interconnected to victimise athletes has been nicely summed up in the aftermath of the LaTasha Jenkins case, by legal expert Michael Straubel:

> The story of *USADA* v *Jenkins*, and the failed appeal by the World Anti-Doping Agency (WADA) that followed, is the story of a lucky win against a multi-headed foe that makes all the rules, then changes the rules when it loses, in a system nearly incapable of addressing the inherent imbalance of power between athletes and their accusers ... those flaws will not be fixed unless the underlying imbalance of power between athletes and those who control sports is changed.
>
> *(Straubel 2009)*

Such issues are essential to understanding, researching and challenging the nature of power in sport. In the next chapters, we review some of the proposals for reform that have already been made, and from there proceed to outlining some new ideas.

References

BBC (2004). "Pantani in suicide link". 19 February. Retrieved 12 January 2018 from http://news.bbc.co.uk/sport1/hi/other_sports/cycling/3490761.stm

BBC (2016). "Liverpool: Mamadou Sakho has doping case dismissed by UEFA". 8 July. Retrieved 12 January 2018 from http://www.bbc.co.uk/sport/football/36752127

Brown, A. (2016). "Meldonium madness, Russia, Sharapova and Rio 2016". Sporting Integrity Initiative, 21 October. Retrieved 12 January 2018 from http://www.sportsintegrityinitiative.com/meldonium-madness-russia-sharapova-rio-2016/

Bull, A. (2016). "Lilly King remains unrepentant over calling out drug cheats". The Guardian, 10 August. Retrieved 12 January 2018 from https://www.theguardian.com/sport/2016/aug/10/lilly-king-unrepentant-calling-out-drug-cheats

Chambers, D. (2010). Race against Me: My Story. Bodmin: Libros.

Cyclingnews (2014a). "Breyne says internet forum comments drove him to suicide attempt". 3 January. Retrieved 12 January 2018 from http://www.cyclingnews.com/news/breyne-says-internet-forum-comments-drove-him-to-suicide-attempt/

Cyclingnews (2014b). "Doping scandals sent Riis into a depression". 9 January. Retrieved 12 January 2018 from http://www.cyclingnews.com/news/doping-scandals-sent-riis-into-a-depression/

Dadds, M. (2016). "Following the herd: The court of arbitration's judgment on Essendon's supplements regime". The Bulletin: Law Society of South Australia 38(2): 30–31.

de Menezes, J. (2016). "Maria Sharapova banned: Jennifer Capriati in verbal attack on disgraced tennis star after failed drug test". The Independent, 8 March. Retrieved 12 January 2018 from http://www.independent.co.uk/sport/tennis/maria-sharapova-banned-jennifer-capriati-in-verbal-attack-on-disgraced-tennis-star-after-failed-drug-a6918426.html

Engelberg, T., S. Moston and J. Skinner (2012). "Public perception of sport anti-doping policy in Australia". Drugs: Education, Prevention and Policy 19(1): 84–87.

Fontecchio, C. (2009). "Tyler Hamilton admits doping, retires from cycling". SB Nation Podium Café, 17 April. Retrieved 12 January 2018 from https://www.podiumcafe.com/2009/4/17/841125/tyler-hamilton-admits-doping

Hamilton, T. and D. Coyle (2012). The Secret Race: Inside the Hidden World of the Tour de France: Doping, Cover-ups, and Winning at all Costs. New York: Bantam.

Haque, O. S. and A. Waytz (2012). "Dehumanization in medicine: Causes, solutions, and functions". Perspectives on Psychological Science 7(2): 176–186.

Hardie, M. (2014). "Making visible the invisible act of doping". International Journal for the Semiotics of Law – Revue internationale de sémiotique juridique 27(1): 85–119.

Hawton, K., C. C. i Comabella, C. Haw and K. Saunders (2013). 'Risk factors for suicide in individuals with depression: A systematic review.' Journal of Affective Disorders 147(1): 17–28.

Kelsall, C. (2016). "Paralympic medallist Jeff Adams is not happy about the Peter Eriksson firing". Athletics Illustrated, 13 December.

Kovacs, M. and B. Garrison (1985). "Hopelessness and eventual suicide: A 10-year prospective study of patients hospitalized with suicidal ideation". American Journal of Psychiatry 1(42): 559–563.

Mackay, D. (2006). "Campbell turns his back on victorious team-mates as protest sours Britain's sole gold". The Guardian, 14 August. Retrieved 12 January 2018 from https://www.theguardian.com/sport/2006/aug/14/athletics.topstories3

Millar, D. (2011). Racing through the Dark: The Fall and Rise of David Millar. London: Hachette UK.

Modahl, D. (1995). *The Diane Modahl Story: Going the Distance The Heartbreaking Truth Behind the Headlines*. London: Hodder & Stoughton.

Newton, T. (2010). *Coming Clean: The Terry Newton Story*. Skipton: Vertical Press.

Overbye, M. (2016). "Doping control in sport: An investigation of how elite athletes perceive and trust the functioning of the doping testing system in their sport". *Sport Management Review* 19(1): 6–22.

Overbye, M. and U. Wagner (2014). "Experiences, attitudes and trust: An inquiry into elite athletes' perception of the whereabouts reporting system". *International Journal of Sport Policy and Politics* 6(3): 407–428.

Rasmussen, M. (2013). *Gul feber*. Copenhagen: People's Press.

Reiterer, W. and B. Hainline (2000). *Positive: An Australian Olympian Reveals the Inside Story of Drugs and Sport*. Sydney: Pan Macmillan Australia.

Sanchez, R. (2013). "Lance Armstrong pleads against 'death penalty' to be allowed to compete again". *The Telegraph*, 19 January. Retrieved 12 January 2018 from http://www.telegraph.co.uk/sport/othersports/cycling/lancearmstrong/9812841/Lance-Armstrong-pleads-against-death-penalty-to-be-allowed-to-compete-again.html

Scott-Elliot, R. (2013). "Ye Shiwen: Marked woman of the pool". *The Independent*, 2 June. Retrieved 12 January 2018 from http://www.independent.co.uk/sport/general/others/ye-shiwen-marked-woman-of-the-pool-8641547.html

Stokes, S. (2008) "Landis case costing WADA $1.3 million", Cyclingnews.com, 11 May. Retrieved 12 January 2018 from http://www.cyclingnews.com/news/landis-case-costing-wada-dollar-1-3-million/

Straubel, M. S. (2009). "Lessons from USADA v. Jenkins: You Can't Win When You Beat a Monopoly." *Pepp. Disp. Resol. LJ* 10: 119.

The Age (2017). "James Hird overdose: Hird had post-traumatic stress disorder 'for years' says Danny Corcoran". 14 January. Retrieved 12 January 2018 from http://www.theage.com.au/afl/afl-news/james-hird-overdose-hird-had-posttraumatic-stress-disorder-for-years-says-danny-corcoran-20170113-gtrdus.html

The Telegraph (2010). "Drug cheat Antonio Pettigrew found dead in car".10 August. Retrieved 12 January 2018 from http://www.telegraph.co.uk/sport/othersports/athletics/7937478/Drug-cheat-Antonio-Pettigrew-found-dead-in-car.html

Voet, W. (2011). *Breaking the Chain: Drugs and Cycling – The True Story*. London: Random House.

Wilson, A. (2010). "Terry Newton, former Great Britain hooker, has been found hanged". *The Guardian*, 26 September. Retrieved 12 January 2018 from https://www.theguardian.com/sport/2010/sep/26/terry-newton-found-hanged-rugby

Wivel, K. (2010). "CAS-seret". *Weekendavisen*, 7 May.

8

PROPOSED ALTERNATIVES TO THE CURRENT ANTI-DOPING STRATEGY

So far, we have shown that the construction of the current anti-doping system is so defective that it cannot be remedied by small adjustments. What is needed is radical reform. This, of course, is easier said than done. In this chapter, we will discuss alternatives to the current approach that have been proposed; propositions, which we will demonstrate, are saddled with their own shortcomings.

Legalisation

The most radical proposal is to lift the ban on doping. That cuts the Gordian knot. This solution would immediately remove the painstakingly difficult problem of how to effectively control that athletes abide by the rules. Even though doping regulations are officially categorised as sports rules they are obviously very different from other regulatory rules in sport. Referees are appointed to administer the rules during games and competitions. It is true that replays often prove that referees can get it wrong. In some sports, this is accepted as part and parcel of the game, in other sports visual technologies are introduced to help referees correct wrong calls. However, because infringements of doping rules take place behind the scenes referees are powerless to this kind of cheating. No technology has yet been invented that can make up for the referees' blindness to doping-rule violations. In comparison with, for example, the Hawk-Eye technology, doping testing is a hopelessly inefficient tool to secure fairness. It goes without saying that the Hawk-Eye would never have been introduced if it only occasionally managed to correct wrong calls, much less if it was uncertain that its calls were indeed correct ones. By removing doping from the rulebook, the uncertainty about potential medical cheating immediately disappears. If the level playing field and fair play serve as guiding principles, allowing what is now considered illegal enhancement methods would thus be the logical solution. But there is at least one serious problem with this solution. If athletes were free to use whatever they want to enhance their performances the competitive nature of elite sport would turn sports into medical arms races. The winners of contests between more or less equally gifted athletes would be the ones who dared to use the most potent cocktail of performance-enhancing means accepting possibly serious health consequences in the short or long term.

Interestingly those who argue in favour of deregulation do not bite the bullet and admit that health hazards are likely consequences of legalised doping. This has been shown at length elsewhere (Møller 2010) so we will restrict ourselves here to give only one paradigmatic example. The authors of an oft-quoted viewpoint article in *The Lancet* elegantly conjure the problem away by simply stating that they do not believe there would be any more deaths or health problems among elite athletes, or that there would be more countries who would facilitate systematic doping in order to gain sporting success:

> If doping was allowed, would there be an increase in the rate of death and chronic illness among athletes? Would athletes have a shorter lifespan than the general population? Would there be more examples like the widespread use of performance-enhancing drugs in the former East-German republic? We do not think so. Only a small proportion of the population engages in elite sports. Furthermore, legalisation of doping, we believe, would encourage more sensible, informed use of drugs in amateur sport, leading to an overall decline in the rate of health problems associated with doping. Finally, by allowing medically supervised doping, the drugs used could be assessed for a clearer view of what is dangerous and what is not.
>
> *(Kayser et al. 2005 p. 521)*

If this is true, there is clearly no reason to ban doping. But the authors do not provide any reason *why* they believe there would be no more fatalities or health damages or more widespread use of doping. They simply proceed with the correct but unrelated observation that only a few of the world's population engage in elite sport. And from here they move further away from explaining why legalisation would not increase usage of doping products and result in an increase in associated health risks by presenting another unsubstantiated conviction – namely that legalisation of doping in elite sport would have an educational effect on amateur athletes. Amateurs would start to use drugs more reasonably, they speculate, without giving any reason why they believe this would be the result. Their final point is no less remarkable as they reiterate what they wrote in their introduction: 'use of doping should be permitted under medical supervision' (Kayser *et al.* 2005 p. 521).

There is only one rational explanation for this proviso, namely that the authors acknowledge that doping can be dangerous if not supervised by responsible experts. But if that is indeed their position it seems more reasonable to argue for the current ban than against it. Because imperfect as the anti-doping test system is, it is still good enough to catch what former WADA Director General, David Howman, called the 'dopey dopers', which translates into athletes who do not have medical expertise to draw on. It is precisely those who are under medical supervision that are not being caught under the current anti-doping regime. It is of course unsatisfactory and deeply unfair, as we have explained in Chapter 1, that athletes with resources can hire doctors who can help them beat the system whilst their less fortunate competitors have not. The current regime leaves the latter with a much higher risk of getting caught if they try to stay competitive. However, from a health-protection perspective it is good that the dopey dopers, who are most likely to run the highest health risk, test positive when they make mistakes so their risky doping practice stops at least for the duration of a lengthy ban. From the same perspective, it is also better that doctors who work with the resourceful athletes know that the testing system is at least so good that there are limits to what they can provide the athletes with without running the risk of having them exposed.

If doping were legal under medical supervision it is not hard to imagine that athletes and doctors with sporting ambition would push the envelope very much like they did in the 1990s when athletes aided by expert doctors like Michele Ferrari used the wonder-drug EPO to increase athletes' haematocrit level up in the danger zone around 60 per cent. And even if the expert doctors used EPO in combination with aspirin or other anticoagulants to lower the risk of blood clotting, athletes who cannot afford the assistance of medical experts might under the pressure of their competitors' performances take their own performance-enhancing drug use to unsafe levels.

The authors want all doping athletes to be medically supervised, but we cannot think of any way this could be guaranteed. What kind of new control system should be established to secure that doping was properly supervised? The moment doping under medical supervision is legalised all athletes can take whatever they want without risking anything but their health. If a medical expert decides he or she only wants to give an athlete doping to a limit he or she considers safe, there is no way to stop athletes from taking extra dosages without the knowledge of the medical supervisor who is supposed to guarantee their health or consulting another expert with a more generous interpretation of what is safe. Sports writer Mark Johnson gives a frank example of this at the team level in relation to the doping practice at Lance Armstrong's U.S. Postal team:

> Spanish doctor Pedro Celeay was brought on to manage the team's use of EPO and other performance enhancers. When Celeya proved too cautious, the team managers replaced him with another Spanish doctor, Luis Garcia del Moral, who prescribed more aggressively than Celeay.
>
> *(Johnson 2016 p. 351)*

So, there is reason to believe that the proposal of medically supervised doping is in effect to ask for complete deregulation of the use of drugs in sport.

Harm reduction

Some propose a harm reduction approach as an alternative to the unconditional legalisation of doping. That is, an acceptance of the use of doping products within safe limits so potential damages are minimised. There is a difference in the reasoning behind the two lines of attack. Whereas outright proponents of legalisation build their argument on libertarianism, harm-reduction advocates take a pragmatic position with health protection as the main concern. However, the proviso we saw in the example above shows how closely related the legalisation and the harm reduction approach are.

Few in favour of legalisation are bold enough to maintain that the health and wellbeing of high-performance athletes is not a concern to them. Instead, they argue that legalisation is, in actual fact, better for athletes' health, maintaining that anti-doping regulations drive doping use underground and push doping athletes away from tried and tested drugs toward undetectable new drugs sometimes not even approved for medical use. This was observed by Ben Johnson's track coach Charlie Francis, who 'argued that without coach and doctor oversight, athletes would put themselves into greater danger by self-medication and by obtaining drugs from street dealers' (Johnson 2016 p. 299). That this was not mere speculation became clear when Italian police raided team hotels during the Tour of Italy in 2001. Among other medications, police 'found the experimental drug RSR-13 made in Denver, Colorado, which enhanced oxygen flow from red blood cells rather than increased the amount of red blood cells as EPO does' (Guinness 2009 p. 285). At the time there was no direct test for EPO but since a maximum haematocrit level of 50 per cent had been introduced in 1997, it is clear why this drug became attractive despite clinical tests on lung and brain cancer patients showing that the drug had serious side effects (Guinness 2009). But the fact that the cycling teams exposed all had physicians in their entourage undermines the argument that if athletes are under doctors' supervision they are in safe hands. It may be true that it is safer to use drugs under the guidance of expert doctors but if doctors are willing to provide drugs to athletes which are not yet approved for human use it is difficult to trust that supervision of expert doctors guarantees athletes against health risks. There is, of course, a theoretical chance that the athletes had picked up the RSR-13 drug without the aid or knowledge of their team doctors. But in that case the conclusion is very much the same, the only difference being that it is not the team doctors' moral deficit, rather their impotence as guardians, that allowed the athletes to use unsafe (quantities of) drugs.

However, the harm-reduction approach builds on public health principles which have proven effective in other contexts (Kayser and Broers 2015). Health clinics' needle exchange programmes have been successful in reducing transmission of HIV and other blood-borne diseases; venereal disease, and unwanted pregnanies have been reduced by providing free condoms. Also, traffic fatalities have been reduced by airbags, speed limits and laws on safety belts, and the construction of roundabouts and traffic lights. Given the current system's lack of success it is understandable why some have started to reason that if the fight against doping is no more winnable than the fight against narcotics, why not replace the zero-tolerance policy and opt for the second-best solution which focuses on reducing harms? Particularly if the consequence of the game of cat and mouse is, as Ken Kirkwood maintains, 'that athletes are chased along the pharmacological frontier, from well-established medications with known manageable side-effects to an ever-increasing supply of experimental substances of indeterminable safety' (Kirkwood 2009 p. 186).

But doping in sport is conspicuously different to other areas where harm-reduction policies have been applied, so it is far from certain that a harm-reduction approach in this field would be successful. Drug addicts want to get high but do not take part in a competition of who can get highest; young women grateful for free condoms, as a means of avoiding pregnancy and venereal diseases, are not looking to beat the birth-giving record; and car drivers want to transport themselves but do not usually race against their fellow road-users. And if they do, they will be punished for speeding. In serious cases, they will lose their drivers' licence and be banned for a lengthy period of time. Thus, it could be argued that the current anti-doping programme is the best possible harm reduction approach one can think of given the nature of the phenomenon at hand. At any rate, it is hard to think of any other surveillance system that would reduce doping athletes' risk further. Kirkwood's assertion may be true that 'athletes move to less-tested and riskier substances as the established substances become more detectable by drug tests' (Kirkwood 2009 p. 188). But the question remains unanswered as to how legalisation of tried-and-tested doping drugs should prevent athletes from using these to excess if that would give them a competitive edge, or move on to new and unsafe drugs if these drugs promise to be more effective than the old ones.

We understand that the idea is that doping control testing under the harm reduction principle should be replaced by health checks to make sure liver enzyme and haematocrit and hormone levels etc. remain within normal range. But if there is no punishment for transgressing reasonable limits other than a no-start rule – as was the case when the UCI in 1997 introduced the 50 per cent haematocrit level to keep the use of the then-undetectable blood-boosting hormone EPO under control – it is hard to see how such a system would decrease the 'risk for long-term health problems related to doping' (Kirkwood 2009 p. 188).

Education

Another strategy proposed to improve anti-doping is to increase the focus on education. Whereas harm reduction is a pragmatic approach the educational approach is an idealistic one, which is already part of the WADA toolkit. The WADC requires 'each Anti-Doping Organization to develop and implement education and prevention programmes for Athletes including youth and Athlete Support Personnel' (WADA 2015a p. 14). It has been noted, however, that in reality WADA does not put much emphasis on this part of its operation. Susan Backhouse draws attention to the fact that only three pages of the 158-page document addresses education and prevention whereas the rest (98 per cent) focuses on the detection-based system. This prioritisation, she maintains, is also reflected in the distribution of the WADA funds. Only a small fraction of the funds is allocated to research and implementation of anti-doping education which, she speculates, may be at least part of the explanation 'why WADA has not been as effective as it could be in pursuing clean sport' (Backhouse 2015 p. 229).

Backhouse is undoubtedly right that there is room for improvement in this regard, and that education needs to be given higher priority. In light of the severe consequences athletes face if they test positive, it is obviously unacceptable if they fail a test because they have taken a substance not knowing that it was banned. We experienced the need of education first hand in 2012 when invited by the Sacred Sports Foundation in Saint Lucia to help undertake an anti-doping education programme funded by UNESCO.

During a lecture for young athletes and coaches, in which the basics of anti-doping were presented, one of the organisers interrupted while a slide presenting some of the most common banned substances was shown on the screen. He asked the audience if they had ever taken any of the drugs mentioned. Even though the recreational drug cannabis, which many young people have tried, was presented on the slide the response was surprising as everyone raised their hands. One of the athletes even raised both hands probably indicating that he was using at least one banned substance regularly. Perhaps even more surprising, one of the trainers came up during the break to ask if the tablets in his hand were banned. They clearly were. The content of the package read among other things 'DHEA' which is a pro-hormone included on WADA's list of banned substances. When asked where he got them he explained: 'The Gym. Everyone in the gym takes them.'

It is true that the beautiful Caribbean island-state has a population of little more than 180,000 and is yet to win its first Olympic medal. Nevertheless, the country is one of over 200 national olympic committees which are WADC signatories. So, the example is at least a reminder that despite the alleged worldwide support of the principles laid out in the Code, in reality there are huge differences between countries when it comes to values, norms, types of problems, and priorities. Given this, it is unsurprising if, from a developing country's point of view, anti-doping and anti-doping education work looks like ill-affordable luxuries in the face of general poverty and serious social problems that needs addressing.

And even if developing countries have the capacity to recruit and train volunteers to become anti-doping educators these volunteers must be extraordinarily good teachers to have any impact because poverty and limited schooling do not impair human beings' use of common sense. This was also a lesson learned from the Saint Lucia lecture. After having explained various sports federations' effort to promote fair competition and anti-doping campaigns such as the International Cycling Union's 'True Champion or Cheat?', the International Ski Federation's cheeky slogan 'Clean as Snow', and the International Ice Hockey Federation's no-less witty 'Doping is not Hockey' the audience was shown a different slide. On the right side of this slide there was an athlete promoting WADA's unmistakable 'Say No to Doping' campaign launched in the lead up to the London 2012 Olympics. On the left a Tour de France podium of athletes who were all later revealed to have doped. After the images had been explained, the audience was asked on which podium they thought athletes preferred to appear. Unsurprisingly the response was unison in favour of the winners' podium. Subsequently they were asked on which podium they would prefer to see themselves? Despite the premise, that they had to run the risk of being caught doping to get there, once again the vast majority chose the winners' podium apparently unconcerned by what they had been told about the winners' means to get there.

It would be wrong to conclude from this that the athletes and coaches attending the lecture would subscribe to a doping programme if given the choice in real life. However, their response indicated that they understood that being a winner of an international sports competition equals wealth and prestige and that this would mean a world of difference to them and their families – a privileged life they could only dream of. If the choice you have to make is between playing true or lifting yourself and your family out of poverty by cutting corners, cheating is a rational choice. This is why education possesses little real anti-doping potential.

The education approach is proposed by fairly well-off upper-middle-class people living in affluent liberal societies where basic education is taken for granted and there are sufficient economic resources to prioritise public health programmes. Anti-doping education will probably have a positive effect on sons and daughters of the same kind of people. But even in the richest countries there are large and growing income differences and increasing poverty rates. This is fertile ground for recruiting athletes willing to make the necessary sacrifices to get the most out of their sporting talent in the hope that this will improve their life conditions. There are plenty of young boys and girls who grow up in wealthy societies where material wealth is paraded before their eyes on a daily basis, yet is out of reach. An illustrious example is, of course, Lance Armstrong who, abandoned by his father when he was two years old, grew up in Plano, Texas, with his mother who was only seventeen when she had him and had to work two or three jobs to make ends meet. At a young age, he discovered his talent for endurance sports. As a teenager he began to win prize money and could contribute to the household (Ballester and Walsh 2004). This kind of practical education seems stronger than theoretical lessons in school about the value of fair play and clean sports. As Andreas Singler poignantly puts it: 'Prevention of risky behaviour will be less effective, or even wholly ineffective, as long as the broader environment remains unchanged' (Singler 2015 p. 241). Young people, who find the school system unappealing and the societal order to work against them, will be less receptive, if not immune, to 'authorities' who teach them upper-middle-class values whereas they will be open to people who tap into their ambitions and prove willing to help them succeed. So, social psychology dynamics work effectively against the educational approach. But, as Singler further observes, it is much more difficult to improve broader social and cultural processes and this may explain why:

> a simple and exclusive call for education [...] is an approach that necessarily underestimates the complexity of the doping problem and therefore involves a gross oversimplification of the problem involved in preventive work.
>
> *(Singler 2015 p. 241)*

All possible should be done to make athletes aware of the potential risks of doping, but in light of the complexity of the problem it is wishful thinking to believe that education is a potent weapon. It is unlikely that ethics lessons and introduction to sporting virtues and vices will change the mindset of ambitious and single-minded athletes particularly not the poor who do not see any alternative paths to the sunny side of life.

Criminalisation

Since improved testing methods, increased number of tests, stricter surveillance measures, and longer bans for doping positives, have not brought doping to an end, it is understandable that people who think doping is an intolerable scourge get impatient. Unwilling to turn their back on sport and give up the fight, unable to reconcile themselves with the pragmatic approach which looks at possible ways to minimise the adverse effects of doping, and unconvinced that anti-doping education is powerful enough to change athletes' attitudes in the long run, some take the position that sport is not able, and will never be, to clean up its own act. Hence they call for state intervention and criminalisation of doping (Hoberman 2011).

Sports leaders fear this approach, not only because it means they lose control. More importantly, because it will tarnish sports' commercial value if successful sports stars, their main product, are seen handcuffed and put behind bars. Ahead of the 2006 Turin Winter Olympics, Italy criminalised the use of doping. This led the IOC to push for a moratorium during the Games. Then WADA President Dick Pound explained that the 'sports system would prefer that the final arbiters on sports matters not be criminal courts' (Goldman 2005). When asked if the IOC's opposition to the tough Italian policy did not contradict WADA's own zero-tolerance policy he conceded 'the difficulty of the communication image that this gives'. There shall be no doubt that he and 'the IOC remains fully committed to getting drugs out of sports', he maintained before entertaining an incautious analogy that proved the difficulty of the position he was out to defend: 'Let's say you don't count a stroke in a game of golf. I mean, what do you do? You send somebody to jail or ...' (Goldman 2005). Canadian cross-country skier and Olympic athlete Becky Scott, observed in response: 'taking banned substances goes way beyond a little cheating on the golf course.' In her opinion, Italy's criminalisation of doping offenses was justifiable because as she explained, in 'the world of sport and particularly Olympic sport, doping is very much a criminal offense. You're defiling the sponsors, you're defiling your fellow athletes and you're defiling the public' (Goldman 2005). The most surprising issue here is not that Scott is able to pinpoint Pound's careless comparison, but that she favours criminalisation despite having to suffer the consequences if she herself tested positive. However, Scott, who in 2012 was appointed to the executive committee of WADA, is not the only athlete who holds the view that doping is a criminal offence. The former British marathon runner Mara Yamauchi, who came sixth in the 2008 Beijing Olympics, argues that doping amounts to stealing money by deception which 'is a criminal offence in many situations and it should be in sport. It's clear that the current system of punishments is not sufficient. It is totally unacceptable that people can steal money and face no punishment' (Ingle 2016).

The view presented by Yamauchi seems to have receptiveness in politics. In 2005 only five countries had national laws specifically targeting doping, but in 2012 the number had increased to 18 (Lowther 2015). So there seems to be a trend towards criminalisation, particularly in Europe. In 2016 Germany passed a law that makes doping a criminal offence. As a result, athletes may now face up to three years in jail if they fail a drug test. The law does not only apply to German athletes but also to those caught doping within the country's borders.

It is understandable if clean athletes who did not make it to the winners' podium think their chance of winning has been stolen from them if they learn that those who beat them improved their performance by illegal means, and see it as a criminal offence. Particularly if the winner has made a fortune from endorsements and prize money. In such cases it is no wonder that rivals wish to see the cheating athletes held to account in the same way as any other fraudster. Once again, the Lance Armstrong case is illustrative. During his career he earned more than $218 million (Levinson and Novy-Williams 2013). Most professional cyclists only earn a fraction of this amount. Riders who are hired by World Tour teams, the highest level of professional cycling, are guaranteed a minimum wage of €36,300 per year. If the rider is neo-professional the amount is even less, namely €29,370 as per the 2014 UCI regulations (Stokes 2014). So, there is a world of difference between star riders and support riders even though they train and race the same. The economic inequality is a strong incentive for athletes to consider using banned means that can take them from the anonymous to the lucrative end of the sporting hierarchy. As long as doping is interpreted solely as a sporting rule violation, albeit resulting in a lengthy ban, athletes can see doping as a gamble. A shift in conception of doping from a rule infraction to a criminal act would remove the excuse that doping is part and parcel of being a true professional (Christiansen 2006). If athletes' self-perception is that they are not criminals but take banned substances because it is a prerequisite to be competitive, the prospect of incarceration may be influential. As Claire Sumner, one of those who argue in favour of criminalisation of doping offences, speculates. Despite the fact that:

> any period of incapacitation imposed by a criminal sanction is unlikely to exceed any period of suspension of the Code [...] the stigma attached to a criminal record is greater than that attached to any regulatory offence and may act as a more powerful deterrent to athletes.
>
> *(Sumner 2017 p. 7)*

Sumner wants the United Kingdom to follow the example of France, Italy, Spain, Austria, and Germany and stresses the deterrence effect of criminalisation by mentioning the long-term consequences it has to have a criminal record in the United Kingdom. For instance, people who have been imprisoned for up to six months must disclose this to potential employers for the next seven years after being released, and even those who get away with just a fine are still under the disclosure obligation for a five-year period. So, the deterrence effect is far-reaching. It might even be educational in another meaning of the word than discussed above, because 'punishment can have a subconscious effect on society and provide an educative deterrent'. This, according to Sumner, has been the case with drink-driving since it was made a criminal offence 30 years ago. 'Criminalising doping could create such an educative deterrent over time', she envisions (Sumner 2017 p. 7).

However, Sumner's enthusiasm about all the good consequences that she thinks will result from criminalisation makes her unreceptive of WADA's arguments why 'the Agency does not believe that doping should be a criminal offence for athletes' (WADA 2015b). Instead she finds it encouraging that among the world's governments 'there is a growing appetite for the criminalisation of doping and a recognition that this would act as a deterrent' (Sumner 2017 p. 9). Before we get too excited about governments' growing appetite for criminalisation of doping it might be worthwhile to consider if WADA's opposition to criminalisation is solely based on sports organisations', not least the IOC's, lack of appetite for government interference with their business or WADA actually has good reasons to be sceptical. So, let us look at potential negative effects of criminalisation.

An immediate problem is the vague definition of doping. WADA's 'definition' of doping 'as the occurrence of one or more of the anti-doping rule violations set forth in Article 2.1 through Article 2.10 of the Code', is not a solid basis for putting people behind bars. More precision is needed. The violations described in Article 2.1 through 2.10 are better suited to guide judges, but we only need to run through the first of these to demonstrate that it is unlikely that these violations would be satisfactory for a judge to put an athlete away. Rule violation 2.1 concerns the 'Presence of Prohibited Substances or its Metabolites or Markers in an Athlete's Sample'. This is the typical anti-doping rule violation. If a urine or blood test flags a prohibited substance the athlete faces suspension. However, it is unlikely that a judge will pass sentence on an athlete on the basis of a positive sample if the athlete pleads innocent and there is no evidence that the athlete intentionally took the substance. The crucial pillar in anti-doping is the acceptance of strict liability. This is not applicable in criminal law where the presumption of innocence is a crucial principle, as is the prosecutor's obligation to prove the defendant guilty beyond reasonable doubt. It goes without saying that if jail time is on the cards athletes will be even more determined to claim innocence. A likely scenario is therefore that athletes who are handed a potential career-ending four-year ban by the Court of Arbitration for Sport, will be found not guilty in the criminal court. Such outcomes would undermine the credibility of sport's anti-doping regulations. Moreover, criminalisation is up to the different states to implement and enforce. Athletes who live in countries where anti-doping is given high priority have often complained that their rivals in other countries are not subjected to a similarly rigorous anti-doping system implying that there is not a level playing field (Hanstad et al. 2010). Criminalisation, if not implemented globally as the WADC has been, adds to the uneven conditions under which athletes compete. Finally, criminalisation of doping could be counter-productive because it may have the effect that athletes begin to think differently about anti-doping and their unions to lobby for better legal protection, demanding threshold values where there are currently none, and higher where there are. Such improvements of athletes' legal protection would result in a less effective and deterring anti-doping system.

Having considered the various proposals that have been put forward to solve the anti-doping crisis we find none of them ideal. So, in the next chapter we will outline a different approach which is radical in the true sense of the word as it goes to the root of the problem.

References

Backhouse, S. (2015). "Anti-doping education for athletes". In V. Møller, I. Waddington and J. Hoberman (eds), *Routledge Handbook of Drugs and Sport*. London: Routledge.

Ballester, P. and D. Walsh (2004). *L.A. Confidentiel – Les secrets de Lance Armstrong*. Paris: La Martinière.

Christiansen, A. V. (2006). "'A clean amateur makes a good professional': On deviance, professionalism and doping in elite sport – illustrated by the case of Danish cycling". In G. Spitzer (ed.), *Doping and Doping Control in Europe: Performance Enhancing Drugs, Elite Sports and Leisure Time Sport in Denmark, Great Britain, East and West Germany, Poland, France, Italy*. Oxford: Meyer & Meyer Sport.

Goldman, T. (2005). "Italy's strict anti-doping laws clash with Olympic rules". Retrieved 25 January 2017 from http://www.npr.org/templates/story/story.php?storyId=5044688

Guinness, R. (2009). *What a Ride: From Phil Anderson to Cadel Evans An Aussie Pursuit of the Tour de France.* Crows Nest, NSW: Allen & Unwin.

Hanstad, D. V., E. Å. Skille and S. Loland (2010). "Harmonization of anti-doping work: myth or reality?" *Sport in Society* 13(3): 418–430.

Hoberman, J. (2011). "Athletes in handcuffs? The criminalisation of doping". In M. McNamee and V. Møller (eds), *Doping and Anti-Doping Policy in Sport: Ethical, Legal and Social Perspectives.* London: Routledge.

Ingle, S. (2016). "IAAF has betrayed athletes but law to jail doping cheats carries risks". *The Guardian*, 10 January. Retrieved 25 January, 2017 from https://www.theguardian.com/sport/blog/2016/jan/10/iaaf-athletes-law-jail-doping-cheats

Johnson, M. (2016). *Spitting in the Soup: Inside the Dirty Game of Doping in Sports.* Boulder, CO: Velopress.

Kayser, B. and B. Broers (2015). "Doping and performance enhancement: Harms and harm reduction". In V. Møller, I. Waddington and J. Hoberman (eds), *Routledge Handbook of Drugs and Sport.* London Routledge.

Kayser, B., A. Miah and A. Mauron (2005). "Legalization of Performance-Enhancing Drugs." *Lancet* 366: S21.

Kirkwood, K. (2009). "Considering harm reduction as the future of doping control policy in International sport". *Quest* 61(2): 180–190.

Levinson, M. and E. Novy-Williams. (2013). "Armstrong's cheating won record riches of more than $218 million". Bloomberg, 21 February. Retrieved January 25 2017 from https://www.bloomberg.com/news/articles/2013-02-20/armstrong-s-cheating-won-record-riches-of-more-than-218-million

Lowther, J. (2015). "Effectiveness, proportionality and deterrence". In V. Møller, I. Waddington and J. Hoberman (eds), *Routledge Handbook of Drugs and Sport.* London: Routledge.

Møller, V. (2010). *The Ethics of Doping and Anti-Doping: Redeeming the Soul of Sport?* London: Routledge.

Singler, A. (2015). "Doping prevention – demands and reality: Why education of athletes is not enough". In V. Møller, I. Waddington and J. Hoberman (eds), *Routledge Handbook of Drugs and Sport.* London: Routledge.

Stokes, S. (2014). "How UCI minimum wage regulations are being broken" Retrieved 15 February 2017 from https://cyclingtips.com/2014/11/how-uci-minimum-wage-regulations-are-being-broken-by-some-pro-teams/

Sumner, C. (2017). "The spirit of sport: the case for criminalisation of doping in the UK." *The International Sports Law Journal* 16(34): 1–11.

WADA (2015a). *The World Anti-Doping Code.* Montreal: World Anti-Doping Agency.

WADA. (2015b). "WADA statement on the criminalization of doping in sport." Retrieved 15 February 2017 from https://www.wada-ama.org/en/media/news/2015-10/wada-statement-on-the-criminalization-of-doping-in-sport

9

RECOMMENDATIONS FOR RADICAL REFORM

It should be clear from the previous chapters that the anti-doping campaign launched in order to secure the integrity of sport and athletes' health has proven unsuccessful. The pursuit of a level playing field has even been counterproductive. Today the playing field is more uneven than it was in 1999 when the French minister for sport and youth Marie-George Buffet brought the doping problem to the forefront of the public agenda by ordering police and customs to raid the Tour de France. We have since learned that nations, teams, and athletes invest in sophisticated doping programmes and state-of-the-art expertise. Some countries prefer sporting success to doping-free sport and do little more than paying lip service to the anti-doping campaign, while other countries do their utmost to promote clean sport by generous funding of their national anti-doping organisations. Some nations even go so far as to pass laws that deem doping a criminal offence. It is also true that some sports are targeted more than others despite WADA's obligation to secure harmonisation across sports. Even within individual sports some athletes are tested much more frequently than their rivals. The fundamental reason why anti-doping has been a fiasco is that it has fought symptoms while the root of the problem has been left untouched. Because it was designed with the primary aim to catch athletes who took advantage of doping it was doomed to fail (Hermann and Henneberg 2014). In this chapter we will review some of the critical issues that must be addressed if anti-doping shall be anything but an image enhancing public relations enterprise that regularly sacrifices careless, ill-advised or unfortunate athletes and at the same time scapegoats almost as many athletes (four out of ten) who have not intentionally cheated (de Hon 2016).

Back to amateurism

Any anti-doping endeavour ought to begin by considering the incentives to start doping in the first place. It goes without saying that if there were no incentives to dope, nobody would do it and as long as there are sufficiently strong incentives there are people who will. Anti-doping testing is supposed to discourage athletes from doping; the anti-doping sanction system is to outweigh the incentives. However, the risk of receiving a two-year suspension for first-time offences was apparently not effective enough to deter athletes from doping. So, in the 2015 revision of the WADC the maximum sanction for first time offences was increased to four years. This increase was a signal of intent but at the same time a forceful admission of the failure of the current approach. Criminologists have known for years that, while certainty of detection and punishment has a strong and consistent negative association with crime rates, the length of sanctions has not (Tittle 1969). In light of this, it is naïve to believe that the risk of receiving a four-year ban will be able to bring about a behavioural change that the risk of a two-year ban could not. A more promising approach is therefore to discourage doping by reducing the incentives as much as possible.

An obvious incentive to begin doping is the will to win and, since the pursuit of victory is the *raison d'être* of elite sport, you cannot remove this fundamental incentive to dope without transforming sports competitions into futile pastimes. Prize money, endorsement deals, size and length of contracts etc. all contribute to doping behaviour. If we trust that EPO, steroids etc. have performance-enhancing effects of such significance that it is important to oppose their use in order to secure fair competition, other things being equal, those who dope are those who win. Hence, in the current situation it is the athletes who most likely have used doping who get the lion's share of the money, while those who most likely have not doped must feed on crumbs. That is, the professional sports system is established in such a way that it bestows glamour, prestige and wealth on athletes who use the very drugs which the same sport system apparently finds unacceptable. On the other hand, athletes who do not resort to doping get little reward and recognition despite working to the best of their natural ability in the spirit of sport as defined by WADA. It is clear why such a system continues to breed dopers and why it is necessary to radically change the anti-doping paradigm if the ambition is to remove doping from sport. And if our diagnosis is correct, the remedy should be evident.

We are of course aware that politicians, sports leaders and athletes alike may find the remedy unpalatable. Nevertheless, the first step is to reform the financial reward system. Ideally sports should return to its amateur roots, and reinvigorate the Olympic spirit as emphasised by Pierre de Coubertin who said: 'In these Olympiads, the important thing is not winning but taking part. The important thing in life is not victory, but struggle: the essential thing is not to conquer but to fight well' (Coubertin 2000 p. 587). Anyone who immediately refutes the idea of returning to amateur sport should bear in mind that in the first half of the twentieth century it was normal that sport was played for the love of the game whereas professional athletes were considered pariahs. Indeed, as noted in Chapter 2, anti-doping ideas emerged directly from amateurism. The derogatory word 'shamateur' was coined as an expression of contempt for athletes who were not openly professionals but found roundabout ways to make money from their sport while pretending to be amateurs (Llewellyn 2011). It was not until 1988 that the IOC decided to allow full-time professional athletes to participate in the Olympic Games. Thus, it should be clear that the current sporting system is a construction that could be changed if there was political will to do so.

If amateurism were to be re-established it would be less painful to lose to a doped rival and the athlete who doped to win would have less pleasure from the victory. There would be nothing to lose but the satisfaction from crossing the finish line first and the 'winner' would not win anything but an honourless victory. In this scenario, the number of athletes who find doping worthwhile will in all likelihood be significantly reduced. And those who would still be tempted by enhancement products would probably not be willing to take as big health risks as they would under the current money-oriented system. Finally, those who still would be so obsessed with winning that they would use drugs regardless of any long- or short-term health risk might suffer sudden death. As sad as this would be, the victims would only have themselves to blame. In the process, they would not have taken anything material away from their rivals. Consequently, there would be little reason to uphold the invasive anti-doping regime which today burdens elite athletes en masse.

Those who immediately rebuff this suggestion by claiming it to be a nostalgic dream impossible to achieve in our time and age, or an unacceptable method in a capitalist market economy should ask themselves what matters most to them: to fight doping in order to protect fair competition and athletes' health or to protect the obscenely lucrative sport business.

The strongest argument against re-establishment of the amateur model of sport is that whilst it still allows sports organisations to profit from arranging events the athletes will not get a share. Thus, the amateur model increases the economic exploitation of athletes. Another valid counterargument is that it may be unjustifiable that in order to demotivate fraudulent athletes from taking drugs honest athletes will no longer be allowed the opportunity to make a living from their hobby. It could also be argued that it goes against the idea of a level playing field that only the affluent few will be able to devote all their time to make the most of their sporting talent. So instead of returning to the old amateur model, it is worth considering an alternative solution, namely to reform the business model.

Reform of the business model

It is paradoxical that doping is opposed because it gives athletes a better chance of winning while, at the same time, it is accepted that winners, who are the most likely dopers, are rewarded much more handsomely than their most likely non-doping competitors. The current distribution of money in sport is possibly the strongest motivation for athletes to use illegal performance-enhancing means. This motivation could be diminished significantly without discarding professionalism. Moreover, the proposal is in accordance with the aforementioned Olympic dictum: the most important thing is not winning, but taking part. And the solution is simple. Money should be shared equally between participants in a given competition. If we take the much-maligned professional cycling as example, the International Cycling Union (UCI) has currently in their regulations a minimum contract salary for professional riders. In 2013 the minimum salary per year for established and new UCI Pro-Team riders (first-tier) was €36,300 and €29,370 respectively. For established Professional Continental Team riders (second-tier) the minimum salary was €30,250 whereas new ones were guaranteed a minimum of €25,300 (AIGCP-CPA 2013). These minimum wages were negotiated between the Association of Professional Cyclists (CPA) and the International Association of Professional Cycling Groups (AIGCP). However, there is no maximum salary included in the joint agreement. As a result, there are huge income differences. Good support riders are estimated to make between €40,000 and €100,000. Star riders on the other hand make anything between €1,000,000 and €3,000,000 per year (Cyclingtips 2010). Such salary gaps are clearly counterproductive to anti-doping. Hence governments and responsible organisations that advocate doping-free sport should push for regulations that level out the income between the athletes. There is nothing in principle that rules out rigid income regulations. Alberto Contador, speaking at a press conference during the Vuelta a España 2017, actually proposed the introduction of salary caps in cycling for the sustainability of his sport rather than for anti-doping purposes, saying:

> I think there should be a salary cap. You have to decide what the amount should be, for example 15 million Euros on rider's salaries. Because if budgets start to go through the roof, we're going to find it hard to attract sponsors at all.
>
> *(Fletcher 2017)*

In a number of countries salary caps have been introduced in various sports leagues, including the capitalist nation par excellence, USA's National Basketball Association (NBA), National Hockey League (NHL), and National Football League (NFL) (Zimbalist 2010). The rationale behind salary caps is that it prevents the wealthiest teams from capturing all the very best players by outbidding the less wealthy teams, which ultimately would kill the competition and render the leagues uninterestingly redundant. It is true that salary caps in these leagues were not introduced to prevent income differences. There are still huge gaps between players in the league and also within teams because the caps only limit the leagues' teams overall spending on players' salaries. However, the salary caps show that even in countries where strong antitrust laws prevent businesses forming cartels (and similar arrangements) to artificially limit demands for employees the business of sport is an exception. The reason why sport is treated differently is that the product of the enterprise is competition. If competition between teams' boardroom tycoons were left unrestricted the essential product – on-field competition – would suffer with the end result being that the entire industry would lose value (Pagels 2014). So, the acceptance of salary regulations is due to the protection of fair competition and that is exactly what anti-doping should be all about.

It is worth noting that a cornerstone in anti-doping is the assumption that sport, although being an occupation for professional athletes, is not work in the ordinary sense of the word. This is a much more radical and dubious interpretation of professional sport than the one that paved the way for the acceptance of salary caps. However, if athletes were supposed to be protected by workers' rights, like ordinary employees, they could not be tested in their spare time, during vacation etc., so out-of-competition testing would be impossible. Likewise, if athletes should enjoy the same legal protection as ordinary employees, strict liability in doping cases which result in a four-year job suspension for first-time offences would be dismissed if there were no more substantial evidence than a positive test result. Former WADA president Dick Pound has explained the rationale emphatically:

> [Sport] is governed by rules that, however, artificial or arbitrary they may be, are freely accepted by the participants. Why a race is 100 or 200 or 1,500 meters does not really matter. Nor does the weight of a shot… the number of members on a team or specifications regarding equipment. Those are the agreed upon rules. Period. Sport involves even more freedom of choice than participation in society. If you do not agree with the rules in sport you can opt-out, unlike your ability to opt-out of the legal framework of society. But if you do participate, you must accept the rules.
>
> *(Teetzel 2007 p. 46)*

By the same token, if sports organisations decide that the athletes who take part in a given sport should be given the same salary irrespective of their placing, athletes who find this unacceptable are free to opt out and find another – a proper – vocation. If the proposal of economic equality in sports is unrealistic it is only because stakeholders are unwilling to promote it. If sport's leaders wanted to implement it, it could be done. It is true there are lots of practicalities that need to be thought through in order to create a fair and equal payment system. We will not be surprised if critics contest our proposal with all kinds of scenarios such as: Should a person who abandons a race be given the same amount as those who make it all the way to the finish line? Should injured athletes have the same income as those who play? Should those who play in the first division have the same annual salary as those who play in the second and third divisions? We will not try to foresee and answer all potential problems and dilemmas that may occur in relation to a more even income distribution in sport but be content with the fact that any such issue can be determined by the governing bodies much the same way as other changes to sporting rules are. Instead we will focus on the most important principal objections.

If there is no income differentiation between the top and the bottom of the professional hierarchy it could be argued that athletes who put in next to no effort benefit unfairly from the extreme effort put in by the dedicated ones at the top end. These objections are indeed relevant and we concede that for the system to be reasonable and fair there should be room for differentiation between first-, second- and third-tier professionals and reduced payment to athletes who withdraw from competitions or are unable to compete due to injuries. But the acceptance of a differentiation of maximum salaries between tiers, which, as mentioned above, is already in place in cycling in relation to minimum salaries, does in no way compromise the purpose of the initiative, namely to bring an end to the exorbitant doping incentivising income differences between winners and losers. Obviously, this only holds if endorsement contracts are included in the same solidarity system. But there is nothing in principle that rules that out either. Winners will still appeal to companies that find it attractive to have sports idols showcasing their products, and athletes should be allowed to take advantage of that so long as the income was put into a professional athletes' foundation established with an obligation to distribute the revenue to the common good of the athletes in their respective tier. For instance, as a post-career pension. Whether athletes want to accept the role of poster boys and girls should be their own decision, but if individual athletes insist on their right to sign endorsement deals privately and thus oppose the anti-incentivising doping rule, sport's governing bodies should be equally free to exclude these athletes from the professional community and effectively terminate their careers.

A more challenging concern would be the incitement to use doping in order to qualify to become a member of the professional league in the first place and subsequently to move up into the more lucrative tier. Doping could also be a temptation for those who want to prolong their careers or maintain their capacity to compete in the more lucrative tier they qualified for during their prime years. We acknowledge that a much more equal income distribution will not eliminate the attraction of becoming a member of the privileged group of athletes who make a decent living from sport. Maximum salary caps that allow for nothing more than a decent upper-middle-class living, together with an equal distribution of income irrespective of the athletes placing in competitions, would undoubtedly make doping less attractive to athletes from affluent Western countries who have opportunities to pursue other career paths. However, athletes from poor countries would still see sport as an attractive way to achieve wealth that, even under the proposed restriction, will be much better than in their home countries. So, it could be argued that the proposal will not eliminate the temptation of doping. However, it would be too hasty to rebut the proposal on the grounds that there will be athletes who continue to dope.

A qualitative study – supported by the Australian government with the purpose of identifying pragmatic starting points to develop effective and sustainable policies to govern professional cycling – addressed the sport's social structure. The researchers wanted to find out if it is possible for the peloton to constitute a sustainable and principled community in relation to doping or if cooperation within cycling was perceived by the riders as no more than a necessary means to fulfil their personal interest. During the process of analysing the interviews they made the observation that 'there is evidence that appears to confirm the existence of an ethical code or community of practice' (Hardie *et al.* 2010 p. 125). This community of practice, dubbed 'the social peloton', is a potential force of self-regulation that has little chance of thriving under the current system where the winner takes it all. However, implementation of the equality model would make athletes self-policing more likely. Athletes are pretty good at working out who is doping. They can identify a donkey even if it begins to perform as a thoroughbred. So, if there is no reason to begin doping other than to make it into the top tier, there is more chance for the athletic communities' ethical code (in the case of cycling 'the social peloton') to work. Because the true thoroughbred athletes will have a vested interest in protecting the integrity of their sport by freezing out the 'enhanced donkeys' or blow the whistle on them.

The idea of equal income distribution will of course provoke opposition from those who swear by the free market and value the view that everyone is the architect of his or her own luck. But anti-doping is not a liberal endeavour in the first place. On the contrary, anti-doping is paternalistic and thus essentially the opposite of liberalism. That is, anti-doping proponents have already opted against free-choice liberalism and step-by-step introduced new paternalistic tools to intensify the fight against doping. The regulation of sport's payment structure would be just another element in the patronising of athletes.

WADA-accredited medical staff

We have no doubt that equal distribution of income would be a big leap forward in the attempt to de-incentivise doping, but anti-doping organisations could further change sport's doping cultures by breaking with the tradition of privately engaged (sports) doctors.

Athletes who compete at international elite level should be forbidden to choose their own doctors. Instead they should be compelled to choose doctors approved by WADA. Critics of this proposal might argue that this is another encroachment on athletes' freedom and privacy rights. However, this addition is negligible compared with the obligations already accepted, such as the demand to allow into their house a doping control officer who rings the doorbell, provide urine and blood samples whenever required, and to expose their private parts so the officer can see the required fluid leave the athlete's body.

The reason why we propose WADA-accredited doctors is that doping scandals often involve private doctors. Prominent names include Spaniard Eufemiano Fuentes and Italian doctors Francesco Conconi and Michele Ferrari. Conconi was a pioneer in developing a doping culture among Italian Olympic athletes. He was the one who helped Francesco Moser break the World Hour Record by introducing him to blood doping. Later he served as a private physician for a number of highly successful cyclists in the 1990s. Michele Ferrari was an apprentice of Conconi (Paoli and Donati 2014). He became equally successful in administering doping and training programmes to elite-level athletes, among which Lance Armstrong probably is the most renowned. And Fuentes became world famous in 2006 when his blood doping clinic, in which he assisted hundreds of athletes from a whole host of sports, was exposed in relation to Operación Puerto (Hardie 2011). But there are many more. As sport historian John Hoberman writes: 'After 25 years of nonstop doping scandals involving elite athletes such as cyclists and sprinters, the major role physicians have played in these doping cultures has received much less attention than it deserves' (Hoberman 2014 p. 570). The crucial role of doctors was also observed by sport sociologist Ivan Waddington who, in an interview during the Play the Game conference in Copenhagen 2002, maintained that more and more doctors' involvement in elite sport:

> has meant that doping research is an increasingly important part of their work .... The development of sports medicine began long ago, but over the last three decades it has increased in pace – and at the same time the medical reasoning has altered. ... It is no longer about using sport as just one of many ways to understand the body. Sports medicine has now become an eternal search to win and set new records ... at the same time, it now appears that today's doctors are not particularly affected by ethical considerations ... Instead of doctors attempting to protect their athletes ... athletes are often simply seen as patients who are required to perform better and better.
>
> *(Toft 2002 p. 25)*

Waddington's claims in the interview are too general. There are surely many doctors who are genuinely concerned and outspoken about the misuse of medicine for athletic enhancement purposes (Gaehwiler 2017). This caveat aside, Waddington is correct to say that doping has been facilitated and advanced by physicians and these doping doctors must be prevented from working with athletes for anti-doping to have any chance of success. The solution is easily organised.

Physicians who are not authorised by WADA should not be granted access to athletes during competition. Instead athletes in need of medical examination or assistance should require this from a group of WADA-approved doctors appointed for the competition. This model mirrors the working of a hospital in which appointed experts take care of whoever turns up with a health issue within their area of expertise. If teams find it necessary to appoint professional doctors so their athletes can get continuous medical attention from a doctor who knows the athletes' injury history, this need could be met so long as the doctors are recruited from the WADA-approved list.

For everyday purposes, that is outside competition, athletes should be allowed to choose any general practitioner in their home city who has WADA-accreditation. It is true that many athletes travel to train in a lot of different places and may be in need of medical assistance when away from home. In such cases they will have to inform WADA about their whereabouts and it would be easy for WADA to return a message with addresses and contact details of WADA-approved doctors in the area.

The benefit of the proposed system is twofold. First, the WADA-approved doctors will not identify as strongly or be so emotionally attached to teams or individual athletes as they would be if they are paid members of teams' or athletes' entourage. This makes them less likely to be willing to contribute to the teams' or individual athletes' success by whichever enhancement means they possess than they would be if they were directly recruited by individual athletes or teams. Second, the support of only WADA-approved doctors will reduce the athletes' risk of being accidentally provided drugs from doctors who are not up-to-date with the banned list.

Unfortunate situations like the one involving the world champion in women's cross-country skiing, Therese Johaug, who tested positive in 2016 would be avoided. Johaug had a lip sore and was treated by the Norwegian ski-team doctor with a steroid cream containing costebol. This resulted in a failed doping test. The team doctor took full responsibility and resigned. Nevertheless, Johaug was handed an 18-month suspension. Improbable as it may be, if a similar situation happened with a WADA-approved doctor, the WADA system rather than the athlete would be at fault. Consequently, the doctor, not the athlete, should be suspended.

Discard therapeutic use exemptions

In the aftermath of the 2016 Rio Olympics the Russia-based hacker group Fancy Bears hacked into WADA's database and published an extensive list of high-profile athletes who held TUEs. After the exposure of Russia's flawed anti-doping programme, which led to the suspension of Russian track and field athletes from international competition and subsequently led to exclusion of Russian athletes from the Games, Fancy Bears' revelations fuelled a debate about the trustworthiness of the international anti-doping system. The revelations raised suspicion that Western athletes exploited the TUE system with WADA's blessing. In response, WADA's TUE Expert Group published an 'independent opinion' on the WADA website that univocally defended the integrity of the TUE system (Gerrard 2016). However, Richard McLaren, the independent investigator in charge of the investigation that resulted in a damning critique of RUSADA, admitted that Fancy Bears' revelation of the many high-profile athletes who hold TUEs raised cause for concern that the system was being exploited: 'One would have to conduct investigations on specific sports as to whether or not too many TUEs are being used with respect to particular substances. One of the common TUEs is for ADHD medication – there may be abuse there', McLaren maintained (BBC Sport 2016).

If WADA-accredited physicians were introduced, the TUE system would undoubtedly be harder to exploit. Independent doctors detached from athletes' and teams' competitive ambitions would be harder to convince that an athlete should be granted a TUE than a doctor appointed for good money in the hope that their expertise will make the athletes under their supervision stay competitive and successful. Even if WADA-accredited team doctors were allowed under the reformed system, they would have gone through interviews, signed up to the Code, and after thorough assessment given the green light to work as team doctors. In other words, they would be adopted by the WADA family and the chance they would stay loyal and act in accordance with the WADA cause would be much higher. But even if the introduction of WADA-accredited doctors would reduce the risk of exploitation, we would argue that the TUE option should be removed as it undermines the anti-doping rationale.

It is worth keeping in mind that a TUE means that an athlete who allegedly suffers from a disease is allowed to make use of a performance-enhancing drug that healthy athletes are not allowed to use. The performance-enhancing capacity of the drug benefits the sick athlete so they are in effect granted an advantage over their healthy rival. An argument in favour of the current system is that sick athletes are not getting an advantage by using the prescribed drug, as they are only allowed to use the drug in a quantity that brings them on par with their healthy competitors. However, this argument is delusional. It is impossible to administer a drug precisely so it results in a physiological balance that is exactly the same as if the person did not suffer from the illness. There is clearly a chance that the drug will enhance the sick athlete's performance capacity beyond what it would have been had the person not been ill. So, no matter if athletes are granted permission to use a banned substance for a valid reason or not the TUE system compromises the ideal of a level playing field.

Another pro-TUE argument is that if the possibility of getting dispensation to use a banned drug was removed altogether a vast number of asthmatics, allergy sufferers, and other athletes with chronic conditions would be excluded from sports. However, there are better solutions to this than the TUE system. The most harmless and least performance-enhancing drugs to treat the diseases in question could simply be removed from the banned list. If this is not enough to solve the situation because some athletes need more potent drugs to combat their illnesses, threshold values for those drugs could be introduced. This would mean that all athletes could benefit from the use of these drugs within certain (safe) limits. However, if these drugs were so dangerous and their performance-enhancing effect so significant that, from an anti-doping perspective, they would be unacceptable to allow everyone to use even in limited amounts, then they should also not be allowed for competitive athletes even if it means they would be unable to compete. As sad as this would be for the sick individuals, they would simply have to accept that regardless of their talent, their constitution was not made for elite sport. They cannot legitimately blame the sport system that will not allow them using a drug that will provide them with a competitive advantage over healthy athletes. Their situation compares to the talented basketball players who were so unfortunate that nature equipped them with a body too short to be competitive in this particular sport, and the talented cyclists whose natural haematocrit levels are subpar which prevents them from being competitive. One of the prominent anti-doping arguments is that sport should be about athletes' natural abilities and not aided by advances in medicine. If no asthma medication were invented asthmatics would not be able to compete anyway. Accordingly, there is no more reason to complain as an asthmatic person that they are unable to be competitive without medical aid than it is for all other athletes who could be competitive if they were allowed to use medicine that could bring them on par with naturally advantaged athletes.

Another argument why TUEs should be banned is that incapacitating injuries are bodily signals that the athlete should stop, rest and recover. Medicines are given to athletes to speed up the healing process unnaturally with potential side effects. For instance, cortisone is one of the drugs often administered to athletes on the basis of a TUE, but has potential side effects including joint degradation and weakened tendons which could lead to higher risk of ruptures. So, if anti-doping took health protection seriously it would not allow injured athletes such potentially damaging shortcuts back to competition. That is, discarding the TUE system will both improve equality, fair play and health.

Health checks before major competitions

The de-incentivising initiatives we have introduced above: economic equality among competitors that will mobilise athletes' self-policing ability; WADA-accredited medical staff that will exclude independent doctors from working with elite-level athletes; and removal of the TUE system will surely reduce the doping prevalence so that it no longer makes sense to uphold the extensive anti-doping testing system we have today. Instead resources should be spent on comprehensive health checks of athletes before major competitions including haematologic scrfeening, hormone levels, electrolytes, vitamins, enzymes, etc. If an athlete's biological data is outside agreed parameters, they will not be allowed to participate for health and safety reasons until they are back to normal, have been properly diagnosed and deemed fit enough to return to competition (by WADA-accredited doctors). In the event that a health check raises concern that an athlete is doping this should activate target testing until the athlete is cleared of suspicion. This would significantly improve the health protection of athletes.

It would increase the relevance of doping testing and bring an end to the ever-growing number of futile tests which are a recurrent annoyance to athletes and which serve no other purpose than to demonstrate to all athletes that doping control takes place, even if it does so rather unsuccessfully. The bottom line is that whereas the current system leads to highly paid doping doctors monitoring athletes to avoid testing positive; our system would involve accredited doctors monitoring athletes to ensure they are healthy, and thus is more rational and humane.

The alternative programme we propose can be opposed with the argument that it is contrary to libertarian values, because it will prevent athletes from the chance to earn fortunes at the expense of less-talented or less-hard-working athletes, and because it takes away athletes' freedom to choose the physician they prefer. It can also be accused of being unfair because it will in effect exclude athletes suffering curable illnesses from pursuing their sporting ambitions because it will prevent them from competing if they make use of the medicine they need. However, the doping regulations currently in place are based on similar paternalistic principles. The current system sacrifices a large number of athletes who have been unintentional victims of the doping test regime either because they have been negligent, poorly advised, unknowingly treated with a doping product, subject to contamination, a false positive or flawed laboratory processes. Moreover, the paternalism of the current regime is much more intrusive than the one we propose. It excludes athletes from their livelihood for a lengthy period of time if they have a positive test without having intentionally doped. A first-time anti-doping rule violation (ADRV), regardless if it is intentional or not, may result in a four-year ban which in effect can be career ending. It sanctions athletes if they have forgotten to (re-)apply in time for a necessary TUE. It requires knowledge of athletes' whereabouts 24 hours a day, every day, all year around. It sanctions athletes if control officers visit them during the daily one-hour time period they have intended to be available but for whatever reason are not located in the right place. With this in mind, it is hard to build a consistent argument on the basis of paternalism against a system that de-incentivises doping in order to protect the integrity and health of athletes in favour of the current system. The limitations to athletes' earnings from sport is a regulation that appears much less restrictive and offers athletes much more freedom and protection than the system we have today.

So, those who want to reject our proposal because of its paternalism must, in order to be forceful, oppose any paternalistic anti-doping system including the current one. In other words, anti-paternalistic critics must bite the bullet and promote the libertarian alternative: legalisation of performance-enhancing drugs in sport. Legalising doping would not be incompatible with the ideal of fair play and a level playing field. However, it would involve a change of the health-protection strategy from paternalism to empowerment of athletes.

Information and education

Education is allegedly one of the central pillars of WADA's anti-doping programme. However, the material produced by the organisation for the purpose of education is not educative in the ordinary sense of the word, but is in fact propaganda and indoctrination. The official WADA leaflet *Dangers of Doping: Get the Facts* is an obvious example of this. The leaflet targets adolescents and is not in the least balanced or level-headed, as documented by the following few examples 'All medications have side effects – but taking them when your body doesn't need them can cause serious damage to your body and *destroy* your athletic career' (WADA 2009). The leaflet does not mention that all prescription drugs have been tried and tested in a process that takes years before they eventually are approved for use in humans because that might lead rational young people to assume they are safe. After all, the pills are meant to cure ills. If the old, the sick, and the weak can tolerate the medicine healthy young athletes will probably survive with good health as well.

'Steroids may make your muscles big and strong, BUT they may: Give you acne. Make you bald. [...] Make you suicidal. Guys you may also look forward to: Shrinking testicles. Breast growth. Reduced sex drive and even impotence' (WADA 2009). Again, there is no information about prevalence of these side effects in steroid users, or the excessive dosages it takes to induce them. As regards sex drive, those who have experienced a reduction in relation to steroid use did so when they stopped taking the drugs, while they experienced increased sex drive during periods on the drug (Hoberman 2005). The most striking example of misinformation in the leaflet is the assertions made about EPO. While it increases oxygen uptake, the leaflet maintains:

> BUT... why risk it when it may lead to death? Using EPO may make your blood more like honey – thick and sticky – than water. Trying to pump this thick blood trough your veins may: Make you feel weak – not good when you are trying to train hard! Give you high blood pressure. Make your heart work so hard that you have a heart attack or stroke (even at your age).
>
> *(WADA 2009)*

The claim that EPO makes blood sticky and thick like honey is absurd to put it mildly. That EPO gives users lethally high blood pressure is also stretching the limits of truth. It is correct that both short- and long-term EPO use increases blood pressure (Rasmussen *et al.* 2012). However, the increase is not as dramatic as the leaflet indicates. 'The metabolic and hormonal and renal effects of EPO do not seem to range beyond acceptable limits and are reversible. Taken together, EPO seems safe to use for experimental purposes in healthy volunteers' (Lundby and Olsen 2011 p. 1265). If this is true, the remark about the risk of death at a young age is a gross exaggeration which seems to tap into the EPO myth deconstructed by Bernat López (López 2011).

All material on WADA's Education and Prevention website can be best described as propaganda, which is unsurprising giving the nature of the enterprise. This is paternalistic and ideological. A liberalistic or libertarian approach requires proper education in accordance with the German philosopher Immanuel Kant's understanding of enlightenment as a process of liberation so people learn to make use of their own intelligence instead of being dependent on authoritarian guardianship (Kant 1784). That is, athletes' education should build on reason and scientific knowledge instead of emotion, myth and subjective values. It should present up-to-date facts about the effects and side-effects of new and old drugs, and make them aware of the particular risk related to the use of unapproved drugs, so the athletes become sufficiently informed to make rational choices of their own.

Educating athletes in a sports world without doping control will in all likelihood have positive outcomes. Some athletes will probably decide not to pursue a sports career knowing that drug use is necessary to be competitive at elite level and make do with recreational sport, which is better than suffering the disappointment of defeat in a naively perceived drug-free competition. Another likely outcome is that athletes who want to take advantage of performance-enhancing remedies will choose the most potent drugs with the least side-effects and seek expert advice about dosages etc. to optimise the benefits and minimise risks. In other words, education will in many cases increase risk awareness and health protection. However, legalisation would not be a simple panacea. There will be athletes who want to go all in on drugs and consume lethal quantities. Those who want a libertarian approach must accept this. If athletes have been properly informed about the risk involved in over-use of drugs and they still take them, so be it. A few may die on that account, but they will not have died in vain. Their deaths will be practical examples for other athletes of the consequences. If sporting success was directly proportional with the amounts of drugs taken, this would clearly pose a challenge to the libertarian approach as it would mean those who accepted doping as part and parcel of sport would be forced to adopt similarly hazardous regimes in order to be competitive. Fortunately, this is not so. Potentially lethal dosages are not necessarily more effective than safe ones. It is with drugs, as it is with training, diet and all other aspects of sporting preparation, not a question about who dares take the most but who is able to take the optimal quantum. So, legalisation does not mean that athletes have to engage in a medical arms race on the verge of death. But in the likely event that deaths happen this will surely make the remaining athletes use drugs even more vigilantly.

A potential objection to this athletes' empowerment model is that it hands responsibility to immature athletes. Many elite-level athletes are not of legal age. Reckless coaches may urge them to use performance-enhancing means and downplay the risks involved. In light of this, it would be irresponsible to suggest that minors should be able to digest anti-doping information sufficiently to make considered decisions whether to dope or not. There are two possible answers to this. First, if athletes are below legal age the responsibility for their protection and wellbeing is their parents. Thus, parents' written consent should be a prerequisite for minors to enter the world of elite sport. Second, if the sports' governing bodies are concerned about the immaturity and potential abuse of underage athletes they could decide to exclude them from professional sport and the Olympics until they reach legal age.

24 hours a day chaperone

However, if there are too many problems with the model that promotes solidarity and equality between athletes, and the alternative which focuses on the empowerment of athletes so they can make rational choices of their own without the patronising roles of anti-doping custodians, then the final efficient solution we can imagine is the introduction of a 24 hours a day chaperone system. That is, the current surveillance system based on unannounced random and target testing should be replaced by a direct surveillance system that would make direct doping testing superfluous.

The idea is simple. Athletes who, under the current system, are part of the registered testing pool should instead be required to have WADA-employed chaperones with them day and night during their career. The chaperones would follow the athlete as discreetly as a police officer follows a person under police protection. After an initial clearance of the athlete's house for banned products, the chaperones would not have to enter the athlete's premises again. Visitors must of course agree to be checked to make sure no doping products are brought to the house. But this is a procedure everyone who flies has experienced. When the athletes leave for training, go shopping or dining, the chaperone will follow as a bodyguard follows a king or a queen. This solution would make it as good as impossible for athletes to dope and eliminate the problem, at least at elite level.

We envision there will be objections to this proposal as well. It may be argued that this system violates athletes' privacy rights. This objection is rather weak if it does not take into account the violation of privacy rights already accepted in relation to the current anti-doping system. A single house search, a discreet anti-doping bodyguard, and a requirement that visitors should be checked in order to secure no doping products are smuggled to the athlete do not seem to violate the athletes' privacy any more than the current system does. Today athletes are forced to provide whereabouts information so everyone with access to the Anti-Doping Administration Management System (ADAMS) can see where the athlete is at any given time. The athletes are also required to stay put in a specific place for one hour every day and in addition to this be available for testing from 6am to 11pm throughout the year. They must accept complete strangers into their house and urinate in front of them. They also must accept having a needle put in their arm to collect blood from them. They can be notified in a restaurant and have to go through the testing procedure in the public toilet if they do not want to cancel the evening and go home with the control officers to get the test done. Although this system has proven inefficient it seems to be much more invasive on athletes' privacy than the 24 hours a day chaperone system does. When anti-doping officials mention privacy issues in relation to anti-doping they rarely, if ever, seem concerned by the grave inroads on athletes' privacy they have already forced through. It appears rather as a way to pretend they are concerned about preventing cheating. An illustrative example of the disrespect for athletes' privacy was given when Mike Miller, chief executive of the World Olympians Organisation spoke at a Westminster Media Forum in 2017. Miller said that anti-doping authorities should be ready to implement new radical measures in order to secure clean sport. Soon the technology will be in place to implant microchips in athletes' bodies that makes it possible to detect the use of banned substances immediately. This would be a great step forward and he brushed aside any concerns as follows:

> Some people say we shouldn't do this to people. Well, we are a nation of dog lovers; we chip our dogs. We're prepared to do that and it doesn't seem to harm them. So why aren't we prepared to chip ourselves?
>
> *(Robershaw 2017)*

The interesting thing is not just that Miller openly proposes the dehumanisation of athletes but rather the response made by chief executive of UKAD Nicole Sapstead who spoke at the same event. Where one would expect a forceful response defending athletes right to, if not bodily integrity which is already violated by the current regime, at least a body uninvaded, she raised concerns about the quality of the imagined chip! There needs 'to be assurances that the microchips could not be [tampered with]'. It is true, she also raised 'concerns about whether the technology could be an invasion of athletes' privacy.' Whether?! 'We welcome verified developments in technology which could assist the fight against doping' she continued. 'However, can we ever be sure that this type of thing could never be tampered with or even accurately monitor all substances and methods on the Prohibited List?' (Robershaw 2017). The obvious interpretation of this is that if it could not be tampered with and if it could monitor all substances Sapstead would accept it. This interpretation is supported by her second mentioning of the privacy issue: 'There is a balance to be struck between a right to privacy versus demonstrating that you are clean,' she says reassuringly, before she returns to her anti-doping equals anti-privacy agenda: 'We would actively encourage more research in whether there are technologies in development that can assist anti-doping organisations in their endeavours' (Robertshaw 2017). In light of this, our proposed chaperone system appears more respectful of athletes' privacy rights.

Another likely objection is that appointing chaperones to follow athletes 24/7 will be unacceptably expensive. If this is true, the only reason is that clean sport is not sufficiently prioritised. And this may be the kernel of the problem. But if that is true the conclusion is straightforward: anti-doping is not supposed to be anything more than an image-protecting engagement that was never supposed to be so efficient that it had negative impact on athletic performance levels. In that case anti-doping is about striking the right balance between the image of sport as healthy and fair and the attraction of sport as high-level entertainment in order to facilitate the continuous growth of the sport economy.

Transparency of sanctions

If we assume that wholesale reforms of the sports industry to address the motivations for doping are not acceptable, and our proposals regarding doctors, education or chaperones are discarded as utopian, we conclude by proposing solutions that at least address and diminish the injustices and social stigma athletes experience under the current regime. Perhaps there is a more efficient and just way to improve the equity of outcomes for athletes who test positive.

The WADC makes injustice inevitable because there is no differentiation between types of athletes or types of offences. An ADRV leads to a sanction regardless of any mitigating circumstances (except for cocaine contamination from nightclub liaisons which, even then, has been inconsistently applied). It is vital that the future of anti-doping policy shifts focus towards differentiation and proportional enforcement: punishments that fit the crime, decided in a way that is appropriate, fair, humane, transparent and consistent.

In order to address this, we propose a scoring system based on a graded sliding scale of violation types integrated with a scale which assesses the athletes' ability to manage their dietary practices in accordance with the WADC. This proposal may initially appear dauntingly complex, and critics may react by saying that it is too complex and impractical. However, there already exists highly sophisticated models for measuring other sports issues, most notably the system for classification in disability sports, and the system for defining the serious of cases under football's Financial Fair Play regulations. Outside of sport, the tools used to assess students' work in universities requires making judgements on a series of marking criteria. And, as will be explained, the classification of illegal drug offences in the UK.

Our proposal would require a revision of the WADC to define categories of athletes, in consultation with international federations, to suit the developmental pathways of their specific sport. In fact, the WADC already distinguishes between international, national and recreational, so this proposal is merely an extension and improvement upon the existing system. We draw inspiration from a system already in place within the legal environment, namely the judgements made in cases of drug use in England and Wales (Sentencing Council 2012). Guidelines were put in place in 2012 to promote consistency in cases, but allow clear differentiation based upon specific criteria in an eight-step process. Step 1 is called: 'Determining the offence category' and considers the offender's culpability and the harm caused by the offence. The most serious offences would involve the defendant have a 'Leading' role (i.e. supplier or abusing a position of trust), as compared to a 'Significant' role (i.e. involvement in dealing) and 'Lesser' role (i.e. engaged by pressure, coercion, intimidation).

Importantly, these are set against 'Category of harm' which lists drug types and quantities: Category 1 includes, among other drugs, heroin and cocaine (5kg), ecstasy (5,000 tablets). On a sliding scale, we find that Category 4 includes by comparison: heroin and cocaine (5g) and ecstasy (20 tablets). Thus, the first step is about identifying the individuals and their context, and detailing the seriousness of the drugs they were in possession of.

Step 2 in the process is to define punishments. For example, a defendant placed in Category 1 for type of drug and quantity and had a Leading role, would face 12–16 years custody. An example of a lesser sentence might be for a Category 3 case with a Lesser role: 3 years 6 months to 5 years custody. There are lighter punishments for the least serious cases, that include curfews and community service. This part of the process therefore focuses on differentiating punishments.

There are a further six steps but we are most interested in Steps 3 and 4. The former considers 'any factors which indicate a reduction, such as assistance to the prosecution'. The latter considers 'Reduction for guilty pleas'. The current anti-doping legal process includes some confusing attempts to deal with these two aspects. The WADC encourages 'substantial assistance' but requires the information provided to lead directly to an anti-doping rule violation decision being made against another person. In other words, this lacks flexibility and presumes that a third party using doping products could be caught through target testing. The admission of guilt is usually encouraged early in the sanctioning process, but there are no clear guidelines on the impact that might have upon the sanction imposed.

We propose that a similar system could be constructed for anti-doping. The obvious place to start would be age: a 12-year-old should not be treated the same as an experienced mature athlete. A second focus would be upon levels of anti-doping education: an athlete who has not had the opportunity for rigorous anti-doping education should not be expected to understand all the procedures and rules. It may be that federations set entry-level education requirements to pass from one category to the next; this would compel a more structured approach to athlete education than is currently in place. For example, if a football player signs for a higher-league club they must pass an anti-doping assessment accordingly. Third, we propose to differentiate athletes according to their financial resources: someone who plays sport for fun should not have to face the same legal costs as the highest paid professionals. Of course, this might not always be straightforward as an amateur athlete might be a millionaire from other sources of income. However, it would give the opportunity to fine athletes for sanctions in certain situations and their money can be used to support anti-doping education and testing. It also allows consideration of athletes living in poverty to have a sanction more suitable. Last, the level of sports medicine support offered by the athletes' support personnel should be considered. A hobby-sport athlete would not know about TUEs or how to batch test supplements; these are services offered to elite athletes. This might not always be an easy assessment as athletes could pay directly for advice, but what is important is whether the sports organisations they are part of have offered medical and nutrition support to pre-empt the use of supplements, banned medicines, or more potent drugs. Using these criteria there could be classifications of athlete types, using a point scoring system of 1–10.

For example, a 15-year-old swimmer might score 2/10 for age, 3/10 for education, 3/10 for resources, but if she is a successful competitor she might score 8/10 for levels of support, dependent on their team environment. If in this exemplar case the athlete scores 16/40, she is then ranked according to the overarching model, which might look like:

Category 1: 1–10
Category 2: 11–20
Category 3: 21–30
Category 4: 31–40

Once these categories are agreed upon, the rules should then be applied differentially. The full imposition of sanctions could remain in place for Category 4 athletes. However, some new sets of rules could be constructed. For example, Category 1 athletes do not need to be in a registered testing pool, do not need TUEs for over-the-counter medicines, would not be tested for social drugs, would have free access to legal support to challenge a sanction paid for by sports federations, and their case does not need to be made public. In most cases, a ban from future sport would not be necessary, but they might be compelled to undertake more education and to help educate others in their immediate environment. They might be treated more generously in cases where accidental use has occurred or where contamination seems a possibility. As athletes move up the ladder in their particular sport, the sports federation is responsible for their accreditation process through anti-doping education and support from doctors, coaches and administrators, as we cannot expect the level of anti-doping awareness from all types of athletes to be the same, and thus policies should be responsive to such variability.

Of course, there may be concerns that such a system could be manipulated by some unscrupulous coaches and doctors to deliberate dope young or inexperienced athletes and avoid a ban. History tells us that such behaviours are probably inevitable, and there is probably no system that is completely watertight.

The second part of this proposal would be to classify violations according to context and significance. Again, we could have a points system using certain criteria. Central to this classification would be the already established criteria of fair play and health. Here we also suggest subcategories. First, would be the potency of the substance or method used: taking a cocktail of EPO, steroids and growth hormone might score 10/10, but levomethamphetamine might score 1/10. Second, could be the intention to cheat and the potential impact: an athlete who wins a race and used a powerful drug in the lead up to the race might score highly, but an athlete who is low down the rankings and/or has only been caught with low amounts of the substance in their system taken out-of-competition might get a lower score. This is not to suggest lower-ranking athletes should be allowed to take more health risks, simply that a sanction should relate to the competitive advantage gained in association with health risks. A third criteria in this regard might take into account the context: being given tablets by a trusted team doctor, or anyone member of their club or federation, might score lower than in a case where an athlete has bought steroids on the internet with the express purpose of doping.

Again, we could have a framework which differentiates outcomes:

Category 1: 1–10
Category 2: 11–20
Category 3: 21–30

This score could be matched to the athlete definition category to create an overall score out of 70. An exemplar outcome might be:

A young amateur athlete with little anti-doping education and at a non-elite level might score 6/40 for athlete type. They might have used steroids which they bought from a street drug dealer, so their score for context and significance might be 15/30. Their overall score is 21/70. The punishments should be graded accordingly, with lower scores quite simply leading to shorter periods of disqualification. 21/70 might lead to a six-month ban and compulsory service to local sports clubs, along with attendance at educational workshops.

By comparison, an athlete with a long career of international sport who is caught using EPO and testosterone would naturally face a tougher sanction because they are a Category 4 athlete (for example, score of 33), and have consumed drugs for deliberate performance reasons that are unhealthy (for example, score of 25). This leads to an overall 58/70 which is in the region of a three-year ban with compulsory youth-education work. However, we would include a caveat here to ensure that even elite athletes who fall victim to contamination or a flawed laboratory process have the right to request full exoneration.

Then there is the question of multiple sanctions. At present, two ADRVs of any nature usually lead to a lifetime ban. However, the cases of Efimova and Gatlin show that the rules are not always applied in ways that everyone understands. Under the system proposed here, athletes would carry forward their scores from previous cases. For example, two violations would be scored out of 140: if the first was 20 and the second was 50, then the 70/140 would be set against previously established framework for second or third offences. A 70/140 might lead to an additional two-year ban on top of the normal ban for their second offence.

The other complicating factor is 'substantial assistance' which currently can lead to a reduction, but only if the information leads directly to another person being charged with an ADRV. Under our new proposal, the score of 70 could be the initial sanction. Thereafter, any substantial assistance is given a graded percentage score that is applied to the sanction. For example, lower-level types of information might be the website from which the athlete bought the banned substance, perhaps a 10 per cent reduction in the period of disqualification. But significant information that leads to criminal investigation of suppliers could bring a 50 per cent reduction in the disqualification period.

Athletes would have the option of whether to allow their case to be announced publicly, thus potentially avoiding the stigma associated with being labelled a doper. All cases regarding athletes under the age of 18 should be kept confidential. However, the decision in their case should be published with the names and other information removed to establish transparency through case law. This means that both the prosecution and the athletes' legal representatives could refer to previous similar cases to help make decisions in a more efficient and uniform way. This would improve international harmonisation if all cases were held on an easily accessible database searchable by athlete type, drug type and sanctions; integrated with the overarching framework for decision-making.

At the same time, athletes in definition Categories 1 and 2 would have their cases settled locally, for example by their national governing body (NGB). WADA would take the role of occasional auditor of processes and decisions to ensure harmonisation and standardisation between different countries (the NADO is responsible for ensuring standardisation between different sports). Athletes in Categories 3 and 4 would face a NADO tribunal and then, if they wish to appeal, take their case to the CAS. In this way, decision-makers become more specialised as they are dealing with a narrower range of cases. Also, Category 1 and 2 would face no legal fees and their cases would be decided by a panel of volunteers (which could include fellow athletes, sports doctors, pro bono early-career lawyers, or sports law interns). It is only elite athletes who have sufficient financial resources and whose sanction will affect their future earnings that would need to pay for arbitration.

A final point to be made here is that international governing bodies would have some influence on the specific details of the two types of categorisation so that they are appropriate for the sport in question. Strength sports might put more emphasis upon drugs that build muscle, endurance sports might focus on blood boosting products and methods, skill-based sports might wish to ensure their athletes do not use drugs to reduce their anxiety. This approach might also mean that the Prohibited List is adjusted depending on the sport, which would in turn improve the efficiency of the testing system by reducing the cost for each test thus allowing more tests for the same amount of money.

While the above might seem potentially too complex and bureaucratic, perhaps even open to abuse, it does require the various relevant organisations to explore mechanisms that would be more nuanced and receptive towards understanding the athletes' context. If the purpose is fairness, proportionality, humanity, transparency and consistency, then there is no reason to avoid complexity and debate. Anti-doping should be constructed to serve the interests of athletes, not to make life easier for WADA, IOC and other powerful sports institutions. Although, in many ways, the desire for simplicity that underpinned the 2003 WADC has clearly not delivered a simple, clear and fair set of outcomes. If WADA can concede there is a need for change, we propose the above as an initial launching point for discussions, but with the insistence that these discussions are not held behind closed doors. Athletes, sponsors, clubs, doctors, lawyers, managers, fans and journalists should all be allowed to contribute to a democratic and just system. Moreover, if such a system can be successfully implemented in the British judicial system and in other sports regulations, there seems no reason why it cannot be used for anti-doping purposes, and might be extended to include more specific guidelines for athlete support personnel and suppliers.

In this final chapter, we have outlined a few ideas for reforming the system which address the major problems identified in this book. We are aware that they are not exhaustive, but at least they offer a fairer and more rational and humane alternative to the current system. We do this not as idealists but as rationalists, recognising that the fundamental problem remains that the vision of anti-doping is unachievable, anachronistic and paternalistic, based on moral panic, fear and the drama of high-profile scandals. Reform should include revision of the foundational principles not just tinkering with the procedures for implementation.

References

AIGCP-CPA. (2013). "Joint agreement". Retrieved 6 April 2017 from http://webcache. googleusercontent.com/search?q=cache:2Jndj_RKHV8J:www.uci.ch/mm/ Document/News/Rulesandregulation/16/26/52/JointAgreements2013-ENG_ English.pdf+&cd=2&hl=da&ct=clnk&gl=dk&client=firefox-b-ab

BBC Sport. (2016). "TUE system can be abused by athletes – Dr Richard McLaren". Retrieved 28 June 2017 from http://www.bbc.com/sport/37382825

Coubertin, Pierre de (2000). *Olympism: Selected Writings*. Lausanne: International Olympic Committee.

Cyclingtips. (2010). "How much money do pro cyclists make?" 1 November. Retrieved 6 April 2017 from https://cyclingtips.com/2010/11/how-much-do-pro-cyclists-make/.

de Hon, O. (2016). "Striking the right balance: Effectiveness of anti-doping policies". PhD thesis, Utrecht University.

Fletcher, P. (2017). "Contador proposes salary caps for pro cycling". Retrieved 28 October 2017 from http://www.cyclingnews.com/news/contador-proposes-salary-caps-for-pro-cycling/

Gaehwiler, R. (2017). "Anti-doping and the physician's role: How do we overcome the challenges in elite sport?" BMJ Blogs. Retrieved 11 January 2018 from http://blogs. bmj.com/bjsm/2017/02/03/anti-doping-physicians-role-overcome-challenges-elite-sport/ 2017

Gerrard, D. (2016). "Independent opinion from WADA's TUE Expert Group." Retrieved 28 June 2017 from https://www.wada-ama.org/en/media/news/2016-09/independent-opinion-from-wadas-tue-expert-group

Hardie, M. (2011). "It's not about the blood! *Operación Puerto* and the end of modernity". In M. McNamee and V. Møller (eds), *Doping and Anti-Doping Policy in Sport: Ethical, Legal and Social Perspectives*. London: Routledge.

Hardie, M., D. Shilbury, I. Ware and C. Bozzi (2010). *I Wish I was Twenty One Now. Beyond Doping in the Australian Peloton*. Geelong: Auskadi Samizdat.

Hermann, A. and M. Henneberg (2014). "Anti-doping systems in sports are doomed to fail: A probability and cost analysis." *Sports Medicine and Doping Studies* 4(5): 1–12.

Hoberman, J. (2005). *Testosterone Dreams: Rejuvenation, Aphrodisia, Doping*. Berkeley, CA: University of California Press.

Hoberman, J. (2014). "Physicians and the sports doping epidemic." *AMA Journal of Ethics* 16(7): 570–574.

Kant, I. (1784). "Beantwortung der Frage: Was ist Aufklärung?" *Berlinische Monatsschrift* December: 481–494.

Llewellyn, M. P. (2011). "The curse of the shamateur". *The International Journal of the History of Sport* 28(5): 796–816.

López, B. (2011). "The invention of a 'drug of mass destruction': Deconstructing the EPO myth". *Sport in History* 31(1): 84–109.

Lundby, C. and N. V. Olsen (2011). "Effects of recombinant human erythropoietin in normal humans". *The Journal of Physiology* 589(6): 1265–1271.

Pagels, J. (2014). "Are salary caps for professional athletes fair?" Retrieved 10 April 2017 from https://priceonomics.com/are-salary-caps-for-professional-athletes-fair/

Paoli, L. and A. Donati (2014). *The Sports Doping Market: Understanding Supply and Demand, and the Challenges of Their Control*. New York: Springer.

Rasmussen, P., Y.-S. Kim, R. Krogh-Madsen, C. Lundby, N. V. Olsen, N. H. Secher and J. J. van Lieshout (2012). "Both acute and prolonged administration of EPO reduce cerebral and systemic vascular conductance in humans". *The FASEB Journal* 26(3): 1343–1348.

Robershaw, H. (2017). "Athletes should be implanted with microchips in order to catch drug cheats, says Olympians' chief". *Cycling Weekly*, 11 October. Retrieved 28 October 2017 from http://www.cyclingweekly.com/news/latest-news/athletes-implanted-microchips-order-catch-drug-cheats-354767

Sentencing Council from England and Wales. (2012). Drug Offences: Definitive Guidelines. Retrieved 12 January 2018 from https://www.sentencingcouncil.org.uk/wp-content/uploads/Drug_Offences_Definitive_Guideline_final_web1.pdf

Teetzel, S. (2007). "Respecting privacy in detecting illegitimate enhancements in athletes". *Sport, Ethics and Philosophy* 1(2): 159–170.

Tittle, C. R. (1969). "Crime rates and legal sanctions". *Social Problems* 16(4): 409–423.

Toft, J. (2002). "Doping doctors". *Play the Game* 2002: 25. Retrieved 20 December 2017 from http://www.playthegame.org/upload/play-the-game-magazine-2002.pdf

WADA. (2009). *Dangers of Doping – Get the Facts*. Retrieved 15 July 2017 from https://www.wada-ama.org/en/resources/education-and-prevention/dangers-of-doping-get-the-facts

Zimbalist, A. (2010). "Reflections on salary shares and salary caps." *Journal of Sports Economics* 11(1): 17–28.

INDEX